Mastering PostCSS for Web Design

Explore the power of PostCSS to write highly performing, modular, and modern CSS code for your web pages

Alex Libby

[PACKT] open source

PUBLISHING

community experience distilled

BIRMINGHAM - MUMBAI

Mastering PostCSS for Web Design

Copyright © 2016 Packt Publishing

First published: June 2016

Production reference: 1240616

Published by Packt Publishing Ltd.
Livery Place
35 Livery Street
Birmingham B3 2PB, UK.

ISBN 978-1-78588-589-1

www.packtpub.com

Credits

Author
Alex Libby

Reviewer
Michael Ebbage

Commissioning Editor
Wilson D'souza

Acquisition Editor
Larissa Pinto

Content Development Editor
Riddhi Tuljapurkar

Technical Editors
Chinmay Puranik

Jayesh Sonawane

Copy Editor
Safis Editing

Project Coordinator
Sanchita Mandal

Proofreader
Safis Editing

Indexer
Monica Ajmera Mehta

Production Coordinator
Manu Joseph

Cover Work
Manu Joseph

About the Author

Alex Libby's background is in IT support—he has been involved in supporting end users for almost 20 years in a variety of different environments; a recent change in role now sees Alex working as an MVT test developer for a global distributor based in the UK. Although Alex gets to play with different technologies in his day job, his first true love has always been the open source movement, and in particular, experimenting with CSS/CSS3, jQuery, and HTML5. To date, Alex has written 10 books on subjects such as jQuery, HTML5 video, SASS, and CSS for Packt and has reviewed several more—*Mastering PostCSS Web Design* is Alex's eleventh book for Packt.

I would like to thank my family and friends for their support throughout the process and the reviewers for their valued comments; this book wouldn't be what it is without them! I would also particularly like to thank Andrey Sitnik for his work in producing PostCSS and being really helpful and patient in answering questions about some of its more complex parts. My grateful thanks also to Ernie Salazar from NPM, who helped with issues with publishing the plugins created for this book, and David Clark for his assistance with getting me back on track with the postcss-bem-linter plugin, also used in the book. Thank you all—I couldn't have finished the book without your help!

About the Reviewer

Michael Ebbage is a software architect who specializes in e-commerce and Java technology-based web applications. He created his first web page almost two decades ago — since then, he's gone on to develop hundreds of websites for some of the UK's biggest companies (many featuring on the FTSE 100 and 250), as the tools and techniques used to do so have continually changed and evolved.

He has a background in software development and holds a BSc (Hons) in computing and information systems. He is also one of the top contributors to Stack Overflow, where you'll regularly find him answering questions on a wide range of web-related languages and technologies.

I'd like to thank the author, Alex, for the opportunity to be involved with this book. It's been a great learning experience, and I now have a renewed admiration for the amount of knowledge and effort that goes into it. I would also like to thank my beloved wife and son for their patience and support during the time I spent working on reviewing it.

www.PacktPub.com

eBooks, discount offers, and more

Did you know that Packt offers eBook versions of every book published, with PDF and ePub files available? You can upgrade to the eBook version at www.PacktPub.com and as a print book customer, you are entitled to a discount on the eBook copy. Get in touch with us at customercare@packtpub.com for more details.

At www.PacktPub.com, you can also read a collection of free technical articles, sign up for a range of free newsletters and receive exclusive discounts and offers on Packt books and eBooks.

https://www2.packtpub.com/books/subscription/packtlib

Do you need instant solutions to your IT questions? PacktLib is Packt's online digital book library. Here, you can search, access, and read Packt's entire library of books.

Why subscribe?

- Fully searchable across every book published by Packt
- Copy and paste, print, and bookmark content
- On demand and accessible via a web browser

Table of Contents

Preface

As a developer, I'll bet you have a perfect workflow — you either write styles using plain vanilla CSS or use one of the current processors, such as SASS or Less, to create them. You'll add vendor prefixes using the likes of Autoprefixer — either manually or using a tool, such as Grunt or Gulp.

Sounds familiar? Why would you want to disturb something if it works for you, right?

Trouble is, a friend or colleague has started talking about a new processor by the name of PostCSS — they've piqued your interest sufficiently to want to find out more about what it is and how it works.

Well, welcome to the fast-growing ecosystem that is PostCSS! By itself, the tool doesn't do anything, but when paired with the right plugins (and there are hundreds available for use), it has the potential to become a really powerful processor for you. Gone are the days when we have to depend on a monolithic library such as SASS or less. Instead, we can pick and choose exactly which plugins to use based on our project requirements. PostCSS is an immensely quick processor to use; the question is, are you ready for the ride?

Here's hoping the answer is yes; if so, let's make a start.

What this book covers

Chapter 1, Introducing PostCSS, kicks off our journey with an introduction to the world of PostCSS, exploring its features and how we can use this ecosystem to transform basic code into valid CSS styles that we can use within our projects. You will discover the benefits of using this ecosystem and how its architecture and modular approach allows us to put together a processor that is tailored specifically for our needs.

Chapter 2, Creating Variables and Mixins, takes a look at some of the basic concepts that are familiar to users of existing processor technologies, such as variables and mixins. You will learn how to transition them to PostCSS and discover how the benefits of using these techniques can transition through to using PostCSS.

Chapter 3, Nesting Rules, explores how existing processors, such as SASS or less, take advantage of concepts such as nesting to reduce the amount of code we need to write and how we can replicate the same functionality within our PostCSS processor.

Chapter 4, Building Media Queries, walks us through the basics of adding responsive support to websites using PostCSS and media queries. You'll learn how to retrofit support for older websites and browsers, and explore how we can take things further with the advent of CSS4 media queries and provide support today within PostCSS.

Chapter 5, Managing Colors, Images, and Fonts, examines the plugins available for handling and manipulating images, colors, and fonts within PostCSS. We will work through a number of examples to illustrate how both images and colors can be manipulated within PostCSS, such as creating image sprites or altering colors using palettes within the system.

Chapter 6, Creating Grids, takes us on a journey through constructing the skeleton of a website using grids—we will explore the basic concept behind using grids and discover some of the plugin options available for creating them within PostCSS. We will work through some examples using the Bourbon Neat grid system, before replicating the examples with PostCSS-equivalent plugins and adding responsive capabilities to the resulting code.

Chapter 7, Animating Elements, begins with a quick recap of using JavaScript to animate content, before switching to using CSS for animation, and how you can transition through to using PostCSS. We will explore using some of the more well-known libraries, such as Animate.css, before creating a quick demo using PostCSS and learning how to optimize our animations using PostCSS.

Chapter 8, Creating PostCSS Plugins, teaches us how plugins can be used to extend PostCSS, and takes us through a journey of exploring the typical architecture of such a plugin. You will then take a look at some example plugins before working through creating your own plugins using the boilerplate code available and before testing and making the plugins available for download by users from the Internet.

Chapter 9, Working with Shortcuts, Fallbacks, and Packs, starts by examining some of the shortcut plugins and packs available before exploring how we can supplement them with creating our own shortcut plugins. You will also discover how you can lint and optimize your code using one of the plugin packs available for PostCSS and learn how to provide fall-backs to PostCSS code to help maintain support for older browsers.

Chapter 10, Building a Custom Processor, pulls together some of the techniques we've covered thus far in the book to produce a custom processor that we can use as a basis for transforming code in our projects. You will explore how to optimize the output before adding source map and vendor prefix support and then testing it on a website. You will then round off the chapter with a look at extending the processor to use the CSStyle framework to allow you to write code that works for both SASS or PostCSS.

Chapter 11, Manipulating Custom Syntaxes, introduces us to writing custom syntaxes using the API and explores some of the options available for parsing code written using syntaxes such as SASS or less. We work though some examples of parsing code using PostCSS before converting the output into something that can be displayed on screen or saved to a file. We will also add in support for highlighting our code using the midas library.

Chapter 12, Mixing Preprocessors, shows us how we can begin to mix processors as an aid to make the transition to using PostCSS. We will take a look at the Pleeease library before installing it and using some of its features. We will then set up a compilation process before using it to make changes to a standard WordPress theme.

Chapter 13, Troubleshooting PostCSS Issues, takes a look at some of the more common issues we might experience when using PostCSS, such as the "taskname not in our gulpfile" error. We will also take a look at what to do next if all else fails. We will cover the methods for getting help with an issue or logging details of a bug within either the core PostCSS system or one of its plugins.

Chapter 14, Preparing for the Future, covers some of the possible options for supporting future style standards from what people know as CSS4. You will also explore some of the risks involved and how you can replicate support using existing plugins available today or extend them to increase support for new CSS4 selectors.

What you need for this book

All you need to work through most of the examples in this book is a simple text or code editor, a copy of NodeJS (for your platform), Internet access, and a browser. I recommend installing Sublime Text 3; it works well with Node and Gulp, which we will use throughout the book.

Some of the examples make use of additional plugins; most (if not all) can be installed directly from within NodeJS. Details are included within the appropriate chapter along with links to view the plugin source code and documentation.

Who this book is for

The book is for frontend developers who are familiar with HTML5 and CSS3, but want to master PostCSS as part of simplifying their development workflow or remove the dependency on existing processors, such as SASS or Stylus. To get the most out of this book, you should have a good knowledge of HTML, CSS3, and JavaScript, and ideally, have some experience of using preprocessors such as SASS, Less, or Stylus.

Conventions

In this book, you will find a number of text styles that distinguish between different kinds of information. Here are some examples of these styles and an explanation of their meaning.

Code words in text, database table names, folder names, filenames, file extensions, pathnames, dummy URLs, user input, and Twitter handles are shown as follows: "We'll start by installing the relevant plugins required for this demo: we'll need the postcss-nested, autocomplete, and postcss-scss plugins."

A block of code is set as follows:

```
gulp.task('rename', ['styles'], function () {
  return gulp.src('dest/example.css')
    .pipe(postcss([ cssnano ]))
    .pipe(rename('example.min.css'))
    .pipe(gulp.dest("dest/"));
});
```

When we wish to draw your attention to a particular part of a code block, the relevant lines or items are set in bold:

```
var sourcemaps = require('gulp-sourcemaps');
var rename = require('gulp-rename');
var cssnano = require('cssnano')
```

Any command-line input or output is written as follows:

```
npm install --save-dev cssnano
npm install --save-dev gulp-rename
```

New terms and **important words** are shown in bold. Words that you see on the screen, for example, in menus or dialog boxes, appear in the text like this: "When we view the page and select the **Images** tab, after a short delay we should see six new images."

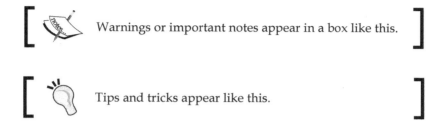

Warnings or important notes appear in a box like this.

Tips and tricks appear like this.

Reader feedback

Feedback from our readers is always welcome. Let us know what you think about this book—what you liked or disliked. Reader feedback is important for us as it helps us develop titles that you will really get the most out of.

To send us general feedback, simply e-mail feedback@packtpub.com, and mention the book's title in the subject of your message.

If there is a topic that you have expertise in and you are interested in either writing or contributing to a book, see our author guide at www.packtpub.com/authors.

Customer support

Now that you are the proud owner of a Packt book, we have a number of things to help you to get the most from your purchase.

Downloading the example code

You can download the example code files for this book from your account at http://www.packtpub.com. If you purchased this book elsewhere, you can visit http://www.packtpub.com/support and register to have the files e-mailed directly to you.

You can download the code files by following these steps:

1. Log in or register to our website using your e-mail address and password.
2. Hover the mouse pointer on the **SUPPORT** tab at the top.
3. Click on **Code Downloads & Errata**.

4. Enter the name of the book in the **Search** box.

5. Select the book for which you're looking to download the code files.

6. Choose from the drop-down menu where you purchased this book from.

7. Click on **Code Download**.

You can also download the code files by clicking on the **Code Files** button on the book's webpage at the Packt Publishing website. This page can be accessed by entering the book's name in the **Search** box. Please note that you need to be logged in to your Packt account.

Once the file is downloaded, please make sure that you unzip or extract the folder using the latest version of:

- WinRAR / 7-Zip for Windows
- Zipeg / iZip / UnRarX for Mac
- 7-Zip / PeaZip for Linux

The code bundle for the book is also hosted on GitHub at https://github.com/PacktPublishing/Mastering-PostCSS-for-Web-Design. We also have other code bundles from our rich catalog of books and videos available at https://github.com/PacktPublishing/. Check them out!

Downloading the color images of this book

We also provide you with a PDF file that has color images of the screenshots/diagrams used in this book. The color images will help you better understand the changes in the output. You can download this file from http://www.packtpub.com/sites/default/files/downloads/MasteringPostCSSForWebDesign_ColorImages.pdf.

Errata

Although we have taken every care to ensure the accuracy of our content, mistakes do happen. If you find a mistake in one of our books—maybe a mistake in the text or the code—we would be grateful if you could report this to us. By doing so, you can save other readers from frustration and help us improve subsequent versions of this book. If you find any errata, please report them by visiting http://www.packtpub.com/submit-errata, selecting your book, clicking on the **Errata Submission Form** link, and entering the details of your errata. Once your errata are verified, your submission will be accepted and the errata will be uploaded to our website or added to any list of existing errata under the Errata section of that title.

To view the previously submitted errata, go to https://www.packtpub.com/books/content/support and enter the name of the book in the search field. The required information will appear under the **Errata** section.

Piracy

Piracy of copyrighted material on the Internet is an ongoing problem across all media. At Packt, we take the protection of our copyright and licenses very seriously. If you come across any illegal copies of our works in any form on the Internet, please provide us with the location address or website name immediately so that we can pursue a remedy.

Please contact us at copyright@packtpub.com with a link to the suspected pirated material.

We appreciate your help in protecting our authors and our ability to bring you valuable content.

Questions

If you have a problem with any aspect of this book, you can contact us at questions@packtpub.com, and we will do our best to address the problem.

1
Introducing PostCSS

A key part of any website is styling—it doesn't matter if this is for a simple element tag or a complex animation; a website is not a website without color and action. Building styles for any online presence takes time and effort—we can reduce development time by using a preprocessor to automate the creation of styles, automatically apply vendor prefixes and the like, but the extra dependency of a library can be like using a sledgehammer to crack a nut!

Enter PostCSS—its unique modular style allows us to create a leaner, faster CSS processor, with no external dependencies. In this chapter, we look at installing PostCSS, understanding its architecture, and learn how to use its speed and power to compile code into valid CSS. We will cover a number of topics throughout this chapter, which will include the following:

- Considering the benefits of creating our own preprocessor
- Introducing PostCSS and exploring its features
- Setting up a development environment using PostCSS
- Creating a simple example using PostCSS
- Exploring how PostCSS works and its architecture

Let's make a start...!

 All of the exercises in this book are written for the Windows platform; please adjust accordingly if you use a different operating system.

Discovering the art of processing

A question: what do SASS, Stylus, Haml, and Less all have in common?

The answer is, they are all compilers, source to source compiling, or **transpilers** (to give them their official name), that have been around since the 1980s. They have appeared in many different formats, with Digital Research's XLT86 being one of the earliest versions, dating from 1981.

More recently, the well-known SASS processor arrived in 2006; this was followed by Less, created by Alexis Sellier in 2009. Both work in a similar fashion: they take a set of rules and compile it into valid CSS. We can extend CSS with all manner of features, such as variables, mixins, functions, and more. Although processors may not help cut down the physical number of lines we have to write, they help us reorganize code into more manageable blocks that we can reuse in future projects, which helps make CSS easier to maintain.

But, as is nearly always the case, there are some drawbacks to using processors:

- There is nearly always a dependency involved, in some form or other — with SASS, it's Ruby; if you're using Less, it's a library, even though it is written in JavaScript
- Our project may only use a small amount of preprocessed code, yet we are forced to rely on what can be a large library, such as SASS
- Processing style sheets using a preprocessor is slow; it may only be a few seconds, but this builds up over time to become a significant amount of time spent waiting for processes to complete

Hmm, this doesn't make processing so attractive! But what if there were a way to alleviate all of these issues, and remove the need for dependencies at the same time?

Well, there is: let's build our own processor! Okay, this might sound a little crazy, but as someone once said, there is method in this madness, so bear with me while I explain why this may be a better option.

Introducing PostCSS

At the beginning of this chapter, I mentioned that we would focus on creating our own preprocessor, right? Well, I have a little confession to make: we're not. Hold on, what gives?

Well, we will create a preprocessor…but we will also create a postprocessor too. Let me explain why — our alternative "option" allows us to create both at the same time. Our alternative option is PostCSS, which can be downloaded from `https://github.com/postcss/postcss`. PostCSS is used by some major companies, such as Twitter, Google, Bootstrap and CodePen, and even WordPress (in a limited capacity).

PostCSS was built as a Node.js module, so will work with any number of the existing plugins already available for Node.js — we will be using a number of these plugins throughout the book. Let's take a moment to explore some of the benefits of this tool.

Exploring the benefits of using PostCSS

What do we mean by PostCSS? In a nutshell, it can be used to refer to one of two things — the PostCSS core tool or the plugin ecosystem that is powered by the tool. On its own, it doesn't actually do a lot; once we start adding plugins, we can achieve a great deal. Let's explore what this means in practice:

- Its modular architecture means we can pick and choose what we use; this allows us to keep the size of the library very small and responsive.

- Existing processors tend to fall into one of two camps — pre- or post-processing — which is a limiting factor when choosing which to use. PostCSS allows us to perform both operations within the same process, meaning we get the benefits of both worlds of processing!

- PostCSS comes with seamless support for all of the common task runners such as Gulp, Grunt, or Broccoli; we can combine it with a number of other tasks that can be automated.

- There are no dependencies for compiling, PostCSS is written entirely in JavaScript, so no need for Ruby, or libraries such as `libsass`, in order to compile code. The only dependency (as such) is Node.js — many developers will likely already have this installed.

- There is no need to learn any new languages; every developer will be familiar with JavaScript, and use it in their development process.

- We can change any plugin in use for something else when needed; we do not get this choice when using a larger library.

- Its relatively low barrier of entry means we can create any plugins we need very easily, or potentially modify existing ones to better suit our needs.

- PostCSS is quick — in a test using the `postcss-benchmark` plugin (available from `https://github.com/postcss/benchmark`), which contained parsed code, nested rules, mixins, variables, and math, PostCSS came out a clear winner:

```
PostCSS:     36 ms
Rework:      77 ms    (2.1 times slower)
libsass:    136 ms    (3.8 times slower)
Less:       160 ms    (4.4 times slower)
Stylus:     167 ms    (4.6 times slower)
Stylecow:   208 ms    (5.7 times slower)
Ruby Sass: 1084 ms    (30.1 times slower)
```

- Perfect — no need to continually update SASS, or have to download a new version of the `libsass` library, right?

Considering some of the pitfalls

Well, there are some considerations to using a custom processor; the key thing to remember is that PostCSS is neither a pre- nor post-processor, but more of a Swiss Army Knife of a toolbox that we can use to process our CSS code. Let's take a look at some of these drawbacks:

- Although we don't need to learn a new language in order to use PostCSS, creating a custom processor will add a layer of complexity to our development process.

- Its flexible approach means some may treat PostCSS as either a preprocessor or a postprocessor; this short-sighted approach means that you will miss opportunities, so it is crucial to keep an open mind in terms of what PostCSS can offer your development process.

- Converting code from an existing preprocessor to using PostCSS can be painful; this process only works if we don't try to convert explicitly, but use it as a basis for progressively moving to using PostCSS.

- PostCSS requires syntactically correct CSS from the start; although we could use any syntax (as PostCSS files are just plain text), compilation can easily fail, even through use of a single line comment!

- The real benefit of using PostCSS, though, is in its seamless integration into tools such as Gulp — imagine this scenario if you will:

You already develop sites using a preprocessor such as SASS. You can compile code using a standalone processor, but normally prefer to use Node.js and Gulp to complete the task. Sound about right? What about making the move to using PostCSS?

No problem, we can include a section for processing CSS files using PostCSS. The key here is to not use PostCSS to perform the initial compilation, but to perform the post-processing, such as adding vendor prefixes or minifying the results. Once this is established, we can start to incorporate some of the plugins available for PostCSS that allow us to replicate functionality, such as from within SASS. Once we've adjusted existing code to use the format required by the plugins, we can then switch to using PostCSS, and begin to remove our dependency on using SASS.

Clearing up some misconceptions

At this point, it is worth spending a few minutes to help clear up some common misconceptions about PostCSS, although many associate it as being a preprocessor, or even a postprocessor, this isn't what was intended:

- Classing PostCSS as a postprocessor, as opposed to a preprocessor (such as Less or SASS) is misguided; PostCSS is capable of compiling in a variety of different use-case scenarios, working on code compiled using any preprocessor, or just plain CSS.

- PostCSS should not be classed as a tool that should be tied in to any one process (such as writing SASS-based loops or conditionals). There are plugins available to do both, but this is just a small part of the role that PostCSS can play in your development workflow.

- If you find yourself in a position where "PostCSS" doesn't appear to perform as expected, it is unlikely to be PostCSS itself, but more likely to be a plugin being used that is causing the issue. Although PostCSS is still relatively young, there are plenty of plugins available, so it is worth trying alternatives if you can as a first port of call.

Okay, let's move on, I think it's time for less chat and more action, right? Let's get stuck in to producing something; there's no better time than now to get PostCSS installed and ready for use.

Preparing for exercises in this book

Before we do so, we just need to cover a couple of requirements. First, we need to set up a local web server. It's not critical, but gives a better effect. I personally use WAMP Server (for PC, from `http://www.wampserver.com/en`), otherwise, Mac users can try MAMP (`http://www.mamp.info/en`), or the cross-platform Apache web server (from `http://www.apachefriends.org`). In each case, default settings should be sufficient.

The second requirement is to set up a project area; assuming you have set up a WAMP as a local web server, go ahead and set up a folder called postcss in c:\wamp\www, as shown in this screenshot:

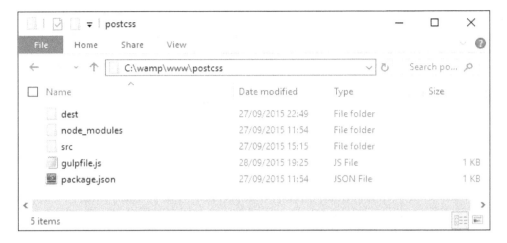

Right, with that out of the way, let's make a start on getting PostCSS installed!

Setting up a development environment

The first step on our journey is to get PostCSS installed — this runs from Node.js; we can use any one of several task runner plugins to install it. For the purpose of the exercises throughout this book, we will use Gulp; if you prefer, alternatives such as Grunt or Broccoli can be used.

When using Node.js, make sure you use the Node.js command prompt, and not node.exe; the exercises will not work when using the latter!

Let's make a start with installing Node and Gulp:

1. We first need to install Node.js; this is available at http://nodejs.org. Make sure you select the right version that is appropriate for your platform:

When installing, accept all defaults; this will be sufficient for the exercises throughout this book.

2. Next, bring up a Node.js command prompt, enter the following command, and press *Enter*:

    ```
    node -v
    ```

    The output shown is the version of Node that is installed; this is a quick check to ensure Node.js has indeed been installed correctly:

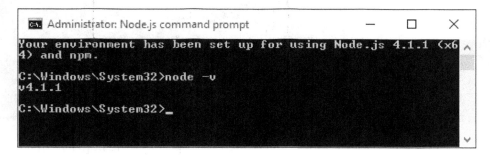

3. Now that Node is installed, we need to create a `package.json` file to store our dependencies for projects. Run this command at the command prompt, and press *Enter*:

    ```
    npm init
    ```

4. Node will prompt for information when creating the package.json file; enter the details as shown in the screenshot, or press *Enter* to accept the given default (shown in brackets, after each question):

```
npm                                                          —  □  ×

c:\wamp\www\postcss>npm init
This utility will walk you through creating a package.json file.
It only covers the most common items, and tries to guess sensible defaults.

See `npm help json` for definitive documentation on these fields
and exactly what they do.

Use `npm install <pkg> --save` afterwards to install a package and
save it as a dependency in the package.json file.

Press ^C at any time to quit.
name: (postcss)

version: (1.0.0)
description: Configuration file for PostCSS
entry point: (gulpfile.js)
test command:
git repository:
keywords:
author: Alex Libby
license: (ISC)
About to write to c:\wamp\www\postcss\package.json:

{
  "name": "postcss",
  "version": "1.0.0",
  "description": "Configuration file for PostCSS",
  "main": "gulpfile.js",
  "dependencies": {
    "cssnano": "^3.2.0",
    "autoprefixer": "^6.0.3",
    "gulp": "^3.9.0",
    "gulp-postcss": "^6.0.0",
    "gulp-rename": "^1.2.2",
    "gulp-sourcemaps": "^1.5.2"
  },
  "devDependencies": {},
  "scripts": {
    "test": "echo \"Error: no test specified\" && exit 1"
  },
  "author": "Alex Libby",
  "license": "ISC"
}

Is this ok? (yes)
```

We now have Node configured and an empty package.json file in place, so let's add our dependencies. We will start by adding Gulp first:

1. Revert back to the Node.js command prompt (or bring up a new one if you closed off the previous session).

2. Go ahead and change the working directory to c:\wamp\www\postcss.

3. At the command prompt, enter the following command, then press *Enter*. This installs Gulp globally and makes it available for use:

```
npm install --global gulp
```

4. Once done, we need to install Gulp for use in our project area — go ahead and run this command, which will add an entry to the `package.json` file we created earlier in step 3 and step 4:

```
npm install --save-dev gulp
```

Once completed, Gulp is now ready for use; we can go ahead and install PostCSS.

 A small point on the use of `--save-dev`: this installs any dependencies required to develop using a specific plugin; if we simply need the dependencies for *running* the plugin (in a production environment), then we can simply use `--save` instead.

Installing PostCSS

We're at the interesting stage now — installing PostCSS. PostCSS is available from `https://github.com/postcss/postcss`, and can be installed into Node using a Gulp plugin. Let's do that now:

1. We'll start by reverting back to the Node.js command prompt session we've just used (or a new one, if the previous one is closed).

2. At the prompt, go ahead and enter this command, then press *Enter*:

```
npm install --save-dev gulp-postcss
```

If all is well, we should see something akin to this screenshot:

```
Node.js command prompt                                    —    □    ×

c:\wamp\www\postcss>npm install --save-dev gulp-postcss
npm WARN package.json postcss@1.0.0 No repository field.
npm WARN package.json postcss@1.0.0 No README data
gulp-postcss@6.0.0 node_modules\gulp-postcss
  ─ vinyl-sourcemaps-apply@0.1.4 (source-map@0.1.43)
  ─ postcss@5.0.8 (source-map@0.5.1, js-base64@2.1.9, supports-color@3.1.1)
  └ gulp-util@3.0.6 (array-differ@1.0.0, object-assign@3.0.0, beeper@1.1.0, arra
y-uniq@1.0.2, lodash._reescape@3.0.0, lodash._reinterpolate@3.0.0, lodash._reeva
luate@3.0.0, replace-ext@0.0.1, minimist@1.2.0, vinyl@0.5.3, chalk@1.1.1, lodash
.template@3.6.2, through2@2.0.0, multipipe@0.1.2, dateformat@1.0.11)

c:\wamp\www\postcss>_
```

On its own, PostCSS doesn't do anything; to make it more useful, we are going to install three plugins. We will explore using plugins in greater detail later in the book, but for now, don't worry too much about what is happening:

1. Enter these commands one by one on the Node.js command prompt, pressing *Enter* after each one:

   ```
   npm install --save-dev autoprefixer
   ```

2. Let's check our `package.json` file; if all is well, we should see something akin to this screenshot:

```
C:\wamp\www\postcss\package.json - Sublime Text          —   □   ×

File  Edit  Selection  Find  View  Goto  Tools  Project  Preferences  Help

   package.json          ×

 1  {
 2      "name": "postcss",
 3      "version": "1.0.0",
 4      "description": "Configuration file for PostCSS",
 5      "main": "index.js",
 6      "scripts": {
 7          "test": "echo \"Error: no test specified\" && exit 1"
 8      },
 9      "author": "Alex Libby",
10      "license": "ISC",
11      "devDependencies": {
12          "autoprefixer": "^6.0.3",
13          "cssnano": "^3.2.0",
14          "gulp": "^3.9.0",
15          "gulp-postcss": "^6.0.0",
16          "gulp-sourcemaps": "^1.5.2"
17      }
18  }
19

Line 1, Column 1                                    Spaces: 2        JSON
```

> To make it easier to view JSON files in Sublime Text, try installing and activating a custom theme, such as MonokaiJSON Plus, available to install from `https://github.com/ColibriApps/MonokaiJsonPlus`.

PostCSS is now installed for use, but if we try to use it, we probably won't get very far, as it needs to be configured for use! Let's take a look at doing that now, by creating a simple example that will add vendor prefixes to some sample CSS rules, and automatically minify the results.

Creating a simple example using PostCSS

PostCSS is a fascinating tool; its modular architecture leaves it wide open to being used in a variety of different use-case scenarios, or even a mix of several! Throughout this book, we'll touch on different uses, before bringing them all together to create a processor that can both pre- and post-process files within the same workflow.

To give you a taste of how well it works, we're going to build a simple processor now; this will automatically add vendor prefixes and spit out minified versions during compilation.

Let's make a start, we've installed the relevant plugins, so let's go create our Gulp task file:

1. In a new file, add the following code, saving it as `gulpfile.js` at the root of our project area:

```
C:\wamp\www\postcss\gulpfile.js - Sublime Text

File  Edit  Selection  Find  View  Goto  Tools  Project  Preferences  Help

gulpfile.js                    ×

1   var gulp = require('gulp');
2   var postcss = require('gulp-postcss');
3   var autoprefixer = require('autoprefixer');
4
5   gulp.task('styles', function() {
6       return gulp.src('src/*.css')
7           .pipe(postcss([ autoprefixer ]))
8           .pipe(gulp.dest('dest/'));
9   });

Line 7, Column 41                    Tab Size: 4        JavaScript
```

2. In the project area, create a folder called `dest`; other folders will be created, but these will be done automatically during compilation.

3. In a new file, add the following code, saving it as `example.css` in the `src` folder of our project area:

```
body {
  display: flex;
  background: green;
}
```

4. Revert back to the Node.js command prompt, then at the command prompt, enter the following command and press *Enter*:

```
gulp styles
```

Gulp will now process the instructions in `gulpfile.js`:

5. Within a matter of seconds (almost instantaneously), we should see a compiled `example.css` appear in the `dest` folder of our project area.

6. We can prove PostCSS has done its job properly; go ahead and open up `example.css` in a text editor: if all is well, we should see this:

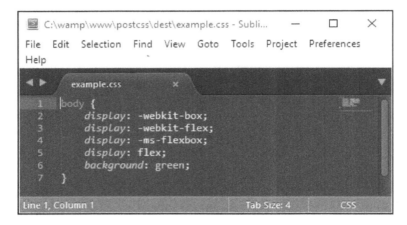

Perfect, we now have a working PostCSS installation; any time we need to add vendor prefixes, we can just fire up our compilation process, and away we go...

Adding source map support

Or do we? Ah, there is much more to PostCSS than simply adding vendor prefixes! Remember how I mentioned that PostCSS is often (incorrectly) labelled as a pre- or post-processor?

Well, there is much more we can do; one of the key benefits of PostCSS is being selective about how we process our code. We're not forced to rely on dependencies (such as Ruby for SASS); we can instead produce something that is very light and quick. In our previous example, we created a task called `styles`; we'll change this to use the task name `default`, which will allow us to run multiple tasks from one command. This means we can simply call `gulp`, instead of needing to supply the task name.

 All of our examples from this point onwards will use this convention by default.

Let's put this to the test and start to expand on our compilation process by adding source map support—we'll use the source map plugin for Gulp by Florian Reiterer, available from `https://github.com/floridoo/gulp-sourcemaps`:

1. We'll start, as always, by installing the plugin using Node—fire up a Node.js command prompt, then change to our project area.

2. Next, enter this at the command line and press *Enter*:

   ```
   npm install --save-dev gulp-sourcemaps
   ```

3. Open up the `gulp` file we created back in the *Creating a simple example using PostCSS* section, then add a reference to `gulp-sourcemaps` as a variable:

   ```
   var autoprefixer = require('autoprefixer');
   var sourcemaps = require('gulp-sourcemaps');
   ```

4. We then need to add the commands to create the source maps—in the same file, alter the code as shown:

   ```
   .pipe(postcss([ autoprefixer ]))
   .pipe(sourcemaps.init())
   .pipe(sourcemaps.write('maps/'))
   .pipe(gulp.dest('dest/'));
   ```

5. Save the results, then from the Node.js command prompt, run this command, and press *Enter*:

   ```
   gulp styles
   ```

6. If all is well, we should see a new source map appear in the `dest` folder, under a subfolder called `maps`.

   We're a step further in the right direction; we now have a map file for our style sheet in the maps folder, created automatically during the compilation process.

It's worth noting that we will make full use of this area—if you see any reference to `project area` throughout the book, this will be our given name for this folder.

But, we can do more: although we only have a small CSS file here, it's still important to compress it to save on unnecessary bandwidth usage. We can easily fix that using PostCSS—let's take a look at how, using the `cssnano` plugin.

Creating minified style sheets

A key part of producing style sheets is minifying the output; this should feature as standard in any developer's workflow. Minifying the results will cut down on bandwidth usage. In an age of broadband or cable use, this is less critical for smaller sites, but should not attract any less importance than for larger sites!

Thankfully, minifying files is a cinch to achieve when working with PostCSS. For this next exercise, we will use the `cssnano` and `gulp-rename` plugins, available from `http://cssnano.co/` and `https://github.com/hparra/gulp-rename`, respectively. Let's go ahead and get them installed:

1. We'll start by firing up a Node.js command prompt, then entering the following and pressing *Enter*:

   ```
   npm install --save-dev cssnano
   npm install --save-dev gulp-rename
   ```

   Don't close the session window, we will use it later in this exercise.

2. Switch to the `gulpfile.js` file we created earlier (it's stored at the root of our project folder), then add the following lines immediately after the last closing `})` on or around line 12:

   ```
   gulp.task('rename', ['styles'], function () {
     return gulp.src('dest/example.css')
       .pipe(postcss([ cssnano ]))
       .pipe(rename('example.min.css'))
       .pipe(gulp.dest("dest/"));
   });

   gulp.task('default', ['styles', 'rename']);
   ```

3. At the top of the file, we need to add two declarations, otherwise our code will fail; go ahead and add the following two lines, as highlighted:

   ```
   var sourcemaps = require('gulp-sourcemaps');
   ```

```
var rename = require('gulp-rename');
var cssnano = require('cssnano');
```

4. Any sharp-eyed readers may now spot a problem — in the last line, we have a reference to `styles`, yet nothing is shown in the code for this! To fix it, we need to change our code. In line 8, change the line as shown:

```
gulp.task('styles', function() {
```

5. Save the file, then switch back to the Node.js command prompt window and enter this command, followed by *Enter*:

```
gulp
```

6. Gulp will now compile:

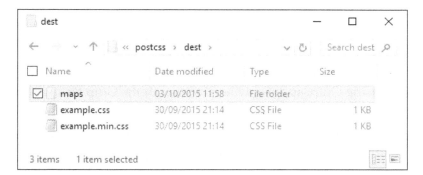

If all is well, we should see the compiled output appear in the `dest` folder of our project area:

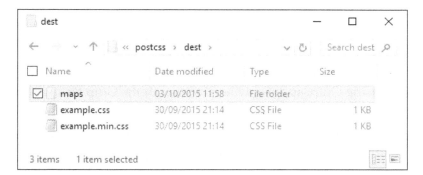

In our project area, we not only have the source map file created under maps, but now also have a minified style sheet, the latter created by renaming the output from `cssnano` (`cssnano` does not do this renaming natively, hence use of the `rename` plugin).

Unfortunately though, we still have one small issue — take a look at the contents of the maps folder: notice anything? Hopefully, you may spot that the source map file is there for the uncompressed version of our style sheet, but not the compressed one! Let's fix that now. To do so, we just need to use the rename task in our Gulp file, as shown:

```
.pipe(rename('example.min.css'))
.pipe(sourcemaps.init())
.pipe(sourcemaps.write('maps/'))
.pipe(gulp.dest("dest/"));
```

Try running Gulp now. If all is well we should see the source map appear for our minified style sheet:

Let's finish off our gulp file; the last stage is to add a watch facility, so that changes are compiled automatically as soon as files are modified.

Altering to compile automatically

Adding a watch facility is simple when using Gulp. It helps reduce the manual effort required when using Gulp, as we only need to fire off the Gulp task file once, and it will continue to apply the tasks each time files are changed.

Unlike other plugins, we don't need to install any plugins for this; simply add the highlighted lines from the following to the gulpfile.js file:

```
gulp.task('default', ['styles', 'rename', 'sourcemaps']);

var watcher = gulp.watch('src/*.css', ['default']);
watcher.on('change', function(event) {
  console.log('File ' + event.path + ' was ' + event.type + ',
    running tasks...');
});
```

We can see the results of the addition to our gulp task file, and how it all comes together, in this screenshot:

At this point, we can save the file then re-run the `gulp` command as before; this time it will automatically recompile any file that has changed, from within the `src` folder. In this instance, we've added an event handler to log an indication into the session so we can tell what is happening; we can easily modify this if needed.

We now have a basic working system; we will begin to add to this over the next few chapters, toward building up our own processor. There is one small thing we should cover though: it's not essential, but a useful tip for developing with PostCSS. I'm talking about linting your code, to ensure it is valid; let's dive in and get this set up for use.

Linting code using plugins

It goes without saying that linting code should be part of any developer's workflow. There are lots of different ways to achieve this, depending on the tools you use. The beauty of PostCSS is that we can easily add a suitable linting capability to our processor, using the `stylelint` plugin for PostCSS (available from `http://stylelint.io/`).

Why would we do this? Easy: we can get a single consistent result throughout. This becomes essential if you work as part of a team; instead as different team members using inconsistent settings, we can set up a central point for processing, to retain a consistent output. Moving the linting process to our central workflow means the server can do the grunt work for us, and provide a consistent result anytime for anyone running the process.

With this in mind, let's take a look at how we can set up our linting capability:

1. We start as always by installing our plugin. For this, fire up a Node.js command prompt, then change to the root of our project area.

2. At the command prompt, enter this command, followed by *Enter*:

   `npm install stylelint`

   If all is well, we should see this appear at the prompt:

3. Next up, we need to install a second plugin — there is a reporter function within `stylelint` that posts any messages to console (or in this case, screen). The plugin is `postcss-reporter`, and is available at `https://github.com/postcss/postcss-reporter`. We can install it thus:

4. With the plugins installed, we need to update our `gulp` file; add the following lines immediately below the last `var` line shown:

```
var cssnano = require('cssnano');
var stylelint = require('stylelint');
var reporter = require('postcss-reporter');
```

5. Immediately, below the rename task in the Gulp file, add this task — this takes care of linting our code, and flagging any errors on-screen:

```
gulp.task("lint-styles", function() {
  return gulp.src("src/*.css")
    .pipe(postcss([ stylelint({
      "rules": {
        "color-no-invalid-hex": 2,
        "declaration-colon-space-before": [2, "never"],
        "indentation": [2, 2],
        "number-leading-zero": [2, "always"]
      }
    }),
    reporter({
      clearMessages: true,
    })
  ]))
});
```

6. Open a copy of `example.css` from the root area of our project folder and change the `color` to `#fff1az`.

7. Back in the Node.js command prompt, enter this command and press *Enter*:

   `gulp`

8. Gulp will begin to process our code; if all is well, it should flag a warning:

It shouldn't take much effort to spot that `#fff1az` is clearly not a valid number! Stylelint has correctly identified it, using the highlighted rule from our configuration:

```
.pipe(postcss([ stylelint({
    "rules": {
      "color-no-invalid-hex": true,
      ...
    }
  })),
```

Let's explore how this plugin works for a moment — the great thing about it is that there are simply dozens of rules available (which you can see at `https://cdn.rawgit.com/stylelint/stylelint/1.0.0/docs/rules.md`). It works by concatenating together what is being checked (in this case, `color`) and the check being run against it (in our case, `-no-invalid-hex`, or checking for invalid hex numbers). We can apply any number of rules in our configuration object, to ensure that the output is consistent for all projects.

If you would like to get a feel for how the rules can be put together, then check out the user guide at `https://cdn.rawgit.com/stylelint/stylelint/1.0.0/docs/user-guide.md`, with more examples of rules available at `https://cdn.rawgit.com/stylelint/stylelint/1.0.0/docs/rules.md`.

Okay, let's move on: we will begin to look at compiling code in more detail from the next chapter, but for now, let's take a look at how PostCSS works in more detail, and how we can begin to make the move from our existing processor to PostCSS.

Exploring how PostCSS works

So far, we've covered the basics of setting up and using PostCSS. It's worth taking a moment to learn about how it works, to better understand how we can use it and develop our own plugins for the platform.

PostCSS is like me on a Saturday morning after a good night out: it does nothing! Yes, it's true, by itself, the application doesn't do anything at all; it's when we add plugins into the mix that it starts to become useful.

The key to PostCSS is treating it as an enabler, it is not meant as a direct replacement for your existing preprocessor, or even postprocessor, but to complement them. It works on the basis of parsing code, processing it with any assigned plugins, and rendering the results:

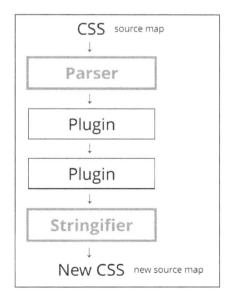

It works by parsing content into an **Abstract Syntax Tree** (or AST) with a series of nodes. Each node in the tree contains a symbolic representation of an element in your code. In other words, if you had a condition statement that pointed to three possible outcomes, then the AST would have a single node, with three branches representing the possible outcomes.

 For an example of an AST, take a look at http://jointjs.com/ demos/javascript-ast, which shows the breakdown of a simple arithmetic function using plain JavaScript.

Our AST is then sent through one or more plugins (we must always use one plugin, but can have many in our gulp file). It then converts the code to a long string, before processing it through any assigned plugins and spitting out the result in the form of valid CSS. We can use this as a basis for creating our own plugins, using the boilerplate code and API that are both available from the main PostCSS site on GitHub.

The trick to the plugin stage is in the mix of plugins we must use to satisfy our needs; the better ones should only perform one role. Any that perform multiple tasks are less ideal, as they are likely to contain excess functionality that we don't need in our projects.

Making the move from SASS

Assuming we decided to use PostCSS, there is almost always one question at the top of everyone's mind: how do we make the move?

In short, the key here is *not* to simply assume existing code can be put through the PostCSS process, as it will likely not work. Instead, we should take an iterative process, and begin to convert low-hanging fruit to using PostCSS. The process will of course require some work, but there are tips on how we can reduce the pain involved in making the switch to PostCSS.

The key to making the transfer is to work out what functionality needs to be processed, then to create the initial framework for a build process (for example, a Gulp or Grunt task file), then to gradually add in plugin support one by one, until you have a fully working compiler.

We can take this a step further, and use plugins that replicate SASS code format into PostCSS; an ideal plugin to start with is Autoprefixer, followed by plugins such as postcss-mixins or postcss-partial-import. We will explore using SASS as a basis for a custom syntax in *Chapter 11, Manipulating Custom Syntaxes*, where we will use these two plugins, and more, to help make the transition process easier and help remove the dependencies on preprocessors such as SASS or Less. Oh, and above all, being based on JavaScript makes it portable; what more could a developer ask for, I wonder?

 Many of the SASS format plugins for PostCSS now come in the PreCSS pack. We will explore using this in *Chapter 10, Building a Custom Preprocessor*.

Okay, on we go. Over the course of the next few chapters, we will take a look at different processor elements that are commonly used to create build processors, such as variables or mixins. We'll see how they might typically be written in processors such as SASS or Less, then work on converting our code to use PostCSS equivalents before processing to produce valid CSS. We will then finish up with pulling everything together to build your own custom processor for use in future projects.

Summary

Writing valid CSS is an art that has been present since the dawn of the Internet; this takes skill, patience, and time to produce and perfect any masterpiece. Processors such as SASS or Less have helped to make the process more efficient, but are not without their drawbacks; PostCSS allows for a more customized approach, but without the extra baggage. We've covered a few key points around PostCSS throughout this chapter, so let's take a moment to review what we've learned.

We began with a brief look at the art of processing, before introducing PostCSS as a tool. We then explored some of the benefits and drawbacks of using it, and how it can fit in seamlessly with your existing development workflow, with a little careful planning.

Next up, we covered the installation of PostCSS along with Gulp as the task runner/host process, before embarking on a simple demo to introduce how the compilation process works, and that with the right choice of plugins, we can take out some of the manual grunt work required to manage our code (pun intended!). With our code compiling, we then turned our attention to adding a watch facility, and automatic support for linting our code, to ensure we maintain consistent standards.

We then rounded out the chapter with a look at how PostCSS works, and understanding something of its architecture, so that we can begin to make the move from using plain CSS or an existing preprocessor, to using PostCSS.

Phew, we've certainly covered a lot; it's time to really get stuck in now, and start to use PostCSS in earnest. Over the next few chapters, we will explore a number of different concepts that are common to existing preprocessors, and explore how we can benefit from making the transition to using PostCSS. We have to start somewhere, so we'll kick off with using variables, functions, and mixins in the next chapter, and see how we can use some of the techniques from processors, but without the associated baggage!

Creating Variables and Mixins

2

A question: how often have you created components such as buttons, where you've used very similar colors multiple times throughout your code? It's a real pain to manually alter. Using a preprocessor such as SASS or Less makes it easier, but with the overhead of a full-sized library.

Can we do it differently? Absolutely; throughout the next few chapters, we'll explore different elements of PostCSS, before pulling it all together to produce a preprocessor application later in the book. We'll begin our journey with a look at using variables and mixins; we'll explore the basics of creating them first, before transitioning to support using PostCSS. In this chapter, we'll cover the following topics:

- An overview of creating variables and mixins using existing preprocessors
- Transitioning to using PostCSS equivalents
- Adding mixin support to PostCSS
- Examining the differences between standard preprocessors and PostCSS

Let's get cracking!

Introducing variables and mixins

So far, we've covered the basics of installing and configuring PostCSS—although there are a few steps involved, it's an easy process to get started with using the processor. To really get to know it though, there is no substitute for using it in anger; it's amazing how much you can automate, with just a little care and planning!

Let's put that to the test and use it to create a couple of simple examples using variables, functions, and mixins. We'll start with creating the original version using SASS, before converting it to use PostCSS plugins. The demos do assume a level of prior knowledge around using SASS, so if you are at all unfamiliar, then you may like to refer to my book, *SASS Essentials*, available from Packt Publishing.

A word of note: we will make good use of the project folders we created back in *Chapter 1, Introducing PostCSS*, where `src` will be our in-tray, and `dest` will contain the compiled code. Make sure you have this open in a window somewhere on your desktop!

Okay, the first step in this process is to get SASS installed, so let's take a look at that now.

Setting up SASS

Setting up SASS is really easy when using Gulp; we can use the same format of command to install it as we do for other plugins. The source code for the plugin is available at `https://github.com/dlmanning/gulp-sass`; it's a lightweight frontend for `node-sass`, which in turn is a Node binding for the C+ library, `libsass`.

Let's dive in and take a look at getting it installed:

1. We start, as usual, with Node. Fire up a Node.js command prompt session, then change to the working directory.

2. At the command prompt, enter the following, then press *Enter*:

    ```
    npm install --save-dev gulp-sass
    ```

3. If all is well, we should see something akin to this screenshot:

```
Node.js command prompt                          —    □    ×

C:\wamp\www\postcss>npm install --save-dev gulp-sass
npm WARN package.json postcss@1.0.0 No repository field.
npm WARN package.json postcss@1.0.0 No README data

> spawn-sync@1.0.13 postinstall C:\wamp\www\postcss\node_modules\gulp-sass\node_
modules\node-sass\node_modules\cross-spawn\node_modules\spawn-sync
> node postinstall


> node-sass@3.3.3 install C:\wamp\www\postcss\node_modules\gulp-sass\node_module
s\node-sass
> node scripts/install.js

Binary downloaded and installed at C:\wamp\www\postcss\node_modules\gulp-sass\no
de_modules\node-sass\vendor\win32-x64-46\binding.node

> node-sass@3.3.3 postinstall C:\wamp\www\postcss\node_modules\gulp-sass\node_mo
dules\node-sass
```

Before we continue, though, I would recommend clearing out or saving the contents of the `dest` folder elsewhere for safe keeping, after each exercise:

1. Next up, open a copy of `gulpfile.js` in Sublime Text; we need to make a number of changes, beginning with adding a reference to the `gulp-sass` plugin (as highlighted):

```
var reporter = require('postcss-reporter');
var sass = require('gulp-sass');
```

SASS will, by default, produce code in unminified format; the addition of
{outputStyle: 'compressed'} in the task will automatically compress the
output code. This makes this line redundant, so go ahead and remove it:

```
var cssnano = require('cssnano');
```

2. We also need to remove the reference to cssnano on or around line 19, so go
ahead and remove this line:

```
.pipe(postcss([ cssnano ]))
```

3. On or around line 10, change the name of the styles task to autoprefixer
and the dependency name to lint-styles:

```
gulp.task('autoprefixer', ['lint-styles'], function() {
return gulp.src('src/*.css')
```

Then remove these two lines:

```
.pipe(sourcemaps.init())
.pipe(sourcemaps.write('maps/'))
```

4. In the rename task, modify the rename task to match this:

```
gulp.task('rename', ['lint-styles'], function () {
  return gulp.src('dest/*.css')
    .pipe(rename('style.min.css'))
    .pipe(sourcemaps.init())
    .pipe(sourcemaps.write('maps/'))
    .pipe(gulp.dest("dest/"));
});
```

5. On or around line 25, we need to add in the lint-styles task — go ahead
and add in this block of code, which will check our styles for consistency:

```
gulp.task("lint-styles", ['sass'], function() {
  return gulp.src("src/*.css")
    .pipe(postcss([ stylelint({
      "rules": {
        "color-no-invalid-hex": 2,
        "declaration-colon-space-before": [2, "never"],
        "indentation": [2, 2],
        "number-leading-zero": [2, "always"]
      }
    }),
    reporter({
      clearMessages: true,
    })
  ]))
});
```

6. We're almost done. Add in the next task; this tells Gulp about how we should compile any SASS files presented to the task runner:

```
gulp.task('sass', function () {
  gulp.src('src/*.scss')
    .pipe(sass({outputStyle: 'compressed'}).on('error',
      sass.logError))
    .pipe(gulp.dest('src/'));
});
```

7. We need to make a couple more changes. The key task that fires off a call to each of the sub tasks needs to be updated, to reflect the changes to our tasks:

```
gulp.task('default', ['sass', 'lint-styles',
  'autoprefixer', 'rename']);
```

8. Our last change is to alter the watch facility to check for SASS files, and not pure CSS; go ahead and change the configuration object as shown:

```
var watcher = gulp.watch('src/*.scss', ['default']);
```

At this point, we have set up our processor to compile SASS files to valid CSS. We can prove this by compiling any SASS file. If all is well, our processor will produce valid style sheets and accompanying source map files automatically. Let's put this to the test as part of our next exercise, where we create an intriguing hover effect for images.

Creating a hover effect example

If you've seen any of my previous books, then you will see I have a thing about flowers, and in particular orchids; indeed, the cover on my first book was that of a phalaenopsis, or moth orchid! We'll use a couple of images of orchids as the basis for our next demo, as shown in the screenshot over the page, where it shows our desired effect in motion for the top image.

 If you prefer using Less, then please skip to the end of this demo for an example using Less CSS.

For this demo, we will need a copy of the tutorial1A folder from the code download that accompanies this book; make sure you dig that out before continuing:

1. Open up a copy of style.scss from the src folder within tutorial1A; let's take a look at its contents.

2. At the top of the file, we have a small handful of variables. These define some of the colors used within the code, and set the `$fullsize` variable to 100%:

```
1   $dark-grayish-green: #868a7b;
2   $very-dark-gray: #333333;
3   $white: #fff;
4
5   $demo-background: $dark-grayish-green;
6   $infobox-background: $very-dark-gray;
7
8   $fullsize: 100%;
```

The sharp-eyed among you will spot that not all colors have been given a value; the reason for this will become clearer later in this chapter.

3. Next up comes an example of a simple mixin, which converts pixel values to their rem unit equivalents, using `16px` as the base equivalent for `1rem` unit:

```
10  @mixin font-size($size, $base: 16) {
11    font-size: $size * 1px; // fallback for old browsers
12    font-size: ($size / $base) * 1rem;
13  }
```

4. To complete the exercise, we need to download a font. The demo uses the Source Sans Pro font available at `http://www.fontsquirrel.com/fonts/source-sans-pro`. Go ahead and download it; you will need to use the **Generator** option available from the black menu to produce a version that can be used online (it creates the CSS we've used in our demo).

5. At this point, go ahead and drop a copy of the `style.scss` file from the `tutorial1A` folder into the `src` folder in our project area.

6. We also need the `img` folder and the `index.html` file — go ahead and copy both across to the root of our project area.

7. Fire up a Node.js command prompt window, then enter this at the prompt and press *Enter*:

`gulp`

8. If all is well, we should see compressed CSS files and source maps appear in the `dest` folder in our project area — copy the `maps` folder and `style.min.css` into the `css` folder of `tutorial1A`.

9. Go ahead and preview the results in a browser. If all is well, we should see two orchid images appear on screen; if you hover over either one, you will see it fly to the left or right, to reveal an information box with information about the orchid:

Interesting effect, huh? It's a simple animation that uses `scale()` to shrink the image to `0.5` (or 50%) of its size and slides it to the right, before sliding in the `infobox` immediately behind it. Take the mouse off the image and the reverse happens—it's the sample principle for the second image—but in reverse; the code sets an `ltr` and `rtl` class to determine which direction the image should move in the demo.

Using Less CSS as an alternative

A copy of this demo using the equivalent code from the Less CSS pre-processor is available in the code download that accompanies this book. It's in the `Tutorial1B` folder if your preference is to use the Less CSS pre-processor; you will need to install the `gulp-less` plugin from `https://github.com/plus3network/gulp-less`, using NodeJS (in the same manner as other plugins that we've installed). An updated copy of the Gulp task file is also included in this folder, along with completed versions of the CSS code.

Transitioning to using PostCSS

Up until now, we've used SASS to build our demo; granted, it's not a particularly complex one, but as I always say, we must start somewhere!

Our demo is a perfect example of how we can introduce PostCSS to provide replacements for the SASS variables and mixins we've used — for this, we will avail ourselves of three plugins, namely `postcss-variables`, `postcss-mixins`, and `postcss-calc`. The first two should be self-explanatory; the third is required in the replacement font mixin that we've used in our code.

Okay, enough chit-chat, let's get stuck in and begin to alter our code; we'll start with adding variable support.

Adding variable support to PostCSS

The beauty of PostCSS plugins is that most (if not all) can be installed using the same method as PostCSS itself, we can use the package manager of Node.js to handle the process.

We'll start with `postcss-css-variables`, which we will use to handle variable support; the source for this plugin is available from `https://github.com/MadLittleMods/postcss-css-variables`. Let's get it installed:

1. Fire up a NodeJS command prompt, then change the working directory to our project area.
2. At the command prompt, enter the following command, then press *Enter*:
   ```
   npm install --save-dev postcss-css-variables
   ```

3. If all is well, we should see the results of the installation appear, as shown in this screenshot:

At this point, Node will have also added an entry to the package.json file for the new plugin. Perfect — we can now put it to good use and switch to using the plugin in place of using SASS. Let's take a look at how to achieve this, as part of the upcoming exercise.

Updating our hover effect demo

If we're altering code to use PostCSS for the first time, it naturally makes sense to start with something simple; incorporating variables and mixins into our code is the perfect place to begin.

For this next exercise, we're going to create a handful of variables to store some values, then add a mixin to handle styles for the fonts used in the demo. Let's make a start:

1. We'll start by opening up a copy of gulpfile.js from the root of our project area — we first need to make some changes to accommodate using the new plugin.

2. In gulpfile.js, add this line immediately below the first block of var statements — this should be on or around line 9:

```
var cssvariables = require('postcss-css-variables');
```

3. We now need to make some changes to our gulp task file — we'll start with the simplest, which is to remove the var reference to SASS, as we will no longer need it:

```
var sass = require('gulp-sass');
```

Now that we have a reference to the postcss-css-variables plugin, we need to make use of it in our tasks. Go ahead and amend the highlighted lines of code in the autoprefixer task, as indicated; this also removes the dependency on the lint-styles task, as this is no longer needed:

```
gulp.task('autoprefixer', function() {
  return gulp.src('src/*.css')
  .pipe(postcss([ autoprefixer, cssnano,
    cssvariables(/* options */) ]))
  .pipe(gulp.dest('dest/'));
```

4. Note that we've also reinstated the `cssnano` command — you will also need to add this line in as a variable declaration, as indicated:

```
var rename = require('gulp-rename');
var cssnano = require('cssnano');
```

5. A little further down, on or around line 25, change the code as highlighted, as we will no longer use SASS to compile our code; we can tweak the order in which each task is run:

```
gulp.task("lint-styles", ['autoprefixer'], function() {
```

6. Next up, we can remove the SASS task in its entirety:

```
gulp.task('sass', function () {
  gulp.src('src/*.scss')
  .pipe(sass({outputStyle: 'compressed'})
    .on('error', sass.logError))
    .pipe(gulp.dest('src/'));
});
```

7. Toward the end of the file, go ahead and alter the default task as indicated — we don't need to call the SASS task, as it has now been removed:

```
gulp.task('default', ['lint-styles',
  'autoprefixer', 'rename']);
```

8. Alter the `gulp.watch` command to look for plain CSS files in the `src` folder — we're not using SASS, so the reference to `scss` format files is now invalid and needs to be changed:

```
var watcher = gulp.watch('src/*.css'; ['default']);
watcher.on('change', function(event) {
```

At this point, if all is well, we should have a working gulp task file that we can now use to compile our code. Let's go ahead and start to convert the code in our orchid demo, to use PostCSS:

9. We'll start by saving a copy of the `Tutorial2` folder from the code download that accompanies this book, locally, to within the project area we created under `c:\wamp\www`, back in *Chapter 1, Introducing PostCSS*.

10. Open up a copy of `style.css` from within the `src` folder of the `Tutorial2` folder. At the top of the file, remove lines 1 to 14 (the variables and mixin code), so that the file starts with the `font-face` declaration.

11. In its place, add the following lines — these are the replacement variable assignments:

```
:root {
  --dark-grayish-green: #868a7b;
  --very-dark-gray: #333333;
  --white: #fff;

  --fullsize: 100%;
}
```

12. Further down, look for the `html, body {` declaration, and alter it as indicated — note the syntax used for the `var` statements; this is not the same as standard SASS. We've changed it to the format supported by the `postcss-css-variables` plugin:

```
html, body {
  width: var(--fullsize);
  padding: 0;
  margin: 0;
  height: var(--fullsize);
  min-width: var(--fullsize);
  max-width: var(--fullsize);
  overflow: hidden;
  background: var(--dark-grayish-green);
}
```

13. We added the `--fullsize` variable at the top of our style sheet — let's make use of it now and update the `img` rule accordingly:

```
img {
  width: var(--fullsize);
  height: var(--fullsize);
}
```

14. The final change we will make is to the `.info` class — go ahead and alter the background attribute as indicated:

```
/* ------ Hover Effect Styles ------ */
.info {
  background: var(--very-dark-gray);
}
```

Our code changes are complete, so go ahead and save the file — once done, fire up a NodeJS command prompt, and change to the project working area.

15. Save the file as `styles.css` into the `src` folder of our project area.

16. Switch to the NodeJS command prompt, then enter the usual command at the prompt, and press *Enter*:

```
gulp
```

17. Copy the compiled code back to the `css` folder within `Tutorial2`. If all is well, when we preview the results in a browser, we should see our demo continue to work as shown at the start of the first part of this exercise.

Phew, there were a fair few steps there! There is a copy of the completed stylesheets, both prior to and post compilation, available in the code download that accompanies this book: they can be found in the `css | completed` folder. You will need to rename the two style sheet files to just `style.css` for them to work correctly.

If you want to see the effects of compiling variables, without committing changes to code, then have a look at the playground offered with this plugin, at `https://madlittlemods.github.io/postcss-css-variables/playground/`. It's a great way to get accustomed to using the `postcss-css-variables` plugin, before diving in and editing production code.

Okay, let's change tack; we've covered a number of key concepts in our demo, so let's take a moment to let the proverbial dust settle, and explore what we've learned through the demo.

Taking it a step further

Over the last few pages, we've created a simple demo, which shows off animated information boxes for a couple of orchid images. There's nothing outrageous or complex about what we've done, but nevertheless, it serves to illustrate some key points about using this plugin, and PostCSS in general:

- Although we used SASS to precompile our CSS code prior to conversion, we could easily have used another pre-processor, such as Less CSS or Stylus. The key here is to work as much as possible within the confines of a task runner such as Gulp, so that we don't need to introduce another technology into the mix.

- It is essential to note that although converting the code *looks* straightforward, the plugin does not compile in the same manner as pre-processors such as SASS would compile. It makes a direct translation from SASS to Less CSS difficult for anything more than simple code.

- In this example, the key to understanding how it works is to follow the CSS Custom Properties Module Level 1 document from the W3C, which is available at `https://drafts.csswg.org/css-variables/`. The trick here is to be aware of CSS specificity, or which element takes precedence over others; in this respect, PostCSS does not simply replace variables with values, but compiles code based on calculating CSS specificity. When using PostCSS, it is likely you will see the `:root` pseudo-element being used frequently — it's worth getting acquainted with how it works!

> For an explanation of how CSS specificity works, please refer to `http://vanseodesign.com/css/css-specificity-inheritance-cascade/`. If needed, we can consider using a plugin to increase specificity — check out the `postcss-increase-specificity` plugin at `https://github.com/MadLittleMods/postcss-increase-specificity`.

- The modular nature of PostCSS means that we can be selective about the plugins we use — in this instance we used the `postcss-css-variables` plugin, which gives more flexibility than others such as `postcss-custom-properties`. As an alternative, we might consider separating our variables into a separate document, and import them in using the `postcss-constants` plugin (which is available at `https://github.com/macropodhq/postcss-constants`).

- If we use the `postcss-css-variables` plugin, we can either store the values in the code itself, or hive them off into the gulp task file; an example of the latter would look like this:

```
var postcss = require('postcss');
var cssvariables = require('postcss-css-variables');

postcss([
  cssvariables({
    variables: {
      '-foo-var': { '100px', isImportant: true },
      '--other-var': { value: '#00CC00' },
      '--important-var': { value: '#ffCC00' }
    }
  })
])
.process(css, opts);
```

In short, we create a reference to each variable within the configuration object for `cssvariables`, as the alias for the `postcss-css-variables` plugin.

Creating an object map using this approach can have mixed benefits. For some, it reduces issues around **separation of concerns**, where we can keep more PostCSS code within the task file, and less within our style sheet. This can make for a task file that is harder to read; it's not a good route to take if you have lots of variables to define. In this instance, we would be better off exporting them to an import file and referencing them at compilation.

If there is one important message at this point, it can be that of flexibility — the modular nature of PostCSS means that we can be free to pick and choose how we proceed; it really is a case of weighing up the pros and cons of using a plugin, and making a decision as to whether this best fits our needs, or if we need to look for an alternative solution.

Setting the order of plugins

At this point, there is a key part of PostCSS we need to cover: the order we use when calling plugins in our task runner file. This might seem a little odd, but there are two good reasons for considering this when developing with PostCSS:

- The first reason is simple — it's about making sure that we maintain a logical order of when tasks are completed at compilation.

- The second is a little more obscure, and will come with experience — some plugins need to be defined in the task file in a certain order, for them to work correctly.

Let's explore what this means:

If we take a look at the gulp task file that we've slowly been building up, you will notice a key difference between lines 13 and 19; and no, it's not the task name, before you ask! The difference is the `['lint-styles']` constraint — this forces Gulp not to run this task until its predecessor has completed:

```
13   gulp.task('autoprefixer', function() {
14       return gulp.src('src/*.css')
15       .pipe(postcss([ autoprefixer, cssvariables(/* options */),
16       .pipe(gulp.dest('dest/'));
17   });
18
19   gulp.task('rename', ['lint-styles'], function () {
20       return gulp.src('dest/*.css')
```

I know this might sound like common sense, and that I am only preaching what you may already know, but getting the order that plugins are called in PostCSS is critical to the successful compilation of your file.

As an example, when researching for this book, I frequently found that either my source map was only being produced for an uncompressed version of my style sheet, or that the minified style sheet wasn't being created at the right point. Simple issues, but tweaking the order can have a serious impact on what happens and when!

Continuing with the theme of order, it is likely you may see notes akin to this when browsing the source site of a PostCSS plugin:

PostCSS plugin for mixins.

Note, that you must set this plugin before postcss-simple-vars and postcss-nested.

This underlines why getting the order of your plugins is essential for an effective result: not only will tasks be completed in the right order and produce the expected results, but some plugins won't even work. This should not necessarily be taken as being a fault; there will be a valid reason that means plugin X must come before plugin Y. The key thing here is that we take any constraints into consideration. It is worth checking, as others may add patch support to remove constraints, or fix it through forking their own version of the plugin.

Okay, time to change focus and take a look at some different functionality: mixins. For the uninitiated, this is a key function frequently used in preprocessors such as SASS, where we can *mix-in* (yes, pun intended!) blocks of code.

The idea here being that we can create anything, from a simple few lines to a complex, dynamic code excerpt that PostCSS will compile into our code and use to produce valid CSS. Let's dive in and take a closer look.

Creating mixins with PostCSS

Our orchid demo so far uses a number of variables to define values in our code. While this works well, it is somewhat limiting; after all, creating lots of variables to handle different values is an expensive use of resources!

A smarter approach is using mixins; this works well when we can group several statements together as a single definition, then clone this definition into multiple rule sets. Users of pre-processors will of course recognize this functionality; the PostCSS team have created a plugin to offer similar functionality within PostCSS.

The plugin source is available from `https://github.com/postcss/postcss-mixins`, and can be installed via Node, using the same method we've covered throughout this chapter. We will also make use of the `postcss-calc` plugin (from `https://github.com/postcss/postcss-calc`) to create a simple mixin that handles pixel fall-back for rem values in our code. Let's dive in and see how it works in action:

1. We'll start—as always—by installing the `postcss-mixins` plugin; for this, fire up a NodeJS command prompt, then change the working folder to our project area.

2. At the prompt, enter each command separately, pressing *Enter* after each:

   ```
   npm install --save-dev postcss-mixins
   npm install --save-dev postcss-calc
   ```

3. If all is well, we should see the results of the output on-screen, as shown in this screenshot:

Updating our hover effect demo

At this point we will have support for mixins within PostCSS installed. Let's make use of them by updating our gulp task file and style sheet. We'll begin with the gulp task file:

1. Let's start by opening a copy of `gulpfile.js` from our project area, then adding the following lines immediately below the block of `var` declarations (on or around line 10):

   ```
   var cssmixins = require('postcss-mixins');
   var calc = require('postcss-calc');
   ```

2. Next, go ahead and alter this line, from within the `autoprefixer` task:

   ```
   .pipe(postcss([ autoprefixer, cssvariables(/* options */),
     cssmixins(/* options */), calc(/*options*/) ]))
   ```

3. Save the file. We now need a copy of the demo files from the code download that accompanies this book — go ahead and save a copy of `Tutorial3` to within our project area.

4. Open a copy of `style.css` from within the `src` folder, then add this block of code immediately after the variable declarations declared in the `--root` rule:

```
@define-mixin fontstyle $size, $color {
   font-size: $(size)px;
   font-size: calc($size/16)rem;
   color: $color;
}
```

5. With the mixin in place, we now need to adjust our code to make use of the mixin; this requires a few changes. The first change is in the `h3` rule declaration:

```
h3 {
   @mixin fontstyle 32, #fff;
   text-transform: uppercase;
```

6. A little further down, go ahead and change the first two lines of the `.info h3` rule, as indicated:

```
.info h3 {
   @mixin fontstyle 20, #fff;
```

7. The third and final change is in the rule for `.info p`. Change it as shown:

```
.info p {
   @mixin fontstyle 12, #bbb;
   padding: 50px 5px;
```

8. Save the file, then copy it to the `src` folder in our project area.

9. Fire up a NodeJS command prompt, then switch to the project area, enter the usual command at the prompt, and press *Enter*:

```
gulp
```

 You may see some option messages from stylelint: these can be safely ignored for now, but we will explore how to optimize this later in the book.

10. Copy the compiled code back to the `src` folder within `Tutorial3`. If all is well, when we preview the results in a browser, we should see our demo continue to work as shown at the start of the first part of this exercise.

Although our demo won't appear any different, there will be a noticeable difference in the code—a quick peek using a DOM inspector such as Firebug shows the use of `rem` values:

```
element {
}
h3    {
✓   font-size: 2rem;
✓   color:    #FFF;
✓   text-transform: uppercase;
✓   letter-spacing: 2px;
✓   width: 232px;
✓   margin-left: auto;
✓   margin-right: auto;
✓   margin-bottom: -20px;
}
```

The use of mixins does raise some important points. Indeed, one might be forgiven for thinking they simply replicate functionality from SASS. The plugin we've used does not follow the same format, even if the principles are the same; let's pause for a moment and take a look at how these stack up against standard processors.

Comparing PostCSS to standard processors

The use of mixins is a great way to automatically insert pre-defined blocks of code, either static or dynamic, into our stylesheet, at the compilation phase.

The key thing to note is that, although the end result may be similar, the similarity is just in name; the mixin plugin we've used was not designed to replicate existing functionality available within SASS. Instead, this plugin exposes the power of JavaScript within PostCSS, and should be used to define function mixins, as a replacement for if or while statements that are not available within PostCSS.

This is particularly true if we need to change any property names within the mixin; an example of this would be when referencing multiple images that each need similar style classes to be applied:

```
require('postcss-mixins')({
  mixins: {
    icons: function (mixin, dir) {
      fs.readdirSync('/images/' + dir).forEach(function (file) {
        var icon = file.replace(/\.svg$/, '');
        var rule = postcss.rule('.icon.icon-' + icon);
        rule.append({
```

```
                prop:   'background',
                value:  'url(' + dir + '/' + file + ')'
            });
            mixin.replaceWith(rule);
        });
    }
  }
});
```

If we were to call this mixin with `@mixin icons signin;` from our code, we would
see this as a result:

```
.icon.icon-back { background: url(signin/back.svg) }
.icon.icon-secret { background: url(signin/secret.svg) }
```

This does pose an interesting question: where should the cut-off point between using
JavaScript in our task file be, in comparison to our CSS? Taking this approach does
mean that we have the benefit of using standard JavaScript, but at the expense of
simplicity!

This is one of the decisions you will need to make as a developer. PostCSS's flexibility
means that not only do we need to choose the right plugin, but that the order they
are all called in can also have an effect on the outcome of our code. In this instance,
an alternative plugin — `postcss-simple-vars` — shares the same syntax as `postcss-
mixins`, but does not support changing of property names.

 We can also consider using the `postcss-nested` plugin if our mixins
are stored within nested statements; this is something we will cover in
the next chapter.

But, to bring it back to our example: we used the classic mixin for providing pixel
fall-back when using older versions of IE.

We could have used an alternative plugin here, in the form of `postcss-simple-
mixins` (available from `https://www.npmjs.com/package/postcss-simple-
mixin`). This is designed to provide simple support for mixins, and doesn't have
the baggage associated with `postcss-mixins`.

 A word of note though: the `postcss-simple-mixins` plugin has
been deprecated, although it is still available for use. It does not
support nesting or the use of arguments.

The key consideration, though, will depend on what you plan to achieve within your
code; choosing the right plugin will reduce the inclusion of redundant functionality
and help keep our custom processor as lean as possible.

There is another reason why choosing plugins is critical: instead of using a mixin to just support older versions of IE, we can use the `postcss-pxtorem` plugin to generate `rem` values during compilation. After all, although most browsers have supported `rem` units for some time, there is always one that is late to the party:

IE	Edge	Firefox	Chrome	Safari	Opera	iOS Safari	Opera Mini	Android Browser	Chrome for Android
								4.1	
8		38	31					4.3	
9		39	43					4.4	
10		40	44	8		8.4		4.4.4	
11	12	41	45	9	32	9	8	44	45
	13	42	46		33				
		43	47		34				
		44	48						

Screenshot taken from the CanIUse site, at `http://www.caniuse.com`

Switching to using this plugin has the added benefit of simplifying our code, as the server can handle the grunt work of replacing pixel values with the equivalent `rem` units. The grunt work can be shifted to a central location, so that anyone using it will receive consistent results.

It's important to also note that the cross over between mixins and functions also exists within PostCSS. We will explore using functions more in *Chapter 5, Managing Colors, Images, and Fonts*, when we learn how PostCSS can be used to make our lives easier when working with colors or media.

Okay, onwards we go. Time to switch topics completely, and take a look at another key part of PostCSS: creating loops. Anyone familiar with SASS or Less will be aware of how mundane it can get when applying very similar styles to identical objects; a perfect example are the classic social media icons that frequently grace posts on a page. PostCSS has a plugin that allows us to mimic this functionality, so let's explore how to use it in action.

Looping content with PostCSS

A question: how often have you come across instances where you have a number of very similar images that share styles, but at the same time need to have individual styles applied? Sound familiar?

I am of course talking about instances such as list items, grid layouts, and the classic social media icons we see littered all over the Internet. We can of course simply write rules to cover each image, but as I am sure you will agree, it's not the smartest approach! Instead, we can use the power of the `@each` statement to iterate through each item and apply each style using string interpolation.

The `@each` plugin, by Alexander Madyankin, is one of two ways to incorporate a facility to loop through content; the source for this plugin is available from `https://github.com/outpunk/postcss-each`. The other plugin, postcss-for (available from `https://github.com/antyakushev/postcss-for`), takes a different approach—the difference between the two is that the former works on objects, while the latter must use a range of numbers to apply styles.

If we take the second plugin for a moment, we have to loop through a consecutive range of numbers in order to produce our result. So, something akin to this:

```
@for $x from 1 to 3 {
  .grid-$x { width: $(x)px; }
}
```

…would produce this, when compiled:

```
.grid-1 {
  width: 1px
}
.grid-2 {
  width: 2px
}
.grid-3 {
  width: 3px
}
```

Seems pretty straightforward, right? Here comes the rub, though: unlike SASS, we can't use variables to define that range by default; this plugin must be defined **before any instance of** `postcss-nested` and `postcss-simple-vars` plugins. In PostCSS, we iterate through **all** of the values inclusively (that is, one to three in our example), which is not the same as in SASS.

It's in cases like this that we must decide between using this plugin on its own, or with `postcss-custom-properties` and `postcss-for-variables`. This is why it is key to fully understand what you need to achieve, and the capabilities of plugins available, so that we can choose the most effective combination to suit our needs. The great thing about PostCSS is its flexibility, speed, and modular design; this modularity and flexibility can also be seen as its Achilles heel, as tweaking the choice and order of plugins can have a real impact on our code!

 We can of course change completely, and use a separate fork of the postcss-for plugin, available from `https://github.com/xori/postcss-for`. This caters for dollar variables.

Let's put some of this into practice. Before we get stuck in to nesting with PostCSS in the next chapter, we'll round out this one with a simple demo that uses a group of social media icons and PostCSS to set up styling automatically for us.

Iterating through @each statements

Staying with the looping theme, but on a different tack, in place of using the `for` statement, we can achieve similar effects with `@each`, but only if the target is an element on the page.

I am of course talking about elements such as buttons or menu items; these elements will share the same styling, but require unique IDs to allow us to interact with them. It goes without saying that we could simply create a shared base class and add multiple classes for each element…

But we can do better than that: most preprocessors have in-built functionality that allows us to iterate through elements and apply CSS styling to each element. Thankfully, PostCSS is no different; we can achieve the same result using the postcss-each plugin, available from `https://github.com/outpunk/postcss-each`. It's a cinch to install, and we can use it to add elements such as social media icons to the foot of a page, and style them. I feel a demo coming on, so let's dive in and take a look:

1. We'll start with installing the plugin, so go ahead and fire up a NodeJS command prompt, and change the working directory to our project area.

2. At the prompt, enter this command to install the `postcss-each` plugin, then press *Enter*:

```
npm install --save-dev postcss-each
```

3. If all is well, we should see the customary confirmation that the plugin is installed:

```
Command Prompt                                    —    □    ×
Microsoft Windows [Version 10.0.10240]
(c) 2015 Microsoft Corporation. All rights reserved.

C:\Users\alex>cd \wamp\www\postcss

C:\wamp\www\postcss>npm install --save-dev postcss-each
npm WARN package.json postcss@1.0.0 No repository field.
npm WARN package.json postcss@1.0.0 No README data
postcss-each@0.7.0 node_modules\postcss-each
├── postcss-simple-vars@1.0.1
└── postcss@5.0.9 (js-base64@2.1.9, source-map@0.5.1, supports-color@3.1.1)

C:\wamp\www\postcss>_
```

With the plugin now in place, let's move on and update our gulp file:

1. We need to make three changes to our gulp file, so go ahead and open a copy from the project area in your usual text editor.

2. First, go ahead and remove lines 9 to 11; they contain the variable declarations for the `postcss-css-variables` and `postcss-mixins` plugins.

3. On or around what is now line 8, we should see the variable declaration for `postcss-calc`. Immediately, below, add the following line:

```
var eachloop = require('postcss-each');
```

4. In the main `autoprefixer` task, we need to alter the `postcss` call; remove this from line 13:

```
cssvariables(/* options */), cssmixins(/* options */),
   calc(/*options*/),
```

We should be left with this (changes have been highlighted):

```
.pipe(postcss([ autoprefixer, cssnano(),
   foreach(/*options*/) ]))
```

At this point, we can save the file. It is now ready for us to process the CSS required for our next demo. For this next exercise, we will need to avail ourselves of some suitable social media icons. I've used the ones by Nathan Brown, available at `http://wegraphics.net/downloads/free-stained-and-faded-social-media-icons/`. We'll use the Twitter, LinkedIn, and YouTube images.

Let's make a start:

1. We'll start with a look at the SASS version of this demo. It's a simple example, but illustrates perfectly how we can use the @each function to iterate through each image and apply the appropriate style:

```
$social: twitter, linkedin, youtube;

.social-icon {
  // shared information here
  background: 50% no-repeat;
  background-size: 100%;
  float: left;
  height: 50px;
  width: 50px;

  // unique information loops here
  @each $network in $social {
    &.#{$network} {
      background-image: url("../img/#{$network}.png");
    }
  }
}
```

2. To compile the code, go ahead and copy the Tutorial4 folder to our project area.

3. Replace the existing gulpfile.js with a copy from the Tutorial1A folder — this contains the appropriate commands to compile the code — we need to use the original version built to compile SASS code, not PostCSS, hence the change.

4. Take a copy of style.scss from the src folder of the Tutorial4 folder, then drop it into the src folder of our project area.

5. Next, fire up a NodeJS command prompt window, then change the working folder to our project area.

6. At the prompt, enter this command, then press *Enter*:

    gulp

    Keep the command prompt window open for now, we will use it again shortly.

7. Once the code has compiled, copy the contents of the dest folder back to the css folder in the Tutorial4 folder.

If all is well, we should have three icons showing, when previewing the results in a browser. Nothing outrageous here: we have the base rule that applies to all of the icons, which is followed by the individual classes required to handle each icon itself:

```
.social-icon {
  background: 50% no-repeat;
  background-size: 100%;
  float: left;
  height: 50px;
  width: 50px;
}

.social-icon.twitter {
  background-image: url("../img/twitter.png");
}

.social-icon.linkedin {
  background-image: url("../img/linkedin.png");
}

.social-icon.youtube {
  background-image: url("../img/youtube.png");
}
```

So, how would this look in PostCSS? Well, surprising as it may be, there isn't a great deal of change needed.

Switching to using PostCSS

We only need to change it in two places within our CSS file. I've also separated the nested code, to make it easier to view:

```
.social-icon {
  // shared information here
  background: 50% no-repeat;
  background-size: 100%;
  float: left;
  height: 50px;
  width: 50px;
}
```

The changes we need to make are highlighted in this block of code:

```
@each $media in twitter, linkedin, youtube {
  . $(img) {
```

```
    background: url('../img/$(media).png');
  }
}
```

Our gulp file also needs to change. Let's work through the steps involved to make the switch to PostCSS:

1. We first need to replace the gulp file — go ahead and delete the copy at the root of the project area, then replace it with a copy from the `Tutorial4` folder in the code download.

2. From the code download that accompanies this book, extract a copy of `style—pre compile.css`, and rename it as `style.css`. Drop it in the `src` folder of our project area.

3. Revert back to the command prompt, then enter `gulp` at the prompt and press *Enter*.

4. If all is well, we should see the compiled style sheets appear in the `dest` folder, along with the source maps.

5. Copy the contents of the `dest` folder in project area to the `css` folder within our local copy of the `Tutorial4` folder.

6. Try previewing the results in a browser; if all is working as expected, we should see these icons appear:

Granted, it is a simple exercise, but then I've always been a fan of keeping things simple! Anyone can write CSS styles, but for me the "step up" is knowing that quantity does not always beat quality, and that there is something to be said for following the *KISS* principle, *Keep It Simple…* Yes, you get the idea!

But, just to show how flexible this plugin is, try this as an exercise:

* Browse to `http://dataurl.net/`, then upload each of the icons in turn, and use the site to generate data-URI equivalent code for each image.

* In the CSS, remove the existing background-image links, and replace them with the code from the `dataurl.net` site.

* Go ahead and compile the code using the same principles we've used throughout this chapter. Looks identical, doesn't it? We've removed the need to pull in separate resources, as we're using a pure CSS solution…

But, there is a catch: when the file has been compiled, check the file size. It should tell you that it is significantly larger than the one which doesn't contain data-URI equivalent code. This is to be expected: it's the trade-off between sizes versus the number of resources we call. It only shows how critical the order of our PostCSS plugins would be, to get the desired results!

Summary

Anyone who has spent time using pre-processors such as SASS will no doubt be familiar with variables and mixins; these make up an integral part of using PostCSS. We've covered a lot of material relating to their use throughout this chapter, so let's take a breather and review what we have learned.

We kicked off with a brief introduction to variables and mixins in SASS, before setting up an example demo in SASS (and Less CSS) as a basis for conversion to PostCSS.

Next up came the start of the transition process to PostCSS. We first looked at adding variable support in, before updating our hover demo to use the new plugin and remove a dependency on using SASS. We then covered some benefits and considerations of using PostCSS, before discovering how a simple tweak in the order of plugins can have a big impact on the end result.

We moved swiftly on with a look at mixins. We covered the install of the postcss-mixins plugin, before using it to update our demo. At this point, we paused for a moment to consider some of the differences between standard processors and PostCSS, and covered how one of the key points to bear in mind is PostCSS's flexibility and power.

We then rounded out the chapter with a look at looping content. We first explored the use of the for statement, before moving on and taking a look at how we can easily style content using the @each function. We then covered its use in a simple demo for styling social media icons. This started in SASS, but finished with the converted results using PostCSS.

Phew, let's move on! Our next stop on this whistlestop tour of mastering PostCSS is a look at nesting, and no, not for our feathered friends, but how we can (dramatically) reduce the content we write, or at least make it easier to read!

3
Nesting Rules

If you have spent any time developing with preprocessors, then you will likely have come across nested properties—instead of writing multiple style rules with repeated references to the same elements, we can use nesting to create concise style rules that compile to valid CSS.

In this chapter, we'll delve into using the power of nesting, show you how you can transition from using preprocessors such as SASS or Less, and explore some of the tricks we can use that are not available with preprocessors such as SASS:

- Exploring the use of BEM (Block, Element, Modifier) or standard nesting
- Creating nested rules and BEM equivalents using existing preprocessors
- Transitioning to using PostCSS plugins
- Understanding the pitfalls of nesting and how we can improve our code

Let's make a start…!

Introducing nesting

The concept of nesting is nothing new when using processors such as Less CSS or SASS; it's a useful technique to help reduce the amount of code we need to write, and to organize code in a more human-readable format.

The flipside of the coin is that it is frequently abused—when using processors for the first time, many developers fall into the trap of thinking that everything should be nested. One can get away with it if the code is very simple; it is more likely to result in fragile code that is difficult to read and easily broken with simple changes to one or more styles in the code.

If nesting is done correctly, then it can be very effective; it helps avoid the need to repeat parent selectors, and allows us to group together rules that apply to the same selector, together. To see what is meant by this, take a look at this simple example for SASS:

```
#main p {
  color: #00ff00;
  width: 97%;

  .redbox {
    background-color: #ff0000;
    color: #000000;
  }
}
```

If this is compiled using a GUI application or via the command line, it results in these styles:

```
#main p {
  color: #00ff00;
  width: 97%;
}

#main p .redbox {
  background-color: #ff0000;
  color: #000000;
}
```

The great thing about this code is that we've not tried to cram in every single rule that applies to the same parent selector, or a descendant; this is something we should consider when working with nesting.

 Notice how, in our SASS example, the nesting was at the end of the code? It's considered good practice to include nested statements at the end, before the closing bracket.

Some developers counsel against using nesting though, as it causes real issues for elements that have been styled in specific contexts; it becomes harder to change the code if we need to change the style. We will explore more of the reasons why nesting is fraught with risks later in this chapter.

Leaving aside the risks of nesting for the moment, we can use the same basic principle of nesting when using PostCSS — for this, we need to use the `postcss-nesting` plugin by Jonathan Neal, which is available from `https://github.com/jonathantneal/postcss-nesting`. To give you a flavor of what nesting looks like in PostCSS, take a look at this screenshot — this is an online playground provided by the author for trialing nested statements, where we can see the results automatically on the right:

The key line is on the left, fifth from the bottom: the `postcss-nesting` plugin uses `@nest &` as the placeholder for nesting code.

To help illustrate how the `postcss-nesting` plugin works, we will use it to create a somewhat unique navigation system. Our navigation will use a mix of jQuery and CSS to style and flip some demo pages, with the animation effects provided by CSS3 styling. Intrigued? Let's dive in and take a look.

Navigating through pages

I've always had a desire to do something a little different; doing the same thing as everyone else becomes so passé! With this in mind, when researching for this book, I came across an intriguing demo by Nikolay Talanov, where pages are flipped over from one to the next, using either CSS3 animation if supported, or falling back to standard jQuery.

You can see the original pen demo at `http://codepen.io/suez/pen/LCH1A`.

This has provided a perfect base for this chapter. For the purpose of the demos, I've stripped back the vendor prefixes (as these will be covered by `Autoprefixer`), tweaked the design of the first page, and switched to just using nesting throughout. The jQuery fall-back code has also been removed, as most modern browsers will support the animations with little difficulty.

Preparing our demo

For our demo, we will have four pages — the navigation will flip between each page, using standard CSS3 animation:

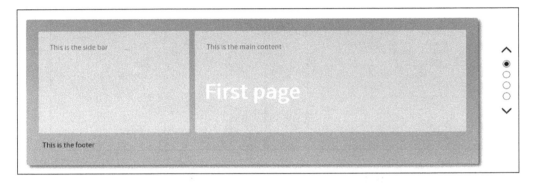

The design may be a little unique, but to help illustrate how it could be used, I've added a simple wireframe sketch to the front page, which could easily be expanded to the remaining pages and developed into something more substantial.

To see it in action, extract a copy of the `Tutorial5` folder from the code download that accompanies this book, then run `index.html` in a browser, and click on the dots or arrow icons to the right — you will see it flip up or down, depending on which direction you click.

Converting from existing processors

At present, our demo is using plain CSS, and nothing is wrong with this, but I suspect some of you will likely be using an existing processor, such as SASS or less CSS. The real benefit of using PostCSS is its ability to mimic existing tools, without the dependencies.

With this in mind, there are copies of the demo, available in the code download, which use Less CSS and SASS. If you prefer using SASS, then go ahead and extract `Tutorial6A` from the code download folder; for Less, use `Tutorial6B`. The code can easily be compiled using the `gulpfile.js` file from `Tutorial1A` in *Chapter 2, Creating Variables and Mixins* (for SASS), or `Tutorial 1B` (for Less CSS, in the same chapter folder).

 You will need to install the plugins listed — most of these will already be present from previous demos, but `gulp-sass` and `gulp-less` will need to be installed using NPM, in the same manner.

Both will produce identical results to the vanilla CSS version, once compiled, and the contents of the `dest` folder have been copied to the `css` sub-folder in the tutorial folder. With the base demo in place, we are now ready to make the conversion — let's make a start by installing the `postcss-nesting` plugin.

Transitioning to using PostCSS plugins

We've seen that adapting code to use nesting is a simple principle, but the real art is getting the balance right, many developers fall into the trap of nesting everything in their code when using the technique for the first time.

With this in mind, let's explore how we can convert our code to using PostCSS. We'll start by installing the `postcss-nesting` plugin, which will perform most of the work for us:

1. Fire up a Node.js command prompt, then change the working directory to our project area.

2. At the command prompt, enter the following command, then press *Enter*:

   ```
   npm install --save-dev postcss-nesting
   ```

3. Node.js will go away and install the plugin — it is ready for use when we see something akin to this screenshot:

```
Node.js command prompt                                        —    □    ×

C:\wamp\www\postcss>npm install --save-dev postcss-nesting
npm WARN package.json postcss@1.0.0 No repository field.
npm WARN package.json postcss@1.0.0 No README data
postcss-nesting@2.0.6 node_modules\postcss-nesting
└── postcss@5.0.10 (js-base64@2.1.9, source-map@0.5.1, supports-color@3.1.2)

C:\wamp\www\postcss>_
```

4. With the plugin installed, we need to configure PostCSS to use it — open up a copy of `gulpfile.js` from the project area, ready for editing.

5. We need to make a few changes — the first is to assign a variable that references the plugin. Add the highlighted line in immediately below the last variable statement:

```
var cssnano = require('cssnano');
var nesting = require('postcss-nesting');
```

6. The `autoprefixer` task needs to be altered — this time around, we will start with compiling our nested code and adding the appropriate vendor prefixes. Alter the first line of this task, as indicated:

```
gulp.task('autoprefixer', function() {
        return gulp.src('src/*.css')
```

7. Next, add in the nesting configuration call:

```
    .pipe(postcss([ autoprefixer,
        nesting({ /* options */ }) ]))
```

8. SASS normally compresses any code on compilation by default — as we're no longer using it, we need to provide an alternative. For this, we will reuse the `cssnano` plugin from *Chapter 2, Creating Variables and Mixins*. Go ahead and add this at line 20:

```
.pipe(postcss([ cssnano() ]))
```

9. The lint-styles task should then run once the vendor prefixes have been added; to make this happen, add the constraint as shown:

```
gulp.task("lint-styles", ['autoprefixer'], function() {
```

10. We no longer have any need for the `sass` task, so go ahead and remove it in its entirety, and from the default task entry — we should be left with this:

```
gulp.task('default', ['lint-styles', 'autoprefixer',
    'rename']);
```

11. Last, but by no means least, go ahead and switch the order of the rename task. Instead of running it immediately after the `autoprefixer` task, we'll run it once the lint-styles task has been completed:

```
gulp.task('rename', ['lint-styles'], function () {
```

At this stage, our gulp task file is now ready for use. We can begin to convert our style sheet to use PostCSS nesting as a replacement for SASS. Let's make a start on converting it, as part of the next exercise.

 If you get stuck, there is a completed version of `gulpfile.js` in the code download that accompanies this book—simply extract a copy and place it in the root of our project area to use it.

Converting our demo to PostCSS

Altering our code to use PostCSS is very simple. Even if it requires a few changes, the format does not change significantly when compared to processors such as SASS; let's take a look at what is involved:

1. We'll begin by opening a copy of `style.scss` from the `Tutorial6A` folder in the code download that accompanies this book—save it to the `src` folder of our project area. Rename it to `style.css`.

2. On line 19, add `@nest` immediately before `&:`, as indicated—this is required to allow the `postcss-nesting` plugin to correctly compile each nesting statement:

   `@nest &:before, &:after {`

3. On line 53, add `@nest &` immediately before `h2`, as shown:

   `@nest & h2 {`

4. On line 61, add `@nest` immediately before `&.`, as shown:

   `@nest` `&.page1 {`

   Repeat step 4 for lines 65, 69 and 73.

5. On line 119, add `@nest` immediately before `&.`, as shown:

   `@nest` `&.invisible {`

6. On line 123, add `@nest` immediately before `ul`, as shown:

   `@nest` `& ul {`

7. On line 125, add `@nest` immediately before `& li`, as shown:

   `@nest` `& li {`

8. On line 136, add @nest immediately before &., as shown:

    ```
    @nest &:after {
    ```

    Repeat the same process for lines 150 and 155.

9. On lines 179, add @nest immediately before &., as shown:

    ```
    @nest &.up {
    ```

    Repeat the same process for lines 183 and 187, then save the file.

Our style sheet is now converted; to prove it works, we need to run it through PostCSS, so let's do that now as part of the next exercise.

Compiling our code

With the changes made to our code, we need to compile it—let's go ahead and do that now, using the same process we saw back in *Chapter 2*, *Creating Variables and Mixins*:

1. Fire up a Node.js command prompt session, or use the one from earlier if you still have it open, and change the working folder to the project area.

2. At the prompt, enter this command, then press *Enter*:

    ```
    gulp
    ```

3. If all is well, we should see something akin to this screenshot:

```
gulp                                                              —   □   ×

Your environment has been set up for using Node.js 4.1.1 (x64) and npm.

C:\Users\alex>cd \wamp\www\postcss

C:\wamp\www\postcss>gulp
[00:07:35] Using gulpfile C:\wamp\www\postcss\gulpfile.js
[00:07:35] Starting 'autoprefixer'...
[00:07:36] Finished 'autoprefixer' after 362 ms
[00:07:36] Starting 'lint-styles'...
[00:07:36] Finished 'lint-styles' after 96 ms
[00:07:36] Starting 'rename'...
[00:07:36] Finished 'rename' after 442 ms
[00:07:36] Starting 'default'...
[00:07:36] Finished 'default' after 47 µs
```

4. A quick peek in the dest folder of our project area should reveal the relevant compiled CSS and source map files, produced by PostCSS.

5. At this point, we need to extract a copy of the `Tutorial7` folder from the code download that accompanies this book – save this to our project area.

6. Copy the contents of the `dest` folder from our project area to the `css` folder under `Tutorial7` – if all is well, our demo should continue to work, but without the dependency of SASS.

 Note, make sure you expand the demo to the full width of the screen to view it properly!

Try previewing the results in a browser – if all is well, we should see the same results appear as before, but this time using PostCSS, and without the dependency on SASS. We can now apply the same techniques to any project, safe in the knowledge that using the postcss-nesting plugin will allow us to compile to valid CSS code – or will it?

Exploring the pitfalls of nesting

It has to be said that although nesting is a simple technique to understand, it can be difficult to get right, as shown in our SASS version of the demo:

```
111    .nav-panel {
112      position: fixed;
113      top: 50%;
114      right: 2%;
115      transform: translateY(-50%);
116      z-index: 1000;
117      transition: opacity 0.5s, transform 0.5s cubic-bezier(0.57, 1.2, 0.68, 2.6);
118      will-change: transform, opacity;
119      &.invisible {
120        opacity: 0;
121        transform: translateY(-50%) scale(0.5);
122      }
123      ul {
124        list-style-type: none;
125        li {
126          position: relative;
127          overflow: hidden;
```

The issues we have here are twofold – the multiple levels of nesting result in a high level of code specificity; if we wanted to change the styling for `.nav-panel ul li` (the compiled version of line **125**), it would likely break the appearance of our front end code. To see what I mean, let's take an example HTML page that any developer might create:

```
<body>
  <div class="container">
```

```
<div class="content">
  <div class="articles">
    <div class="post">
      <div class="title">
        <h1><a href="#">Hello World</a>
      </div>
      <div class="content">
        <p></p>
        <ul>
          <li>...</li>
        </ul>
      </div>
      <div class="author">
        <a href="#" class="display"><img src="..." /></a>
        <h4><a href="#">...</a></h4>
        <p>
          <a href="#">...</a>
          <ul>
            <li>...</li>
          </ul>
        </p>
      </div>
    </div>
  </div>
</div>
</body>
```

Now, before you all scream, *Yuk, I would never do that!* at me, and claim (quite rightly) that we should use semantic elements such as <header>, <section>, <article>, and / or <footer> to provide context and meaning, instead of all of these <div> statements, then stop! There is a point in producing that ugly mix of code. Let me explain:

The example HTML we have just seen is likely to result in this nested CSS:

```
body {
  div.container {
    div.content {
      div.articles {
        & > div.post {
          div.title {
            h1 {
              a {
              }
```

```
            }
          }
          div.content {
            p {  ...  }
            ul {
              li {  ...  }
            }
          }
          div.author {
            a.display {
              img {  ...  }
            }
            h4 {
              a {  ...  }
            }
            p {
              a {  ...  }
            }
            ul {
              li {  ...  }
            }
          }
        }
      }
    }
  }
}
```

Some developers might think this is perfectly acceptable — after all, they know no different, so why should it be an issue, right? Wrong — this code, while it may *technically* fit the styles in our HTML document, has several issues with it:

- **It is awkward to read** at best, and enough to give anyone a headache when trying to decipher it.

- Try compiling it; it will result in a lot of **duplicated parent selectors**, with code stretching to around 20 lines.

- **Rendering performance** is likely to be poor — if for example, a tool such as Google's Page Speed is installed, then it is likely to trigger the **Prioritize Visible Content** rule, where additional round trips are needed to render content on-screen above the fold.

- **Size** is likely to be an issue — even though we live in an age of broadband connections, it is bad manners to take a cavalier attitude to content, and not create something in as small a footprint as possible.

- **Maintainability** will become a problem—our example code has bound styles too tightly, which defeats the purpose of cascading style sheets, where we should be able to place common styles in a parent selector and allow these to cascade down to children, or be overridden as required.

How can we get around it? The simplest answer is to be sensible about the number of levels we use when nesting code—some developers argue no more than four; I would argue from experience that two should be sufficient (which in this case would be `body div.content`, had we compiled our monster CSS style sheet).

There is nothing to stop us from using four levels if we absolutely have no other way of achieving our desired result; if we're doing this regularly, then we clearly need to revisit our code!

Taking a better approach

If, when working on code, we are forced to regularly use nested styles that are more than two or three levels deep, then there are some tricks we can use to reduce both the CSS specificity over time, and the need to use nesting more than two to three levels deep. Let's take a look at a few:

- Can you give yourself the class you need? Specificity can creep in if we're overriding an existing selector:

```css
.section-header {
  /* normal styles */
}

body.about-page .section-header {
  /* override with higher specificity */
}
```

To avoid specificity, can a class be emitted through the use of server-side code or functions, which we can use to style the element instead?

```html
<header class="<%= header_class %>">
```

Which could output one class, or both, as desired:

```html
</header>
```

```css
.section-header {
  /* normal styles */
}

.about-section-header {
  /* override with same specificity */
  /* possibly extend the standard class */
}
```

- The order of your style sheets can play an important role here, even though you might use a single class to override styles:

```
<header class="section-header section-header-about">
...
</header>
```

Your existing class may be overriding your override; both selectors have the same specificity, so the last rule(s) to be applied will take precedence. The fix for this is simply to rework the order in which your style rules are applied, so that overriding classes can be applied later.

- Consider reducing the specificity of the element you're trying to style; can the element be replaced, or removed in its entirety? If, however, it's being used within JavaScript (or jQuery) code, then it is preferable to leave it as-is, and add a second class (or use an existing class already applied, if one exists).

- Where possible, aim to use as flat a structure as possible for your code; it is too easy to style an element such as this:

```
.module > h2 {

}
```

In this example, we're styling all h2 elements that are direct children of the parent .module class. However, this will work until we need to assign a different style for the h2 element. If the markup looks similar to this example:

```
<div class="module">
  <h2 class="unique">
    Special Header
  </h2>
</div>
```

...it will be difficult to apply styles easily, due to CSS specificity creeping in:

```
.module > h2 {
  /* normal styles */
}
.unique {
  /* I'm going to lose this specificity battle */
}
.module .unique {
  /* I'll work, but specificity creep! */
}
```

- To avoid this, using as flat a structure as possible is recommended — it will be worth the extra effort required to set it up:

```
<div class="module">
  <h2 class="module-header">
  </h2>
  <div class="module-content">
  </div>
</div>
```

- Consider using an established pattern library, or atomic design (such as the one at `http://patternlab.io/`), to help guide you through how a site should be built — they are likely to be built using minimal CSS specificity, and with hopefully little need to override existing code.

- Be careful if you decide to use cascading when applying CSS styles — if we apply a base style to an element (or class) that is reused multiple times, this will cause issues. To avoid this, try to avoid using cascading if it isn't really needed; consider limiting it to 2-3 levels only, to reduce risk of odd or unexpected styles being applied.

- Sometimes code is outside of your control — in instances such as this, we have to work with it; we can either try using low specificity selectors where possible, or use the `!important` keyword to override the code. For now, we may have to leave comments in the code to explain why the selectors are set as such; in an ideal world, we would try to contact the authors to see if they can update or alter the code to remove these issues.

- As a last resort, if you must get into the realms of CSS specificity, then try to only apply a light touch, and not take the sledgehammer approach, such as using a selector ID or `!important`.

  We can try applying a single class to an existing tag, but this may not feel right for some; an alternative is to use two classes:

```
.nav .override {
}
.override .override {
}
.nav {
}
```

  The key here, though, is to not use more than one additional class!

- Nesting styles can lead to writing overly specific selectors in our code—some developers discourage its use for this reason, even though nesting can help make our code visually easier to read and digest. Instead of using compound selectors, we can emulate a form of name-spacing by using the ampersand symbol:

```
.somestyle {
    color: darkred;
    &-so {
      color: blue;
      &-ever {
        color: green;
      }
    }
}
```

  …which will compile to this:

```
.somestyle { color: darkred; }
. somestyle-so { color: blue; }
.somestyle-so-ever { color: green; }
```

- If your style is overriding a style that is already an override—stop: Why are you doing this? Overriding a class or selector element can be an efficient way of styling, but applying a second override will only cause confusion.

We've seen a number of ways of avoiding, or reducing CSS specificity issues that are inherent with nesting; the key message, though, is that we are not forced to have to nest our code, and that, to paraphrase the front-end architect Roy Tomeij—nested code doesn't create bad code; bad coders do!

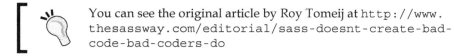
You can see the original article by Roy Tomeij at `http://www.thesassway.com/editorial/sass-doesnt-create-bad-code-bad-coders-do`

There is one method, though, that we've not touched on, and for good reason: it's a route many developers new to using processing will likely take for the first time. Intrigued? It has something to do with using conversion tools, and more specifically, how we use them to convert from plain CSS to code suitable for compiling using PostCSS.

Reconsidering our code

Imagine this scenario, if you will:

You've taken over a website, and are keen to make use of PostCSS to help with maintaining your code. The code uses plain vanilla CSS, so as a step to converting it, you happen to know of a number of sites that will convert plain CSS to SASS. After all, there are some similarities between PostCSS and SASS code, so why not?

You extract the results into a text file, save it, and put it through a SASS compilation process. Out comes some newly compiled CSS, which you drop into the relevant location on your server, and voilà! You have a working site that now uses SASS. A working site, and a perfect basis for converting to PostCSS...or is it?

The short answer should be no, but the longer one is that it will depend on your code. Let me explain why:

Simply pushing code through a conversion process isn't enough—granted, it will give you code that works, but unless it is very simple, it is likely **not to give code that is concise and efficient**. To see what I mean, take a close look at the CSS style sheet from `Tutorial5`—and specifically, the style rules for `.nav-panel`, from around line 132.

 For reasons of space, the style sheet is too long to print in full— I would recommend taking a look at the file from the code download in a text editor!

A conversion process will have no problem processing it to produce valid SASS, but it won't look pretty—as an example, try copying lines 114 to 197 into the converter hosted at `http://css2sass.herokuapp.com/`. Doesn't look great, does it? There is definitely room for improvement—I've already made some changes to the code, but we can do more; let's take a look at what can be done to improve the code.

Updating our code

When using a CSS to SASS convertor, the one key point that should always be at the back of our minds is that the converted code should **not** be considered the final article.

It doesn't matter how simple or complex your code is—it should be the first step in our conversion process. It's just a matter of how little or how much we have to do, once the code has been through the converter! As an example, take a look at this block of code:

```
1   .nav-panel ul .nav-btn.active:after, .nav-panel ul .nav-btn:hover:after {
2     -webkit-transform: translateX(-50%) translateY(-50%) scale(0.7);
3         -ms-transform: translateX(-50%) translateY(-50%) scale(0.7);
4             transform: translateX(-50%) translateY(-50%) scale(0.7);
5     opacity: 1;
6   }
```

It's a direct copy of lines 234 to 239 of the compiled version of the pen by Nikolay, which we used as a basis for our earlier demos. Now take a quick look at the equivalent code that I tweaked from the original and used in my version:

```
162   .nav-panel ul li.active:after, .nav-panel ul li:hover:after {
163     transform: translateX(-50%) translateY(-50%) scale(0.7);
164     opacity: 1;
165     background-color: #000;
166   }
```

Notice any differences? The vendor prefix version of the `transform` attribute has been stripped out — most modern browsers (certainly within the last year to eighteen months), should handle this code without the need for vendor prefixes. The original version also suffered from a high degree of CSS specificity — this will become even more apparent if the code is nested!

To improve it, I've switched in `.nav-panel ul li` as a direct replacement for `.nav-panel ul .nav-btn` — the code is relatively simple in that it does not need a second class to identify elements for styling purposes. The next logical step is to break up the large nesting block within the source file; it is tempting to include a single large block, but this will be at the expense of readability, maintenance, and performance.

We could potentially go even further, and consider removing the leading `.nav-panel`; not only will it make the code infinitely easier to read, but it will also reduce the issues around CSS specificity. Of course, this kind of change will depend on what is in your code; the point here is to examine your code thoroughly, and look to reduce any CSS specificity as much as possible, so that your nesting won't look so bad!

There is an alternative means we can use though, which removes issues around CSS specificity — using **Block Element Modifier** notation (or **BEM** for short). It's a great way to systematically style elements using CSS, and it is worth taking time to get accustomed to how it works. Let's dive in and take a look.

Making the switch to BEM

So what is BEM, and why can it help with reducing or removing CSS specificity issues?

BEM, or **Block Element Modifier**, helps us style elements using a systematic naming convention, which is structured thus:

- `.block`: top-level containing the element we're going to change
- `.block__modifier`: the style assigned when the state of an element is changed
- `.block__element`: an element inside a top-level container
- `.block__element__modifier`: alternate representation of an element, when its state has been changed

The idea behind this style of coding is to make it portable and easier to maintain. The basis for this is that, while standard, non-BEM CSS is more concise, it is harder to infer what each rule does. We frequently have to assign multiple classes to an element, which introduces a degree of CSS specificity, and reduces the reusability of CSS rules. Using BEM allows us to combine the constituent names into one style class name, and remove any concern around CSS specificity.

If we use this concept, we can use it to write style rules such as this:

```
.block {
  &__element {
  }
  &__modifier {
  }
}
```

This will compile to the following:

```
.block {}
.block__element {}
.block__modifier {}
```

The preceding code uses plain BEM format, but from within a processor environment such as SASS to construct BEM rules in PostCSS, we can use the `postcss-bem` plugin (available from `https://github.com/ileri/postcss-bem`) to produce our BEM CSS using `@-rules`. For example:

```
@component ComponentName {
  color: cyan;

  @modifier modifierName {
```

```
      color: purple;
    }

    @descendent descendentName {
      color: darkred;
    }

    @when stateName {
      color: yellow;
    }
  }
```

In this instance, @component signifies our Block, @descendant our element, and @modifier is our modifier. When compiled, our CSS would look like this:

```
.ComponentName {
  color: cyan;
}

.ComponentName--modifierName {
  color: purple;
}

.ComponentName-descendentName {
  color: darkred;
}

.ComponentName.is-stateName {
  color: yellow;
}
```

The beauty of using BEM is that it helps to reduce or even avoid CSS specificity issues—although names are longer, we can combine both element and modifier names into one class, instead of having to apply three or more separate classes. Granted, there may be instances where we might have to apply a second class, but with careful planning we should be able to reduce this to a minimum.

Right, onwards we go: let's get stuck in to coding! Over the next few pages, we will take a look at implementing BEM styling in a simple demo, and see how we can use PostCSS to compile our code.

Creating simple message boxes

For our BEM demo, we're going to work through the CSS rules required to show some simple message boxes on screen, such as for displaying confirmation that a task has completed, or a warning when something isn't right.

 The original version of this demo, by Rene Spronk, is available from http://www.cssportal.com/blog/css-notification-boxes/.

It's a simple demo, but shows off the principles behind BEM CSS perfectly — go ahead and extract a copy of the `Tutorial8` folder, then run `index.html` to get a feel for what we will be producing. This version uses standard CSS; we will use this as a basis for converting to using BEM.

Let's make a start:

1. We'll begin by extracting a copy of the `Tutorial9` folder from the code download that accompanies this book — drop this into our project area.

2. Next, in a new file, add the following CSS statements starting at line 1, and leaving a one-line gap between each — they should be fairly self-explanatory, but we will go through each block in turn.

3. We kick off with the core styles for each dialog — this is a basis style for each dialog box:

```
.dlgBox {
  border-radius: 0.625rem;
  padding: 0.625rem 0.625rem 0.625rem 2.375rem;
  margin: 0.625rem;
  width: 14.5rem
}
```

4. Next up comes a simple style for each `<span>` element — this turns the lead-in caption for each dialog to uppercase and sets it in bold text:

```
span { font-weight: bold;text-transform: uppercase; }
```

5. We now need to add our block element — it's the opening line that forms the basis for our styling:

```
@component content {
```

6. Next up comes the Element part of our style rule. These rules need to be added as nested (that is, indented) rules immediately underneath — using the PostCSS plugin, we add it in as a `@descendent` of our `@component`:

```
@descendent alert {
  font-family: Tahoma, Geneva, Arial, sans-serif;
```

```
    font-size: 0.6875rem;
    color: #555;
    border-radius: 0.625rem;
}
```

7. Up next comes the first of our status messages — we kick off with styling the Error message first; the main rule adds an error icon and styles the border. The :hover pseudo-element reduces the opacity when we hover over the box:

```
@modifier error {
  background: #ffecec url("../img/error.png")
    no-repeat 0.625rem 50%;
  border: 0.0625rem solid #f5aca6;
}

@modifier error:hover { opacity: 0.8; }
```

8. This is swiftly followed by styling for the Success message:

```
@modifier success {
  background: #e9ffd9 url("../img/success.png")
    no-repeat 0.625rem 50%;
  border: 0.0625rem solid #a6ca8a;
}

@modifier success:hover { opacity: 0.8; }
```

9. We can't forget the obligatory Warning message, so here's the style rule for that status:

```
@modifier warning {
  background: #fff8c4 url("../img/warning.png")
    no-repeat 0.625rem 50%;
  border: 0.0625rem solid #f2c779;
    }
  @modifier warning:hover { opacity: 0.8; }
```

10. Last but by no means least, here's the final one, which is Notice; it includes the closing bracket for the BEM nesting:

```
    @modifier notice {
      background: #e3f7fc url("../img/info.png")
        no-repeat 0.625rem 50%;
      border: 0.0625rem solid #8ed9f6;
    }
  @modifier notice:hover { opacity: 0.8; }
}
```

11. Save the file as style.scss into the src folder of our top-level project area (and not into the Tutorial8 folder!).

Our simple demo isn't going to set the world alight in terms of styling. If we were to preview it now, the results will of course not look great; let's fix that by setting up the compilation and linting tasks within PostCSS.

 If you are a SASS user, then you can see a version of this code suitable for that processor on GitHub – the code is available at: `https://gist.github.com/alibby251/45eab822a6a619467279`. Note how similar the results are when you compare the compiled version with the version we'll get in the next exercise!

Compiling and linting our code

Our code is in place, but the boxes won't look particularly appetizing – most of the styles are still written using PostCSS `@-rules`. We can fix that by compiling the code, so let's dive in and take a look at installing support for BEM.

Installing BEM support

Setting up BEM support in PostCSS is a cinch – we can make use of two plugins to compile and lint our code. The plugins we need for this task are `postcss-bem` (available from `https://github.com/ileri/postcss-bem`), and `postcss-bem-linter` (available from `https://github.com/postcss/postcss-bem-linter`). Both can be installed using the same process through Node.js.

Hopefully the process will be familiar by now, so without further ado, let's make a start:

1. We'll begin by firing up a Node.js command prompt, and navigating to our working folder.

2. At the command prompt, enter this command then press *Enter*:

   ```
   npm install --save-dev postcss-bem
   ```

3. Node.js will install each of the elements required; if all is well, we should see this result, to indicate a successful installation:

```
Node.js command prompt                                    —    □    ×

C:\wamp\www\postcss>npm install --save-dev postcss-bem
postcss@1.0.0 C:\wamp\www\postcss
└── postcss-bem@0.4.0

npm WARN EPACKAGEJSON postcss@1.0.0 No repository field.

C:\wamp\www\postcss>_
```

4. Repeat the same process for `postcss-bem-linter`, using this command:

    ```
    npm install --save-dev postcss-bem-linter
    ```

5. Keep the command prompt session open, but minimized. We're going to make use of it again in a moment!

Now that the plugin is installed, we can go ahead and add support to our gulp task file, and begin to parse our code:

1. First, go ahead and remove the existing `gulpfile.js` file at the root of our project area.

2. In a new file, add the following lines and save it as `gulpfile.js`, at the root of our project area. We start with setting a number of variables that call each of the plugins:

    ```
    var gulp = require('gulp');
    var postcss = require('gulp-postcss');
    var bem = require('postcss-bem');
    var bemLinter = require('postcss-bem-linter');
    var reporter = require('postcss-reporter');
    ```

3. The first task in the file checks the code for consistency with BEM standards, and displays any errors on-screen:

    ```
    gulp.task('lint', function() {
      return gulp.src('dest/*.css')
        .pipe(postcss([
          bemLinter({ preset: 'bem' }),
          reporter({ clearMessages: true })
        ]))
        .pipe(gulp.dest('dest/'));
    });
    ```

4. The second task in the file compiles the BEM code to valid CSS:

    ```
    gulp.task('bem', function() {
      return gulp.src("src/*.css")
    ```

```
    .pipe(postcss([bem({
      style: 'bem',
      separators: { descendent: '__' }
    })]))
    .pipe(gulp.dest('dest/'));
});
```

5. This task is the default that is called when we run gulp from the command line; it calls each of the tasks in turn:

```
gulp.task('default', ['bem', 'lint']);
```

6. We finish the `gulpfile.js` with a watch facility, to kick in and compile our code when any changes are made to it:

```
var watcher = gulp.watch('src/*.css', ['default']);
watcher.on('change', function(event) {
  console.log('File ' + event.path + ' was ' +
    event.type + ', running tasks...');
});
```

7. We're going to replace the `package.json` file too — add these lines to a new file, and save it to the root of the project area. These simply tell gulp which versions of our plugins to use when compiling the code:

```
{
  "name": "postcss",
  "version": "1.0.0",
  "description": "Configuration file for PostCSS",
  "main": "index.js",
  "scripts": {
    "test": "echo \"Error: no test specified\" && exit 1"
  },
  "author": "Alex Libby",
  "license": "ISC",
  "devDependencies": {
    "gulp": "^3.9.0",
    "gulp-postcss": "^6.0.0",
    "postcss-bem-linter": "^2.0.0",
    "postcss-reporter": "^1.3.0"
  }
}
```

8. From the code download that accompanies this book, go ahead and extract a copy of `style.css` from the `css - completed version` folder under `Tutorial9` — save this to the `src` folder under our project area.

9. Revert back to the Node.js command prompt session we had before, then at the prompt, enter this command and press *Enter*:

```
gulp
```

10. If all is well, the code will be checked, and the results displayed on screen. You may see errors appear, such as those shown in this screenshot. If they do, they can be ignored for now (we will explore this in more detail later):

```
gulp                                                    —    □    ×

C:\wamp\www\postcss>gulp
[21:39:31] Using gulpfile C:\wamp\www\postcss\gulpfile.js
[21:39:31] Starting 'bem'...
[21:39:31] Starting 'lint'...
Container#eachAtRule is deprecated. Use Container#walkAtRules instead.
Node#removeSelf is deprecated. Use Node#remove.

dest\style.css
2:1      !!  Invalid component selector ".dlgBox" [postcss-bem-linter]
9:1      !!  Invalid component selector "span" [postcss-bem-linter]

[21:39:31] Finished 'bem' after 133 ms
[21:39:31] Finished 'lint' after 113 ms
[21:39:31] Starting 'default'...
[21:39:31] Finished 'default' after 47 µs
```

11. Go ahead and copy the contents of the dest folder into the css folder underneath Tutorial9 — if all is well, we should see something akin to this screenshot when previewing the results in a browser:

Our simple demo shows some useful message boxes that we can use as a basis for something more complex; it illustrates perfectly how we can use BEM to style our code, while keeping issues around CSS specificity at bay. We've covered a few useful techniques throughout this exercise, so let's take a moment to explore them in more detail.

Exploring our changes in more detail

It is worth taking time to really get familiar with BEM styling principles. This is one of those areas where not spending time can easily dissuade you from using this technique; the principles are easy to understand but can take time to implement! Let's take a look at our code in more detail.

The key principle around BEM, when using the PostCSS plugin, is that of nesting — in this instance, we create our core component content, which results in an empty style rule at the top of our style sheet. Indented to the next level is our @descendant — this indicates that our message boxes are being styled as alerts. We then use a number of @modifiers to style each type of alert, such as success, warning, error, or notice (that is, information). This includes a separate style rule to cover each instance of the hover pseudo-element used in our code.

What does this mean for us? It means we have to not just consider each element (for instance, a message box) as a single entity to which we simply apply lots of classes; instead, we should consider the constituent parts of each element and apply a single class to each. Hold on, does that not mean we still have three classes in use (as we might have here)?

 To learn more about BEM naming conventions, take a look at the useful article posted at `https://en.bem.info/tools/bem/bem-naming/`.

Well, the answer is yes, and no: the trick here is that PostCSS will combine each nested style into valid CSS; for example, this extract (adapted from our demo):

```
@component content {
  @descendent alert {
    font-family: Tahoma, Geneva, Arial, sans-serif;
    font-size: 0.6875rem;
    color: #555;
    border-radius: 0.625rem;

    @modifier error {
      background: #ffecec url("../img/error.png")
        no-repeat 0.625rem 50%;
      border: 0.0625rem solid #f5aca6;
    }
  }
}
```

When compiled, this will appear as this CSS:

```
.content {}
.content__alert {
    font-family: Tahoma, Geneva, Arial, sans-serif;
    font-size: 0.6875rem;
    color: #555;
    border-radius: 0.625rem;
}
.content__alert_error {
    background: #ffecec url("../img/error.png")
       no-repeat 0.625rem 50%;
    border: 0.0625rem solid #f5aca6;
}
```

The sharp-eyed among you will have spotted that we still have errors being generated when our code is compiled:

It's always disconcerting to see errors, but there are valid reasons for them. We can safely ignore the two deprecation warnings (these should be fixed in a future version), but the two errors are of more concern.

Fixing our errors

The two errors are being caused by `postcss-bem-linter`, which is not recognizing the two styles as valid BEM notation. This raises a question: can we alter our code to remove the issues?

To answer this, we would need to weigh up how much code is affected against the time and effort required to alter it. In our demo, there is very little code affected; to resolve it, we would need to alter the `.dlgBox` and `span` styles to equivalent BEM naming.

Is this worth the effort? In a small demo such as ours, it is likely that the answer is no, for a larger demo, we would look to alter these two styles. Instead, we can add a simple directive at line 48, thus:

```
48    /* postcss-bem-linter: ignore */
49    .dlgBox {
50        border-radius: 0.625rem;
51        padding: 0.625rem 0.625rem 0.625rem 2.375rem;
52        margin: 0.625rem;
53        width: 14.5rem;
54    }
55
56    span {
57        font-weight: bold;
58        text-transform: uppercase;
59    }
60
```

When the code is recompiled, the errors are removed:

```
C:\wamp\www\postcss>gulp
[15:15:09] Using gulpfile C:\wamp\www\postcss\gulpfile.js
[15:15:09] Starting 'bem'...
[15:15:09] Starting 'lint'...
[15:15:09] Finished 'lint' after 26 ms
Container#eachAtRule is deprecated. Use Container#walkAtRules instead.
Node#removeSelf is deprecated. Use Node#remove.
[15:15:09] Finished 'bem' after 130 ms
[15:15:09] Starting 'default'...
[15:15:09] Finished 'default' after 54 µs
```

Purists may say this is cheating. It's true, our code is still *technically* not all BEM. In defense though, it's up to each developer to make that decision; there may be elements that have to remain as standard CSS, which we can't convert. In this case, it may be sensible to import these styles using the PostCSS import plugin — we will explore using this more in *Chapter 10, Building a Custom Preprocessor*.

It's worth noting that the `postcss-bem-linter plugin` will not display the results of any errors by itself — for this, we need to use a plugin such as `postcss-reporter` (available at `https://github.com/postcss/postcss-reporter`, for command line), or postcss-browser-reporter (from `https://github.com/postcss/postcss-browser-reporter`, displays content in the browser window). Both have a number of options that are worth investigating to help fine-tune what is displayed when the code is processed through PostCSS.

Summary

Over the years, developers have had to frequently write code that duplicates all or part of a selector—a perfect example is styling lists or navigation items. It's a real pain to have to write so much extra code; instead we can use nesting principles to help remove some of this code. We've covered a number of techniques around nesting in PostCSS throughout this chapter, so let's take a moment to review what we've learned.

We kicked off with an introduction to nesting, to help bring us up to speed, before launching into using the `postcss-nesting` plugin to create nested styles within PostCSS. We then moved on to creating our nesting demo. We began with preparing a plain vanilla CSS version, before taking a look at converting to existing processors such as SASS.

Moving on, we then took a look at converting our code using the `postcss-nesting` plugin, before exploring some of the pitfalls that are associated with nesting, and some of the tips and tricks we can use to reduce CSS specificity, one of the key issues associated with nesting.

We then rounded out the chapter with a look at BEM, and how it can be used in PostCSS. We covered some of the basic principles of this methodology, before applying it to a simple example. We also learned why it won't always work for every instance; for those where it is suitable, we took a brief look at how we can set PostCSS to automatically lint our BEM code.

Phew, a real whistle stop tour there! Hang on to your hats though, as it won't stop: in our next chapter, we're going to take a look at writing media queries, and how PostCSS can help with compiling them into valid CSS.

4
Building Media Queries

The days of simply using one device to browse an online site are long since gone: responsive sites will work on a range of devices, from smart phones through to digital TVs and laptops. A key element of making sites responsive is the use of media queries. In this chapter, we'll explore how to create them using PostCSS, see how they compare to the likes of Less and SASS, and how the use of PostCSS makes for a more flexible approach in comparison to standard preprocessors. This chapter will cover the following technical topics:

- Revisiting media queries
- Working through the basics of media queries using PostCSS
- Adding responsive support
- Optimizing media queries
- Retrofitting support for older browsers
- Taking things further — exploring the hover feature in CSS4 media queries

Let's make a start...!

Revisiting media queries

If you spend any time viewing sites on different devices, then it will hardly come as a surprise to see media queries in the style sheet — they form the basis for responsive design and declarations allow us to control what is displayed on screen, according to the available screen width.

The principles behind media queries are simple. In a nutshell, we have to define the device or media, and the resolution (or width) at which point the rule (or breakpoint) either kicks in or stops being applied. Take this simple example:

```
@media only screen and (max-width: 768px) {
  /* CSS Styles */
  ...
}
```

Any styles within will be applied only when we're viewing on screen, and our available screen estate is 768px or less. This is a simple example, they can be as simple or as complex as required; it's down to us as developers to work out exactly where our content breaks and to build a suitable breakpoint to manage the change.

> To get a feel for some of the more recent media queries that are possible, take a look at this post by Chris Coyier, who has queries for laptops, PCs, and even wearable devices! The list is available at https://css-tricks.com/snippets/css/media-queries-for-standard-devices/.

Okay, let's make a start: PostCSS makes it easy to manage queries for both text and images; we'll begin our journey with a look at handling images.

Exploring custom media queries in PostCSS

Making the switch to using PostCSS is a cinch, we can use the `postcss-custom-media` plugin for this purpose, available at https://github.com/postcss/postcss-custom-media.

The plugin is easy to install, it follows the same principles as all of the other plugins we've covered, so without further ado, let's get that out of the way now:

1. Fire up a Node.js command prompt, then navigate to the working directory.
2. At the prompt, enter this command, then press *Enter*:

   ```
   npm install --save-dev postcss-custom-media
   ```

3. Keep the command prompt open for now, we will use it in the next few steps.

With the plugin installed, we can now use it, before we get stuck into converting our previous demo, let's work through a simple example, so you can see it in action:

4. In a new file, add the following code, saving it as `style.css` within the `src` folder at the root of our project area:

```
@custom-media --apple-watch (max-device-width: 42mm) and
    (min-device-width: 38mm);

@media (--apple-watch) {
  h2 {
    font-size: 0.8rem;
  }
}
```

5. Remove the existing `gulpfile.js` file from the root of the project area.

6. In a new file, add the following code, this will form a new `gulpfile.js` file; save this to the root of our project area:

```
var gulp = require('gulp');
var postcss = require('gulp-postcss');
var customMedia = require('postcss-custom-media');

gulp.task('default', function() {
    return gulp.src('src/*.css')
    .pipe(postcss([ customMedia() ]))
    .pipe(gulp.dest('dest/'));
});

var watcher = gulp.watch('src/*.css', ['default']);
watcher.on('change', function(event) {
  console.log('File ' + event.path + ' was ' +
    event.type + ', running tasks...');
});
```

7. Revert back to the command prompt session we had open earlier, then enter `gulp` at the command prompt, and press *Enter*.

8. If all is well, we should see this code if we open up the compiled `style.css` from within the `dest` folder of our project area:

```
@media (max-device-width: 42mm) and
    (min-device-width: 38mm) {
  h2 {
    font-size: 0.8rem;
  }
}
```

Believe it or not, this is all that is required to use the plugin; let's take a moment to consider what we've covered through this demo.

At first glance, you might be forgiven for thinking that this plugin doesn't actually do anything to help us—it's a valid point, but there is one key benefit to using this plugin. We can separate out the media breakpoints into separate variable statements, and store these at the top of our style sheet. This means that if we should ever need to update a particular breakpoint, we only need to do it once. Our code is then updated automatically at the compilation stage.

With that in mind, let's get stuck into a demo; we're going to work through the previous plain CSS version of our parallax scrolling example, and convert it to use PostCSS.

Beginning with plain CSS

Over the next few pages, we're going to use a relatively recent technique as the basis for our demo—parallax scrolling. Just in case you've been under a rock, parallax scrolling is a single page application, which allows us to scroll through content whilst showing a number of fixed images behind our content:

We'll be using a demo created by Nick Salloum, which is available at `http://callmenick.com/_development/simple-parallax-effect/` (I've simplified some of the CSS styles used, removed vendor prefixes, and reduced the number of separate files called by the example). We'll start with a plain CSS version of our demo—go ahead and extract a copy of `Tutorial11` to our project area. Try running `index.html`; if all is well, we should see something akin to the screenshot at the head of this section.

It's a great effect when used well, our interest is in the last section of the CSS file, from around line 133; this section contains the media queries we will convert in our next demo.

Altering our demo to use PostCSS

If media queries are used correctly, this can open up a world of possibilities; we can tweak our style sheet for anything from an iPhone through to a printer. In our demo, we've used a couple to adjust how content is displayed on sites where displays are larger than 600px or 960px width; altering these to work in PostCSS is a cinch.

 The CSS3 Media Queries site has a large list of different types of queries that are available; if you check out the site on a target PC or device, it will show you if that query is supported on that device. The full list is available at http://www.cssmediaqueries.com.

We only need to make a couple of changes in the style sheet to switch to using PostCSS, so let's make a start:

Let's make a start on the changes:

1. We'll start by copying the style.css file from Tutorial11 folder to the src folder in our project area.

2. We need to edit the file, to convert our media queries to use the PostCSS plugin—go ahead and add these two lines at lines 4 and 5:

   ```
   @custom-media --small-viewport all and (min-width: 600px);
   @custom-media --medium-viewport all and (min-width: 960px);
   ```

3. Further down, replace lines 161 and 182 with this code:

   ```
   @media (--small-viewport) {
   ```

4. On line 200, replace that line with this code:

   ```
   @media (--medium-viewport) {
   ```

5. Save the file—next, go ahead and replace the current gulpfile.js file with the version from the root of the Tutorial12 folder. It has the same initial PostCSS task, but this has been renamed and extended with additional tasks that we've already used from earlier chapters.

6. Next, go ahead and save a copy of the package.json file from the same location to the root of our project area—this contains updated links to the plugins used in this demo.

   Fire up a Node.js command prompt window, then change the working directory to our project area. At the prompt, enter gulp then press *Enter*.

7. If all is well, we should have a compiled CSS file appear in the dest folder— go ahead and copy this into the css folder of the Tutorial12 folder.

8. Go ahead and run `index.html` in our project area, to preview the results — if all is well, we should not see anything different, but a quick check in the source code should show that we're using the minified version of our code:

```
<head>
  <meta charset="utf-8"></meta>
  <!-- title and meta -->
  <meta charset="utf-8"></meta>
  <meta name="viewport" content="width=device-width,initial-scale=1.0"></meta>
  <title>Simple Parallax Scrolling Effect</title>
  <link href="css/style.min.css" rel="stylesheet"></link>
</head>
```

It's worth noting that in our demo, we used a typical format of media query: we could for example extend or alter our style sheet to work on handheld devices such as Galaxy tablets; the same principles apply, but clearly different width values will need to be used! For details on the values to use, take a look at http://cssmediaqueries.com, which has a useful list of queries to use for recent devices.

If we want to push the boundaries of what is possible, there are a couple of options that we can consider:

- `postcss-media-variables`: This plugin (available at https://github.com/WolfgangKluge/postcss-media-variables) works in the same way, but allows us to use variables in media queries. The benefit of using this plugin is that we can hive off width values into a central `:root` rule; we can potentially use one fixed value, but work out others based on this value:

```
/* input */
:root {
    --min-width: 1000px;
    --smallscreen: 480px;
}
@media (min-width: var(--min-width)) {}
@media (max-width: calc(var(--min-width) - 1px)) {}

@custom-media --small-device (max-width: var(--smallscreen));
@media (--small-device) {}
/* output */
@media (min-width: 1000px) {}
@media (max-width: 999px) {}
@media (max-width: 480px) {}
```

The downside is that it is considered as non-standard, the plugin must be called twice, and if other plugins are used, be called in a certain order — this means it might only suit a specific set of circumstances!

- `postcss-quantity-queries`: This plugin (available at `https://github.com/pascalduez/postcss-quantity-queries`) is based on the SASS quantity queries mixins by Daniel Guillan. This allows us to use rules such as this:

```
ul > li:at-least(4) { color: rebeccapurple; }
```

Which will compile to this:

```
ul > li:nth-last-child(n+4),
ul > li:nth-last-child(n+4) ~ li {
  color: rebeccapurple;
}
```

This is one of four pseudo-selector extensions we can use with this plugin, it's a perfect way to style items such as navigation entries, or if we wanted a numbered list of items with different styles for even or odd numbers.

 For a useful reference article on using quantity queries in CSS, head over to the post by Heydon Pickering at `http://alistapart.com/article/quantity-queries-for-css`.

Let's change tack now, and focus on our content. So far, we've concentrated on the page layout, but we can take it further by making images truly responsive; let's dive in and take a look.

Making images responsive

A key element of making any site responsive has of course to be images—after all, we can always construct a site without images, but how effective would it *really* be?

Sure, one can always use a data **Uniform Resource Identifier (URI)** to convert images to CSS equivalents, but this is at the risk of dramatically inflating our style sheet to the point of it becoming impossible to manage. The reality is that we have to have some form of images—if we are to make them behave, we clearly need to ensure that they expand or contract in size, according to available screen estate.

The easiest way to adapt images for responsive layouts is to set a `max-width` value to `100%`, along with `height: auto` and `display: block`, and remove any attribute that defines either a fixed height or width for that image element. We can make the changes manually, but this is time-consuming; instead, let's take a look at a PostCSS plugin that allows us to set these three values at compilation, by adding one single line of code to each image.

Making an image responsive with PostCSS

Adding responsive capabilities to a site using PostCSS is simple; it will depend largely on your requirements as to how we make the images responsive, but the two key plugins to look out for are `postcss-responsive-images` (available at `https://github.com/azat-io/postcss-responsive-images`), and `postcss-at2x` (available at `https://github.com/simonsmith/postcss-at2x`).

We will cover the use of the `postcss-at2x` plugin in a moment, but for now, let's take a look at using the `postcss-responsive-images` plugin.

Implementing responsive capabilities to images

Making our images responsive requires a single line of code to be added to any image-based rule; let's dive in and add this capability to a copy of the `Tutorial13` folder from the code download that accompanies this book:

1. We'll start, as always, by installing the plugin—for this, fire up a Node.js command prompt, then run the commands as shown in this screenshot:

2. We'll start by extracting a copy of the `Tutorial13` folder from the code download that accompanies this book, then saving it to our project area.

3. Open up `style.css` from the `css` folder within the `Tutorial13` folder, then remove this rule:

```
img {
  width: 584px;
  height: 389px;
}
```

4. In its place, add the following line:

```
#retina img { image-size: responsive; }
```

5. Save the file, then copy it to the `src` folder underneath our project area (not within the `Tutorial` folder!).

6. For this exercise, we're going to replace the Gulp task file — go ahead and add this code to a new file, saving it as `gulpfile.js` at the root of our project area:

```
var gulp = require('gulp');
var postcss = require('gulp-postcss');
var responsiveimages =
  require('postcss-responsive-images');

gulp.task('default', function() {
    return gulp.src('src/*.css')
    .pipe(postcss([ responsiveimages ]))
    .pipe(gulp.dest('dest/'));
});

var watcher = gulp.watch('src/*.css', ['default']);
watcher.on('change', function(event) {
  console.log('File ' + event.path + ' was ' +
    event.type + ', running tasks...');
});
```

Note that we're concentrating on just making our image responsive with this `gulp` file, hence why it is a lot shorter than previous versions we have used to date.

7. Fire up a Node.js command prompt, then change the working directory to our project area — at the prompt, enter `gulp` then press *Enter*.

8. Node will go away and compile our code — if all is well, the compiled code for `#retina img` will look like this:

```
16   #retina img {
17       max-width: 100%;
18       height: auto;
19       display: block;
20   }
21
22   #retina img {
23       padding: 4px;
24       border: solid 1px #bbb;
25       background: #fff;
26       box-shadow: 0 1px 2px rgba(0,0,0,.2);
27   }
```

9. Copy the compiled CSS file from the `dest` folder into the `css` folder of the `Tutorial13` folder.

10. Go ahead and preview the results — try resizing the browser; if all is well, the image will automatically resize the image for us.

Although it's easy enough to install and use this plugin, it works best when referencing images directly in our HTML code, and not through the use of `background:` or `content: url(...)` attributes in our CSS.

What does this mean for us? It's a little limiting, as the purists amongst us may prefer to hive off asset attributes to CSS style sheets such is open source software, though this is one limitation that is bound to be fixed in the fullness of time!

The keen-eyed amongst you will spot that the image presentation clearly needs further work — for example, the paper clip isn't repositioning when the window is resized, and we need to set a minimum width so that there is some white space around the image when we resize it:

The key principles remain the same though, irrespective of the presentation, removing the fixed image sizes and replacing with a `max-width` of `100%` is a good step to making an image responsive.

To get a true responsive image though, we ideally would use the new HTML5 `<picture>` tags — trouble is, PostCSS doesn't yet have a plugin to implement these tags!

If you're interested in some of the more general techniques of making images responsive (and outside of the world of PostCSS), then take a look at `https://jakearchibald.com/2015/anatomy-of-responsive-images/`.

In the absence of any available capability to handle the use of `<picture>` tags within PostCSS, we can instead take a more traditional route and use media queries to help switch between different images, depending on the available screen estate.

We can go a step further, and even switch in images of better resolution if the device supports it—I'm thinking of course of Apple iPads or iPhones, which support retina images. We can easily use this format when working with PostCSS; for this, we need to make use of the `postcss-at2x` plugin by Simon Smith, available at `https://github.com/simonsmith/postcss-at2x`. I feel a couple of demos coming on, so without further ado, let's go explore using this plugin.

Adding support for retina images

Retina images, a term coined by Apple's marketing team, contain up to twice as many pixels in the same space as standard images. This allow us to switch in images of higher quality (or resolution) automatically, provided we're using a device that supports their use.

This might be as simple as an iPhone, or something more substantial like an iPad—Apple's marketing clout means that they are probably two of the most popular portable devices that people own! But I digress...

At a technical level, we have two routes available for adding retina images, before we explore these in more detail, let's just remind ourselves of the basics:

```
@media (-webkit-min-device-pixel-ratio: 2),
  (min-resolution: 192dpi) {
  #retina img {
    content: url("../img/mothorchid@2x.png");
  }
}
```

This code is an extract from the CSS style sheet in the `Tutorial15` folder, which is available in the code download that accompanies this book; try previewing `index.html` in a browser.

 For best results, it is strongly recommended that you use Google Chrome—it's a great browser for simulating the effects of switching between low and high resolution images.

The image displayed displays the text *8-bit version* — to switch, try this:

1. Press *Shift + Ctrl + I* to display the Developer toolbar.
2. Click on the mobile phone icon to enable Responsive Design mode

We can then switch between different devices using the dropdown — try switching to **Apple iPad**; you may need to press *F5* to refresh the display. If all is well, it will switch between 8-bit and 24-bit versions of the orchid image.

Taking the next steps

This is all good, but we're clearly not using PostCSS here — what are our options? Well, we have two that we can use: `customMedia()` or the `postcss-at2x` plugin. We've already covered the basics of using `customMedia` in the *Exploring custom media queries in PostCSS* section; for this, we would use a variable such as this:

```
/* media query for hi-resolution image support */
@custom-media --hi-resolution screen and
  (-webkit-min-device-pixel-ratio: 2), (min-resolution: 192dpi);
```

This would be coupled with a query such as this:

```
@media (--hi-resolution) {
  #retina img {
    content: url("../img/mothorchid@2x.png");
  }
}
```

When compiled, and run in Google Chrome (to take advantage of its responsive design tools), we can see the image switch from 8-bit:

...to a 24-bit version of the image:

A peek at the active style rules view shows the media query update automatically:

```
@media (-webkit-min-device-pixel-ratio:    style.css:47
2), (min-resolution: 192dpi)
#retina img {                              style.css:48
    content: url("../img/mothorchid@2x.png");
}

#retina img {                              style.css:29
    padding: ▶ 4px;
    border: ▶ solid 1px ▨ #bbb;
    background: ▶ ▢ #fff;
    box-shadow: 0 1px 2px rgba(0,0,0,.2);
    content: url("../img/mothorchid.png");
}
```

This is good, but still a manual approach that takes time—instead, we can use a quicker route to achieve similar results. The alternative route, using `postcss-at2x`, is a simpler option—instead of working out what resolution ratio to use, we simply add the term `at-2x` to our style rule:

```
#retina img { background: url("../img/mothorchid.png") at-2x; }
```

This automatically compiles to produce the relative resolution statements for us in our style sheet. It's a useful trick to use when working with iPads and other devices that can support hi-res images.

 Make sure the `src` and `dest` folders at the root of our project area are clear of files before starting this demo, otherwise you might find they have some undesired effects during compilation!

Let's dive in and take a look at this in more detail.

1. We start, as usual by installing the plugin—fire up a Node.js command prompt, then change the working directory to our project area.

2. At the prompt, enter the commands shown in this screenshot, pressing *Enter* after each:

Keep the window handy, we will need it in a few steps!

3. Let's now set up our markup, extract a copy of the Tutorial17 folder from the code download that accompanies this book, and save the folder to our project area.

4. Extract a copy of the gulp file from this folder and use it to replace the existing one at the root of our project area.

5. Extract a copy of style - pre-compile.css from the Tutorial17 folder, then copy it to the src folder at the root of our project area. Rename it as style.css.

6. Switch back to the Node.js command prompt window we had up earlier—at the prompt, enter gulp then press *Enter*.

7. PostCSS will go away and compile our code—if all is well, we should see something akin to this extract in the compiled file within the dest folder:

```
#retina img {
    padding: 4px;
    border: solid 1px #bbb;
    background: #fff;
    box-shadow: 0 1px 2px rgba(0,0,0,.2);
    content: url("../img/mothorchid.png");
}
...
@media screen and (-webkit-min-device-pixel-ratio: 2),
    (-webkit-min-device-pixel-ratio: 2),
    (min-resolution: 192dpi) {
    #retina img {
```

```
content: url("../img/mothorchid@2x.png");
    }
}
```

8. Go ahead and copy the contents of the `dest` folder to the `css` folder within the `Tutorial17` folder.

9. Try previewing the demo—if all is well, we should see that orchid flower as before, and force Chrome to display the hi-res version as we did in our previous demo.

The great thing about this plugin is that it deals with creating the media query for us; all we need to do is add the `at2x` tag to any image where we want to display hi-resolution versions in the browser. There is always a risk that we may end up producing queries that are not 100% optimized (for example, combining identical breakpoints into one block, and so on); we will explore a couple of options to help keep our queries working efficiently towards the end of this chapter.

As an aside, a more concise option for working with hi-res images which is frequently forgotten, is the use of `image-set()`; this performs in a similar fashion, by providing different versions for devices that support high-resolution images. PostCSS provides a fallback option in the form of `postcss-image-set` (available from `https://github.com/alex499/postcss-image-set`), which sets a basic image that will work in those browsers that don't support the use of `image-set()` within a style sheet.

Exploring other media possibilities

So, we've covered a number of key topics around making content responsive, using media queries; what does this mean when using PostCSS? The simple answer is that it opens up a world of possibilities—if your site needs to use media queries, then it is very likely that we can use PostCSS to compile our queries into valid CSS rules. To pique your interest, here are a couple of options to consider:

- Creating a responsive slider using the `bxSlider` plugin, available from `http://www.bxslider.com`. Granted, it uses jQuery to move between each slide, but who's to say you couldn't eventually convert this to an all-CSS option?

- How about using responsive image sprites? A classic use for this is credit card symbols on an e-commerce shopping cart, with a bit of care, we can even make the image adapt to display hi-res versions, if the device being used supports it. We'll cover more of this in *Chapter 5, Managing Colors, Images and Fonts*, if you want to give this a try, take a look at the postcss-sprites plugin, available from `https://github.com/2createStudio/postcss-sprites`.

Okay, we've covered making images responsive using PostCSS, but what about text? Pages won't look good if text doesn't flow properly when content is resized. Thankfully we can apply similar principles to text, using the `postcss-responsive-type` plugin by Sean King—let's take a look at it in action.

Adding responsive text support

The process of making text responsive within PostCSS shares some similarities to the postcss-responsive-images plugin we've already used, in both cases, all we need to add is a simple attribute to make our content responsive.

The plugin we need to use for text though is the `PostCSS-responsive-type` plugin by Sean King (available at `https://github.com/seanking/postcss-responsive-type`); adding font-size, being responsive to a rule in our style sheet is enough to get us started. Of course, we almost certainly want to specify our own rules; for example, we can use something like this:

```
html {
    font-size: responsive 12px 21px; /* min-size, max-size */
    font-range: 420px 1280px; /* range of viewport widths */
}
```

This compiles into two media queries—one at `480px`, and the other at `1280px`; the former sets a text size of `12px`, with the latter setting `21px` as the font size. Without further ado, let's get stuck in and start using this plugin in anger:

1. Fire up a Node.js command and change the working directory to the project area.

2. Enter the command shown in this screenshot, then press *Enter*:

```
Node.js command prompt                                    —    □    ×

C:\wamp\www\postcss>npm install --save-dev postcss-responsive-type
postcss@1.0.0 C:\wamp\www\postcss
└── postcss-responsive-type@0.3.1

npm WARN EPACKAGEJSON postcss@1.0.0 No repository field.

C:\wamp\www\postcss>
```

At this point, the plugin is installed—we can start to use it:

1. Start by extracting a copy of the `Tutorial18` folder from the code download that accompanies this book; save it to the root area of our project folder.

2. In a new file, add the following code—this contains some simple font styling for our demo; save it as `style.css` in the `src` folder of our project area:

```
@font-face {
  font-family: 'robotoregular';
  src: url('Roboto-Regular-webfont.eot');
  src: url('Roboto-Regular-webfont.eot?#iefix')
    format('embedded-opentype'),
      url('Roboto-Regular-webfont.woff') format('woff'),
      url('Roboto-Regular-webfont.ttf')
        format('truetype'),
      url('Roboto-Regular-webfont.svg#robotoregular')
        format('svg');
  font-weight: normal;
  font-style: normal;
}

body {
  font-family: "robotoregular", sans-serif;
  font-size: responsive 12px 21px;
  font-range: 420px 1280px;
}
```

3. Next, open up a copy of the `gulpfile.js` file at the root of our project area.

4. Note how a reference to the `postcss-responsive-type` plugin has been added, as indicated:

```
var at2x = require('postcss-at2x');
var responsivetype = require('postcss-responsive-type');
```

5. The `autoprefixer` task has also been amended—it has a reference to the `postcss-responsive-type` plugin, using the variable that has been declared at the top of the file:

```
gulp.task('autoprefixer', function() {
  return gulp.src('src/*.css')
  .pipe(postcss([at2x(), responsivetype(), autoprefixer]))
  .pipe(gulp.dest('dest/'));
});
```

6. We can now compile the code from a Node.js command prompt, change the working directory to the project area, and run this command:

```
gulp
```

7. Once the code has compiled, copy the contents of the `dest` folder to the `css` folder of the `Tutorial18` folder; if all is well, we should see this when previewing the results in a browser:

Try resizing the window to make it larger or smaller — you should notice that the text size increases or decreases in size, according to the size of the available screen estate. We can then use this as a basis for adding images; if we apply both `postcss-responsive-images` and `postcss-responsive-type` plugins, we can use this as a solid basis for adding responsive capabilities to our sites.

A small point to note though — we've used pixel values throughout our code. Historical convention recommended the use of `em` (or even better `rem`) values, as these scaled better than standard pixel values. However, some developers now argue that this convention is no longer valid; there are occasions when pixel `em` or `rem` values should be used. It's up to us to decide which unit of value to use, and when it should be used!

For a good discussion on the merits of using pixel versus rem values, take a look at this post by Gion Kunz, at `https://mindtheshift.wordpress.com/2015/04/02/r-i-p-rem-viva-css-reference-pixel/`.

Leaving aside what is possible when working with media queries, there are a couple of key topics we should explore—optimizing media queries, and how we can retrofit some form of support for older browsers. We'll start with optimizing queries—PostCSS has a couple of useful plugins available to help with maintaining our code.

Optimizing media queries

Throughout this chapter, we've explored using PostCSS to compile our media queries; while there are plenty of options open to us in terms of what we create, we should be mindful of what we create, to ensure that we're not creating a monster that slows our site down!

PostCSS has a couple of plugins available to help us here. They are:

- `postcss-mq-keyframes`: Available at `https://github.com/TCotton/postcss-mq-keyframes`), this is a simple plugin that moves all keyframes out of existing queries, to the bottom of a style sheet. This allows us to rationalize our keyframe rules—in the event that we have multiple media queries, we can apply the same rule to each of these media queries.

  For example, the highlighted code below would be moved out of the query, and become a rule in its own right:

  ```
  @media only screen and (min-width: 415px) {
    .pace {
      animation: pace-anim 5s;
    }

    @keyframes pace-anim {
      100% {
        opacity: 0;
        }
    }
  }
  ```

- `css-mqpacker`: Available at `https://github.com/hail2u/node-css-mqpacker`), this plugin parses our code and merges any identical rules into one media query rule. It is arguable how much benefit we are likely to get from this plugin; we will likely only see any significant benefit from using it on larger, more complex sites!

Both plugins can be installed using the same process as all of the plugins we've used to date; it's worth noting that we should not overuse our queries. Instead of designing for specific platforms, try designing for instances where content clearly breaks and becomes unusable. The fewer queries we have, the easier it becomes to manage our code; simplicity is absolutely key to a successful site.

Looking further afield, there is one area we should not forget when optimizing our code — what browsers should we support? I'm all for pushing the proverbial browser boat out and using modern browsers where possible. However, some of you may still have to support older browsers (and please don't tell me that includes IE6!). Let's explore an option available in PostCSS to help those of you still having to support applications that really should be put out to pasture, so to speak.

Retrofitting support for older browsers

For those of you who still have to support older browsers, such as IE6-8, then PostCSS can help — we can use the `postcss-mqwidth-to-class` plugin to generate hardcoded class rules, based on the media queries we specify, such as this example:

```
@media (min-width: 1024px) and (max-width: 1298px) {
   .bar { float: left; }
}
```

If we compile it using this plugin, it will produce this result:

```
.min-width-1024px.max-width-1298px .bar { float: left; }
```

Anyone spot the danger here? The code may be *technically* correct, but it suffers from some limitations which make it less attractive: a risk of high levels of CSS specificity, media types are ignored (such as screen or print); and JavaScript may be required if adding classes to the <body> or <html> tags.

Ultimately it is down to us to decide what we need to use, but we should always be mindful that our code doesn't introduce new issues if we have to support older browsers! In this instance, a better alternative to consider is the `postcss-unmq` plugin (the source is available at `https://github.com/jonathantneal/postcss-unmq`); this removes media queries in favor of allowing us to create rules that adhere to specific screen sizes.

Now, whilst browsers such as IE8 should indeed be (forcibly) retired from active service, there is something to be said for considering if we can take it one step further, and start to move away from using responsive design techniques.

For example, conventional wisdom suggests that using rem values were a better alternative than using pixels. There is now a recent shift that suggests a blanket use (as many developers may have done) of rem units is less preferable, and that we should perhaps consider a blend of different units, to ensure content is correctly resized and maintains sufficient clarity. This is an important concept to consider as part of our development work in PostCSS, so let's take a moment to consider what this might mean for us.

Moving away from responsive design

"Moving away from responsive design?? Have you really lost your marbles...??"

In answer to what many might consider a perfectly valid question, the answer is no — or as *Polonius* might have put it in *Hamlet*, *"Though there be madness, yet there is method in't"*.

In short, there is a good reason for considering this topic, as creating breakpoints using PostCSS is a cinch, but working out what they should be is the key to the success of our code. Many developers have blogged online about different types of media queries to use — examples for tablets, desktops, and laptops are widely available, and are frequently updated or replaced, if hardware changes.

Since Ethan Marcotte's popularization of the term "responsive web design" in 2010, many have accepted responsive design as an accepted standard for creating content for multiple devices or platforms. As a concept though, it is starting to lose favor with developers; an inherent weakness is the need to download multiple assets, even though only select versions of those assets may be used (such as larger or smaller versions of images). This of course increases bandwidth usage, and ultimately makes a site slower to navigate.

So, should we not use responsive design at all? Well, not entirely, but it depends on your circumstances. Instead of blindly adding media queries that add a layer of complexity, take a moment to consider if you *really* need that media query.

As an alternative, consider using content specific breakpoints, in place of media equivalents; instead of tying our design to specific devices, we can work out where content can no longer be consumed properly, and build our breakpoint on this, rather than a known device width, which is likely to be changed.

Images, or specifically hi-resolution versions, are no longer an issue; in place of using a low and high res version of each, consider switching to SVG format. This scales beautifully (irrespective of device), and removes any issue with scalability on devices at a stroke. Granted, there are some known issues with support for IE, but most other browsers should be able to handle SVG without causing too many problems!

Fonts are another area where we can begin to reduce our use of media queries — here, we would need to look at using `vw`, `vh`, `vmin`, or `vmax` units; text will automatically resize if the browser viewport is resized. Adapting our code will require some manual changes; we can use the `postcss-vmin` plugin to provide some fallback for older versions of Internet Explorer.

Hopefully this has given you some food for thought—the key message here is that whilst the PostCSS plugin for media queries makes it really easy to implement, we should not blindly go ahead and implement lots of media queries, without considering if there are alternative means to achieve the same results.

Okay, let's move on: time to push the boat out a little; let's take a look at how we can take things further with CSS4 (as it is popularly known). We'll work on an example that allows us to simulate the new greater than or less than operators that can be used as part of CSS level 4 media queries.

Taking things further with CSS4

One of those small pet hates when working with media queries is that the query itself isn't really semantic; most queries will show something like `max-width: 1024px`, when we really mean *...less than...* or *...greater than....*

Thankfully, with the upcoming changes to CSS in what most people call CSS4, we will be able to use `>`, `<`, or `=` symbols to express what we really mean in our code. The beauty about PostCSS is that we can emulate that functionality now, with the `postcss-media-minmax` plugin (available at `https://github.com/postcss/postcss-media-minmax`); the plugin will convert these to the more familiar min- or max- statements that we already know.

It's a really easy plugin to use—we're going to break with convention here though, and use CodePen to demonstrate the plugin in action. CodePen will support a limited number of plugins, of which this is one of them—it's a perfect opportunity to see the effect of our query in action. For our demo, we're going to use the Font Awesome library to create some social media icons—our demo is loosely based on a version by Amey Raut:

You can see the demo at `http://codepen.io/alibby251/pen/wKNMGL`—the code that is of interest to us is from lines 70 to 79—notice the use of `<=` and `>=` in line 71:

```
70  ▼ /* Change the font size of the title */
71  ▼ @media screen and (width >= 500px) and (width <= 1200px) {
72  ▼   h1 {
73          font-size: 1.4em;
74      }
75
76  ▼   .fa {
77          font-size: 1.25em;
78      }
79  }
```

When compiled, it shows this valid CSS:

```
80  ▼ /* Change the font size of the title */
69  ▼ @media screen and (min-width: 500px) and (max-width:
      1200px) {
```

The use of operators such as < or > in media queries is just a small part of what is coming in CSS4; for more details, take a look at the W3C editorial draft at `http://dev.w3.org/csswg/mediaqueries/` — note, it makes for dry reading!

Summary

For anyone creating responsive sites, media queries are a core part of this process — PostCSS can easily help with creating the appropriate media queries that are needed for our projects. We've covered a number of key topics over the last few pages, so let's take a moment to consider what we've covered in this chapter.

For anyone creating responsive sites, media queries are a core part of this process — PostCSS can easily help with creating the appropriate media queries that are needed for our projects. We've covered a number of key topics over the last few pages, so let's take a moment to consider what we've covered in this chapter.

We kicked off with a quick review of standard media queries in CSS, before altering our code to use PostCSS as the basis for our queries. We then put this to good use in making images responsive, with a look first at the options available in PostCSS, before working through an example using PostCSS. We then switched to a common use of media queries for images, with a look at switching in a high resolution version for those devices that support their use.

We then switched to making text responsive, and discovered that it is a similar process that takes place, albeit using a different plugin. We then moved onto look at optimizing queries using PostCSS, before a quick review of some of the options available when retrofitting support for older browsers. We then rounded out the chapter to look at how we can use alternative techniques to make our sites responsive, without the need for media queries, before finishing with discovering a small part of what is available within CSS4, and how PostCSS can be used to make those techniques available today.

Phew, we certainly covered a lot: it doesn't stop there though! The next stop on our journey promises to be just as interesting; every website or online application will use different fonts, images, or colors in some form throughout the site. We'll take a look at how we can use PostCSS to make our lives just that little bit easier....

5
Managing Colors, Images, and Fonts

A website isn't a great website without some form of color, imagery, or fonts—a mix of these will add interest, express content more clearly where words might be insufficient, and generally help maintain visitor engagement.

Users of existing preprocessors will of course be familiar with libraries such as the Compass authoring framework for SASS from `http://www.compass-style.org`; what if we could produce similar effects, but much faster, and without the need for dependencies? No problem, with PostCSS, we can pick and choose which plugins are needed for our site, and begin to build up a processor that suits our needs. We will cover a number of topics throughout this chapter, which will include:

- An overview of plugins available to handle colors, images, and fonts
- Creating image sprites using existing preprocessors
- Adding SVG support using existing preprocessors
- Transitioning to using PostCSS plugins
- Manipulating colors and color palettes using PostCSS plugins

Let's make a start…!

Adding color, fonts, and media to sites

A picture paints a thousand words...

Originally created in the 1920s, this phrase is so apt in the world of digital content—writing a hundred words doesn't have the same appeal if we can replace it with a single image and still convey the same meaning!

A part of any developer or designer's work will be to source the right images or fonts, or choose the right colors, and include them on the site they are building so they can be referenced at the appropriate point. We'll explore some of the plugins and tricks we can use to modify colors, but for now, let's take a look at some of the plugins available for manipulating images and fonts within a site.

Maintaining asset links

When sourcing media for a site, the usual process will be to create a folder for fonts, another for images, and so on, if any part of the process is likely to fail, then it is likely to be with applying incorrect links in our code. The risk of this happening will of course increase if we have a particularly complex folder structure!

Instead, we can take an alternative approach: why not get PostCSS (or a plugin) to do the work for us?

We can use the `postcss-assets` plugin for this purpose; if we specify a name, it will look in the files relative to the source file, then file paths specified in the loadPaths configuration option, and finally search in the URL specified in the basePath config path. The beauty of this is that we can simply reference the image name, and provided PostCSS finds an image with the same name in one of these preassigned locations, then it will substitute in the appropriate path for us at compilation.

If a link needs to change, then no problem, we can either add a new one in, or modify the existing one; CSS styles will be updated at the next compilation. Let's put this into practice, using the `postcss-assets` plugin, in a simple demo.

Automating links to assets

Remember the moody landscape image from *Chapter 4, Building Media Queries*?

In our first example, we're going to rework this demo, but this time use the `postcss-assets` plugin (available from `https://github.com/borodean/postcss-assets`) to automate the insertion of links for all of our assets. We'll focus on images and fonts, but this can equally apply to media such as videos as well.

Here's a screenshot to remind ourselves of that image:

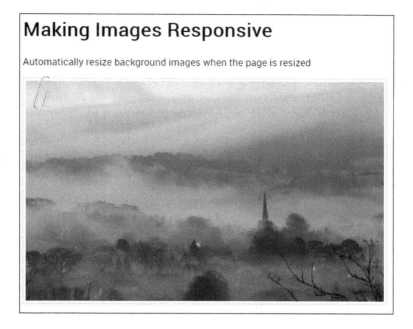

Let's make a start:

1. Go ahead and download a copy of the `Tuturial19` folder from the code download that accompanies this book, save this at the root of our project area. This contains a partially reworked version of the demo from *Chapter 4, Building Media Queries*.

2. Next, go ahead and remove any copies of `gulpfile.js` and `package.json` from the root of our project area — we'll start this chapter with fresh copies from our code download.

3. We now need to install the `postcss-assets` plugin, so fire up a Node.js command prompt session, enter this command, and then press *Enter*:

   ```
   npm install postcss-assets --save-dev
   ```

   Don't close it, we will use it again shortly!

4. We need to extract copies of the `gulpfile.js` and `package.json` files from the code download — go ahead and save them to the root of our project area.

   The sharp-eyed amongst you will note we are not installing any other plugins — we're using ones that we have already installed in earlier exercises; the `package.json` file will include references to these and the `postcss-assets` file.

5. In the `Tutorial19` folder, look for and copy the `styles - pre-compile.css` file to the `src` folder in our project area; rename it to `styles.css`.

6. Revert back to the Node.js command prompt window, then enter gulp at the prompt and press *Enter*.

7. If all is well, we should have a `maps` folder and two CSS stylesheets (one full version, one minified) — if we copy these back to the `css` folder in the `Tutorial19` folder, then run the demo, we should see a familiar image of a landscape with early mist, as shown at the start of this demo.

Okay, the image is displayed, along with the text in Roboto font, but how does it all work? It's worth taking a few moments to explore the code; setting it up correctly will help save you a lot of time!

Most of what is in the gulp file you will recognize from earlier demos — we've included the same linting, renaming, and source map creations as before. In addition to the new assets task (to handle our asset links), we've removed the `autoprefixer` task; we're not calling anything that requires vendor prefixes, so there is no need to use it.

The key process in the gulp file centers on this code — this creates, and substitutes in, the correct asset links. We start with the options configuration object — the `loadPaths` take care of the asset locations, and `relativeTo` tells the plugin to set relative links in relation to the `dest/` folder. In this case, `loadPaths` defines specific folders to use; we use `relativeTo` to make these paths relative:

```
var options = {
  loadPaths: ['img/', 'fonts/'],
  relativeTo: 'dest/'
};
```

The `dest/` folder is used in our creation process — in reality, this would be the location of our CSS style sheets on the production server. This next simple task simply calls the `postcss-assets` plugin, and processes each style sheet found in the `src` folder:

```
gulp.task('assets', function() {
  return gulp.src('src/*.css')
    .pipe(postcss([ assets(options) ]))
    .pipe(gulp.dest('dest/'));
});
```

We then simply call the task, if we were to call gulp from a command prompt, then it will run all of these tasks:

```
gulp.task('default', ['assets', 'lint-styles', 'rename', 'sourcemap']);
```

All in all, a very simple but highly effective tool, it removes the need to insert any links manually, provided we've included them within the configuration object.

Alright…let's move on: we've covered a simple method to ensure we always have the right links for font or image files. There is still an element of manual work required though—do we really need to include all of the lines added for our custom font?

Well, we could always just use a font hosted on Google, but that destroys the point of using PostCSS! Instead, we can simply use the custom font name in our style sheet, but get PostCSS to add in the custom font-face declaration automatically at compilation. Intrigued? Let's take a look at how, as part of our next exercise.

Managing fonts with PostCSS

In our previous demo, we explored a means to automatically add links using PostCSS—it shortcuts the need to worry about providing the right locations for files. The trouble is, when used with custom fonts, it still requires too much work (yes, I know, we humans are inherently lazy!). There is a better alternative:

Enter the `postcss-fontpath` plugin, available from `https://github.com/seaneking/postcss-fontpath`; this is a simple plugin that requires limited information about our custom font, and in return will produce the full font-face declaration at the compilation stage.

So, rather than talk about it, why don't we put it to use? Let's revisit the responsive image demo we covered in the previous demo, and alter our style sheet to use the fontpath plugin to handle our custom font:

1. We'll start by extracting a copy of the `Tutorial20` folder from the code download that accompanies this book, and save the folder to the root of our project area.

2. Next, take a copy of `package.json` and `gulpfile.js` files from the `Tutorial20` folder, and replace the existing versions that are at the root of our project area.

3. Go ahead and fire up a Node.js command prompt, and change the working folder to that of our project area.

4. At the command prompt, enter this command, then press *Enter*:

```
npm install postcss-fontpath --save-dev
```

Although we've installed the plugin explicitly, we can easily install it using just `npm install`; the presence of the `package.json` file in the folder will tell NPM what to install (in this case the missing `postcss-fontpath` plugin). Keep the session open, we will use it again shortly.

5. Take a copy of `styles - pre-compile.css` from the `css - completed version` folder, and save this as `styles.css` into the `src` folder at the root of our project area.

6. Revert back to the Node.js command prompt window, then enter `gulp` at the prompt, and press *Enter*.

7. If all is well, we should see the, by now, familiar style sheets and source map appear in the `dest` folder; copy these to the `css` folder within the `Tutorial20` folder.

At this point, we should now have a working demo; we won't see anything intrinsically different, but know that at compilation, PostCSS has automatically added the right font-face declarations for our font.

The beauty about this plugin is in its simplicity — it needs no more than the addition of a simple command in the main task:

```
gulp.task('fonts', function () {
  return gulp.src('src/*.css').pipe(
    postcss([ fontpath() ])
  ).pipe(
    gulp.dest('dest/')
  );
});
```

There is no need to have to specify any additional configuration elements or rules, the plugin does exactly what it says on the tin, so to speak! Although we've not achieved anything ground-breaking with this example, it does serve to illustrate some key points about using PostCSS:

- PostCSS works best when plugins concentrate on a single task and don't try to achieve everything under the sun in one go. Adhering to the single responsibility principle means we can reduce duplication, make the plugin more robust, and avoid instances where changes can end up breaking functionality elsewhere in our processor! This plugin is perfect — it just provides a font-face declaration for the specified font, and nothing else.

- Sometimes, when choosing the right plugin in PostCSS, there will be occasions when we choose something that later turns out not to work as expected. A case in point is the `postcss-font-magician` plugin (available from `https://github.com/jonathantneal/postcss-font-magician`); it has the right idea of providing font-face declarations, but tries to provide them for Google-hosted fonts, locally hosted fonts, Bootstrap, and so on.

 Unfortunately, the net result is that at the time of writing, not all of the functionality appears to work as expected, so it is at this point where we have to look for alternatives.

If you would like to explore more, then the `postcss.parts` directory (at `http://www.postcss.parts`) has more options available; two that might be of interest are the `Assets Rebase` plugin (from `https://github.com/devex-web-frontend/postcss-assets-rebase`), and the PostCSS `Font Pack` plugin, from `https://github.com/jedmao/postcss-font-pack`. We will cover the latter plugin in more detail in *Chapter 8, Creating PostCSS Plugins*.

Okay, so we have our text in place: it does look a little boring, doesn't it? Well, we can fix that by adding images. So, how exactly can PostCSS help us, I hear you ask?

It can help in a number of ways—instead of using plain colors, we can begin to mix some together, for example. Or how about using image sprites? A pain to create manually, right? Not with PostCSS. I'll bet you've seen some of the image filters you can use on images (such as sepia or tint), but found that they don't work in every browser right?

These are just some of the ways that PostCSS can help us, and we will cover all of these and more throughout this chapter. Let's make a start though on working with images: our first demo will cover the creation of image sprites. We'll start with a quick recap of the SASS process, before switching to using PostCSS.

Creating image sprites

Let's start with something easy: I'm sure that at some point you will either have used or created image sprites, right? If you're a SASS developer, no doubt you will have availed yourself of the sprite mixins from Compass, and used an app such as **Koala** to compile, or compiled directly from the command line.

A copy of the relevant files for creating sprites using Compass can be found in the code download that accompanies this book, in the `Tutorial21A` folder.

The process is relatively straightforward, but you still have to set up a `Compass` project, install a GUI application (if you're using one), and so on, which is a real pain! We could use an online application such as **SpritePad** (`http://spritepad.wearekiss.com/`) instead, but again that's a manual process, and it's prone to error. Instead, we can easily use PostCSS to help us here — over and above the normal variables that we declare at the top of any gulp file, there is very little required in order to produce basic image sprites. Let's take a look at creating one now, using the `postcss-sprites` plugin.

Demo – creating a credit card icon bar

How many times have you bought something from an e-commerce site? If you've bought as much as I have online, then no doubt you will have seen shopping carts with assorted payment card icons. These may be small, but they are nevertheless key to our site — after all, how can we tell if using a particular credit card might fail, if the online retailer doesn't accept Mastercard, for example? Seems obvious, but it's not always easy to tell.

Leaving that aside, it is a cinch to create an image sprite with PostCSS; gone is the dependency on SASS: in its place we can use the `postcss-sprites` plugin (available from `https://github.com/2createStudio/postcss-sprites`) to produce our composite image. Let's dive in and take a look.

For this demo, we will use the credit card icons available at `http://findicons.com/pack/2102/credit_card_debit_card`; please feel free to substitute if you would like to use different icons.

All of the code for this tutorial can be found in the `Tutorial21B` folder, in the code download — we will start afresh by installing the `postcss-sprites` plugin:

1. Go ahead and fire up a Node.js command prompt, and change the working folder to that of our project area.

2. At the command prompt, enter the command shown in this screenshot, then press *Enter*, once Node has confirmed successful installation, and minimize the window, as we will return to it later in this exercise:

3. Go ahead and fire up your text editor, then add the following lines — these represent four credit card icons we would typically add to any online e-commerce site:

```
.amex { background: #fff url(img/amex.png) no-repeat 0 0; }
.cirrus { background: url(img/cirrus.png) no-repeat 0 0; }

.delta { background: url(img/delta.png) no-repeat 0 0; }
.solo { background: url(img/solo.png) no-repeat 0 0; }
```

4. Save the file as `style.css`, and store it in the `src` folder of our project area.

5. In the same folder, create a folder called `img` at the root of our project area; extract copies of the icons stored in the code download that accompanies this book, and save them to the `img` folder.

6. From the code download that accompanies this book, go ahead and extract a copy of `gulpfile.js`, and save this to the root of our project area.

7. Revert back to the Node.js window, then at the prompt, enter `gulp` and press *Enter*.

8. Our code will now be compiled, if all is well, we should see something akin to this when viewing the `style.css` file within the `dest` folder:

```
.amex { background-image: url(../img/sprite.png); background-
position: 0 0; background-color: #fff; }
.cirrus { background-image: url(../img/sprite.png); background-
position: -102px 0; }
.delta { background-image: url(../img/sprite.png); background-
position: 0 -64px; }
.solo { background-image: url(../img/sprite.png); background-
position: -102px -64px; }
```

At this stage, we can then copy the code to our website, along with image — instead of using four separate icons (which each require separate calls to the server), we can cache the single icon. This will result in faster response times with fewer calls to our server. The compiled style sheet can be found in the `dest` folder, with the composite image one level up, in the `img` folder:

Even though this is a simple process, it's worth noting a key point with how our gulp file has been configured — the use of a configuration object for the `sprites` plugin:

```
var opts = {
  stylesheetPath: 'dest/',
  spritePath    : 'img/sprite.png',
  path          : 'src/img/'
};
```

It's not a process we've used to date, but it does not mean that it is any less useful — it simply boils down to a matter of personal preference and readability. It does make it easier to read the calls for each plugin we assign; in this instance, we're only using one, but you can imagine what it will be like with multiple plugins in use:

```
gulp.task('autoprefixer', function() {
  return gulp.src('src/*.css')
    .pipe(postcss([ sprites(opts) ]))
    .pipe(gulp.dest('dest/'));
});
```

Okay, let's change tack and take a look at a different side to using images with PostCSS: using SVG format images. Standard images don't always scale well, particularly when used in a responsive environment; sometimes we might use retina images instead, but an alternative to consider is the use of SVG images.

Working with SVG in PostCSS

The rapidly increasing use of mobile devices makes creating responsive content a must; the traditional route is using something akin to `max-width: 100%` to control the size of an element on screen.

A better alternative is to use SVG—this maintains quality, even when resized; standard image formats will become pixelated if resized to an excessive size. For those of you who have previously used SASS, then there isn't any in-built support for SVG as such; the most we can hope to achieve is efficient nesting within our style sheet.

An example of what we might use can be found in the `sass` folder within the `Tutorial22` folder in the code download that accompanies this book.

If we're a regular user of SVG images within SASS, then it is likely we would use a library such as `sass-svg`, from `https://github.com/davidkpiano/sass-svg`. Moving away from SASS to PostCSS is easy; the PostCSS ecosystem has a number of plugins we can use to manipulate images. Let's take a look at how, using the `postcss-svg` plugin.

Altering icon images using PostCSS

We'll use the `postcss-svg` plugin (from `https://github.com/Pavliko/postcss-svg`), to manipulate some icons from the `Evil Icon` package (available from `https://github.com/outpunk/gulp-evil-icons`), as part of the next demo:

1. We'll begin by extracting a copy of the `Tutorial22` folder from the code download that accompanies this book. Save it to the root of our project area.

2. From within the `Tutorial22` folder, extract copies of the `gulpfile.js` and `package.json` files, and use them to replace any that are currently stored at the root of our project area.

3. Go ahead and extract a copy of `style - pre-compile.css` from the same folder; save this as `style.css` within the `src` folder. Do the same for the `index.html` file as well.

4. In a break to previous demos, we need an additional `css` folder—go ahead and create one within the `dest` folder.

5. Next, fire up a Node.js command prompt, and change the working folder to that of our project area.

6. We need to install the `postcss-svg` plugin, so at the command prompt, enter this command, then press *Enter*:

    ```
    npm install postcss-svg --save-dev
    ```

7. Once completed, enter `gulp` at the command prompt, then press *Enter*.

8. If all is well, we should see the usual two style sheets appear in the `/dest/css` folder, along with a source `map` folder. The HTML markup file will appear in the `dest` folder.

   If you don't see the source map or minified versions appear, then rerun `gulp` — sometimes these files will only appear if a compiled `style.css` file is present.

9. Copy the contents of the `dest` folder to the `css` folder within the `Tutorial22` folder — if all is well, we should see these icons appear when previewing the results in a browser:

Although this is a simple demo, we've covered some useful tips and tricks within; it's worth taking some time to explore how the demo was put together in more detail.

Exploring the results in more detail

There are several key elements to this exercise that are worthy of attention, the use of a CDN link and Node to provide the style sheet and icons for Evil Icons, the compiled HTML file and the references to use within our custom style sheet. We will cover all of these, but first let's explore the gulp file in more detail.

We begin with these two lines:

```
var evilIcons = require("gulp-evil-icons");
var postcssSVG = require('postcss-svg')
```

You should not be surprised to see the latter, but the former is present as the Evil Icons library can be installed using the `gulp-evil-icons` package. There are a number of different options available for installing, but as we're already using Gulp, it makes sense to continue using the task runner.

Next, we spread our work over two tasks — the first compiles the HTML code to assign the relevant icon image to our `<icon>` statements within our markup:

```
gulp.task('icons', function () {
  return gulp.src('src/index.html')
.pipe(evilIcons())
    .pipe(gulp.dest('dest/'));
});
```

To change the colors requires the use of the `postcss-svg` plugin, here referenced by postcssSVG:

```
gulp.task('changecolor', ['icons'], function() {
  gulp.src('src/style.css')
  .pipe(postcss([ postcssSVG() ]))
    .pipe(gulp.dest('dest/'));
});
```

We of course had to update our default task, if we simply call `gulp` at the command line, then it will know to run all of these tasks in turn:

```
gulp.task('default', ['icons', 'changecolor', 'lint-styles' ,
'rename', 'sourcemap' ]);
```

The last step also applies a similar update to our watch facility:

```
var watcher = gulp.watch('src/*.*', ['default', 'icons',
'changecolor', 'lint-styles', 'rename', 'sourcemap']);
```

If we then take a look within the HTML markup, we can see a link to the `Evil Icons` library that was installed using Node.js:

```
<link rel="stylesheet" href="../node_modules/gulp-evil-icons/
node_modules/evil-icons/assets/evil-icons.css">
```

We then put our customizations into a separate style sheet:

```
<link rel="stylesheet" type="text/css" href="css/style.css">
```

These look something like this:

```
1   .icon {
2       display: inline-block;
3       padding: 3rem;
4   }
5
6   .icon--ei-sc-linkedin {
7       fill: green;
8   }
9
10  .icon--ei-sc-github {
11      fill: orange;
12  }
```

At this stage, the CSS styles may look simple, but the HTML markup is anything but; the `postcss-svg` plugin has added an in-line version of our icons to the HTML markup, with the appropriate edits made from our custom style sheet:

```
      1.6-1.1 2.6-1.7 3.1V31c0 .9 1.8 1.6 3.4 2.2 1.9.7 3.9 1.5 4.6 3.11-1.9.7c-.3-.8-1.9-1.4-3.4-1.9-2.2-.8-4.7-1.7-4.7-4v-2
      .6-.3.6-1.1 0-.2-.2-.5-.3-.6l-.4-.4.2-.5s.5-1.6.5-3.6c0-1.9-1.1-3.3-2-3.3h-.6l-.3-.5c0-.4-.7-.8-1.9-.8-3.1 0-5 1.7-5 4.
      0-.3.3-.3.7 0 .5.6 1.1.9 1.3l.4.3v.5c0 1.5 1.3 2.3 1.3 2.4l.5.3v2.6c0 2.4-2.6 3.6-5 4.6-1.1.4-2.6 1.1-2.8 1.6z"></path>
11    <div class="icon icon--ei-sc-linkedin"><svg class="icon__cnt"><use xlink:href="#ei-sc-linkedin-icon" /></svg></div>
12    <div class="icon icon--ei-sc-github"><svg class="icon__cnt"><use xlink:href="#ei-sc-github-icon" /></svg></div>
13    <div class="icon icon--ei-sc-twitter"><svg class="icon__cnt"><use xlink:href="#ei-sc-twitter-icon" /></svg></div>
14    <div class="icon icon--ei-sc-youtube"><svg class="icon__cnt"><use xlink:href="#ei-sc-youtube-icon" /></svg></div>
15  </body>
16  </html>
```

Sometimes, it is easy to wonder if using SVG is worth the extra markup, the main benefit being that if it is added in-line, then we reduce the number of calls to external resources; any content that requires altering can be done, without sacrificing the quality of our images.

Considering alternative options

We concentrated on using the `postcss-svg` plugin throughout our exercise, as a start to manipulating SVG images within the PostCSS system; there are some more options available, which may be of interest:

- `postcss-write-svg`: This plugin (available at `https://github.com/jonathantneal/postcss-write-svg`) allows us to write inline SVGs in CSS.

- `postcss-inline-svg`: Another plugin (from `https://github.com/TrySound/postcss-inline-svg`), which in-lines SVG images and allows us to customize their styles.

- `postcss-svgo`: This plugin (available at `https://github.com/ben-eb/postcss-svgo`) processes inline SVG using the SVG Optimizer Tool for Node.

If you have a need to provide a fall-back position for SVG files, then you can try the `postcss-svg-fallback` plugin, available from `https://github.com/justim/postcss-svg-fallback`— we will use this plugin later, in *Chapter 8, Creating PostCSS Plugins*.

Okay, let's change tack: using SVG images can be a little heavy handed if all we need is a straightforward format for displaying images, right? Well, we could use standard formats, or one which has superior quality while maintaining smaller sizes. I'm talking about the lesser-known WebP format from Google—let's dig in and find out more about this format, and why it deserves more attention.

Adding support for WebP images

Manipulating SVG images is an acquired art, and in some instances, it will clearly be overkill for what we need to achieve.

Instead, for those occasions where we need the detail in our images, we might normally use the JPEG format, or potentially PNG as an alternative. There's nothing wrong with either, but, it's old hat, and I do like to push the boundaries of what is possible! In addition, the JPEG image format is lossy and does not support alpha channels; PNG images are lossless, but suffer from larger file sizes for more complex images. If all we did was simply insert images onto a page, then PostCSS wouldn't be helpful here; instead, how about considering a different format altogether?

Enter Google's **WebP**. You'd be forgiven for thinking "Web...what?", as it isn't a common format! Part of this can be attributed to the lack of take-up; the only browsers to support it natively are Chrome, Android, and Opera. That doesn't mean to say it should be discounted. The format can offer some significant space savings over standard image formats such as JPEG or PNG, while maintaining superior quality. We can even get PostCSS to do most of the work for us, to boot! Let's explore the nuts and bolts of this in more detail, with a simple demo.

Switching WebP images in and out

Image switching is nothing new, we covered one aspect back in *Chapter 4, Building Media Queries*, when we used PostCSS to switch-in hi-res images when supported in the browser.

We can use a similar technique, but this time with image formats, Google's WebP format was designed as a replacement for the myriad of other image formats available for the web. In an ideal world, we would use the new `<picture>` tag to take care of switching images automatically:

```
<picture>
  <source srcset="../img/landscape.webp" type="image/webp">
  <img src="../img/landscape.jpg" alt="The Oslo Opera House">
</picture>
```

It's not supported in all browsers, so instead, we can use a mix of PostCSS and Modernizr to apply the same effect. The plugin we need for this task is the `webpcss` plugin (available from `https://github.com/lexich/webpcss`) — we will need to run `npm install gulp-webp --save-dev` in a Node.js command prompt session to install the plugin. Let's dive in and take a look at it in more detail.

For best results, I would recommend using Chrome throughout these two demos, support can be added for Windows and other browsers, by visiting `https://developers.google.com/speed/webp/`.

Viewing the differences in file sizes

Before we get stuck into using PostCSS, let's take a moment to perform a quick test. The files for this tutorial are in the `Tutorial 23` folder:

1. In the code download that accompanies this book, go ahead and extract a copy of `landscape - original version.jpg`, and rename it as `landscape.jpg`. The size should be around 11.5 MB in size.

2. Save the image to the root of our project area—we also need a copy of `cwebp.exe`, so go ahead and extract that to our project area as well.

3. Fire up a command prompt session, change the working folder to our project area, enter `gulp`, and then press *Enter*.

4. If all is well, we should see the results of our conversion, and the new WebP-format image appear in our project area:

```
Node.js command prompt                                    —    □    ×

C:\wamp\www\postcss>cwebp -q 100 landscape.jpg -o landscape.webp
Saving file 'landscape.webp'
File:        landscape.jpg
Dimension: 4000 x 4949
Output:      7505870 bytes Y-U-V-All-PSNR 51.57 54.71 55.33    52.44 dB
block count:  intra4: 166305
              intra16: 66195   (-> 28.47%)
              skipped block: 0 (0.00%)
bytes used:  header:           1550  (0.0%)
             mode-partition: 121680   (1.6%)
  Residuals bytes  |segment 1|segment 2|segment 3|segment 4|   total
    macroblocks:   |    33% |     0% |     0% |     0% |  232500
      quantizer:   |     0  |     0  |     0  |     0  |
   filter level:   |     0  |     0  |     0  |     0  |

C:\wamp\www\postcss>_
```

5. Try performing the same process with a PNG format image; here are the results of a similar test I performed, with a PNG version of our landscape image:

```
Node.js command prompt                                    —    □    ×

F:\Books\B05194 - Mastering PostCSS WebDesign\Chapters\Chapter 5\Code\Tutorial -
 WebP images>cwebp -q 100 landscape.png -o landscape.webp
Saving file 'landscape.webp'
File:       landscape.png
Dimension: 4000 x 4949
Output:     7496788 bytes Y-U-V-All-PSNR 51.56 54.71 55.33    52.44 dB
block count:    intra4: 165954
                intra16: 66546  (-> 28.62%)
                skipped block: 0 (0.00%)
bytes used:   header:         1557  (0.0%)
              mode-partition: 119071  (1.6%)
  Residuals bytes  |segment 1|segment 2|segment 3|segment 4|  total
     macroblocks:  |      33%|      0%:|      0%:|      0%:| 232500
       quantizer:  |       0 |       0 |       0 |       0 |
    filter level:  |       0 |       0 |       0 |       0 |

F:\Books\B05194 - Mastering PostCSS WebDesign\Chapters\Chapter 5\Code\Tutorial -
 WebP images>_
```

In both cases, the image sizes reduced significantly, the JPEG version dropped from around 12.5 MB to just over 7 MB; the PNG format shrunk from an enormous 25 MB to around the same size!

 To learn more about using the WebP format, take a look at the documentation on the Google Developers site at `https://developers.google.com/speed/webp/`.

Okay, time for another demo! Let's now make use of PostCSS to create our styles for both standard JPEG format, and WebP equivalents:

Switching in WebP images

Automatically switch in WebP images when supported by the browser

For this demo, we'll use the `gulp-webpcss` plugin, available from `https://github.com/lexich/webpcss`:

1. Go ahead and download a copy of the `Tutorial23` folder from the code download that accompanies this book, save this at the root of our project area.

2. Next, go ahead and remove any copies of `gulpfile.js` and `package.json` from the root of our project area; we need to replace them with copies from the `Tutorial23` folder.

3. With these files in place, we still need to install the plugins, in a Node.js command prompt window, change the working folder to our project, then run these commands, pressing *Enter* after each:

   npm install --save-dev gulp-webp

   npm install --save-dev gulp-webpcss

   Note the order of the parameters in these commands, if they are written in a different order, they will not install.

4. Copy the `style - pre-compile.css` file from the `Tutorial23` folder to the `src` folder at the root of our project area, then rename it as `style.css`.

5. Fire up a Node.js command prompt, change the working folder to our project area, then enter `gulp` at the prompt and press *Enter*.

6. If all is well, we should see the code shown in this screenshot when viewing the contents of the compiled file; the converted image will also appear in the `img` folder:

```
50    .js.webp #retina a:before { background: url(../img/paper-clip.webp) no-repeat;
51
52    .js.webp .landscape { background-image: url(../img/landscape.webp); }
```

7. Copy the contents of the `img` folder into the `img` folder within the `Tutorial23` folder.

8. Copy the `style.css` file from the `dest` folder into the `css` folder within the `Tutorial23` folder.

9. Go ahead and run `index.html` in a browser, if all is well, we should see something akin to the screenshot at the start of this exercise.

If we run the same `index.html` in Google Chrome or Firefox, at first we should not see any difference—we'll only see the difference when viewing the compiled source within the Developer Toolbar in Chrome:

```
.js.webp .landscape {                              style.css:52
    background-image: url(../img/landscape.webp);
}
.landscape {                                       style.css:46
    background-image: url('../img/landscape.jpg');
}
```

The real benefit, though, is in the `img` folder within our project area, the original JPEG image we use is 222 KB; however, the WebP is a fraction of this size: it weighs in at just 82 KB. See what I mean about the saving in space?

Okay, onwards we go: time to focus on another area of site building, which is manipulating colors. Colors play a key role within any site, as they make up a part of the message to the end user; let's dive in and take a look at some of the options available when using PostCSS.

Manipulating colors and color palettes

A challenge that any developer or designer will face is which color should be used on a site—a nice shade of red, or how about sea blue, for example? It doesn't matter whether they are responsible for choosing the shade to use, or if they have to pick the right RGB or HEX color to use.

Irrespective of where responsibilities lie, we still have to choose a color, and there is a good chance we won't be choosing one that comes from the default 256-color palette, but one that is likely to be a lighter or darker shade, or perhaps a mix of two colors:

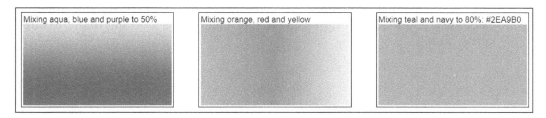

Anyone used to working with SASS will already be aware of functions such as `lighten()`, `darken()` or `saturate()` — the great thing about PostCSS is that we can replicate similar functionality for those who want to move away from the dependency of SASS.

To see how easy it is to use, we're going to combine the power of two plugins for PostCSS — `postcss-color-palette` (available at `https://github.com/zaim/postcss-color-palette`), and `postcss-color-mix` (from `https://github.com/iamstarkov/postcss-color-mix`). The former allows us to choose one or more colors from any of three palettes, while `postcss-color-mix` will mix specific colors to make a new color. There are reasons for using these plugins, which will become clear; for now, let's get stuck in and watch these plugins in action.

Displaying and mixing colors using palettes

In this exercise, we're going to take a look at mixing colors; `postcss-color-palette` allows us to choose multiple colors by name (and not by number!), then converts them to HEX equivalent values. We can then either create gradient-type effects, or simply mix the colors together (using `postcss-color-mix`) to produce a new color.

Let's make a start:

1. We'll start by extracting a copy of the `Tutorial24` folder from the code download that accompanies this book; save the folder to the root of our project area.

2. From the `Tutorial24` folder, copy the `package.json` and `gulpfile.js` files to the root of our project area.

3. We also need our stylesheet, for this, go ahead and copy the `style - pre-compile.css` file from the same folder and drop this into the `src` folder in our project area. Rename it as `style.css`.

4. At this point we need to install the plugin, for this, so go ahead and fire up a Node.js command prompt session, then change the working folder to our project area.

5. At the prompt, enter the command shown in this screenshot, then press *Enter*, if all is well, we should see confirmation that the plugin has installed correctly:

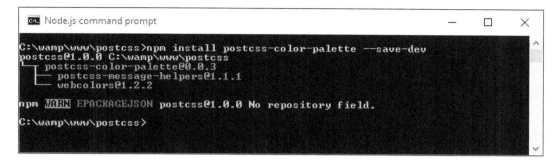

6. Repeat step 5, but this time, run the command shown in this screenshot:

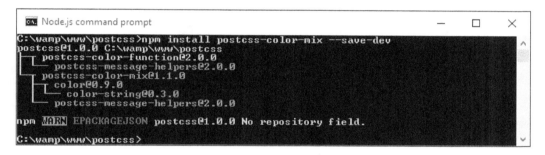

7. At the prompt, enter `gulp`, then press *Enter*—PostCSS will go away and compile the style sheet, and drop the compiled results into the `dest` folder.

8. Copy the contents of the `dest` folder (which will be the uncompressed and minified style sheets, along with a source map file) to the `css` folder within the `Tutorial24` folder.

9. Try previewing `index.html` at the root of our `Tutorial24` folder; if all is well, we should see our mixed colors, as shown in this screenshot:

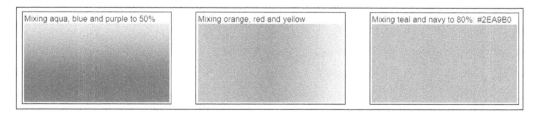

Okay, the colors I've chosen clearly aren't going to win any style awards any time soon, but they help serve a purpose: it is very easy to use proper color names, if preferred, while still allowing PostCSS to compile them into valid HEX values. That aside, let's take a moment to consider the code we've used in this demo — it does raise a few key points, which we should cover, when using these plugins.

Dissecting our demo in more detail

The demo we've created follows similar principles to most other demos we've built so far; we begin with declaring variables to store instances of our plugins, thus:

```
var palette = require('postcss-color-palette');
var colormix = require('postcss-color-mix')
```

The magic then happens in this task, within our `gulp` file:

```
gulp.task('palette', function () {
  return gulp.src('src/*.css')
  .pipe(postcss([ autoprefixer, palette({ palette: 'mrmrs' }),
  colormix() ]))
  .pipe(gulp.dest('dest/'));
});
```

Notice that we've specified a palette to use, the `mrmrs` option is the default, but we can equally use `material` or `flatui` as alternatives. All three reference the `webcolors` plugin from `https://github.com/zaim/webcolors/`; this package could be expanded to include other palettes if desired.

With the links to our two plugins in place, and the task set up, we can then begin to specify rules within our style sheet, which will use the plugins. We've created three, and all three use the `postcss-color-palette` to determine what the HEX value should be for each color; the third and final mixes the two colors together once HEX values have been assigned:

```
#box0 { background: linear-gradient(aqua, blue 50%, purple); }

#box1 { background: linear-gradient(to right, orange, red,
yellow); }

#box2 { background: mix(teal, navy, 80%); }
```

Getting the mix of the color right for the third rule isn't easy, the key to a successful mix is to avoid using colors that are in the same spectrum; the closer they are, the less impact the mix will have!

If you want a quick way to gauge how well colors have mixed, then try `http://jackiebalzer.com/color` — this demo has a `mix()` option in it, which will compile them in the browser and avoid the need to run the compilation process manually.

We've covered some of the plugins that are likely to be more popular; there are more available via the `PostCSS.parts` directory, which may be of interest:

- `colorguard`: Helps maintain a consistent color palette
- `postcss-ase-colors`: Replaces color names with values read from an ASE palette file; this is perfect if you happen to be a user of Adobe PhotoShop, InDesign, or Illustrator
- `postcss-shades-of-gray`: Helps keep grayscale colors consistent to a gray palette
- `postcss-color-pantone`: Transforms Pantone color to RGB.

In the meantime, let's move on: we've explored using palettes to select our colors, before mixing them to create new ones. This is just scratching the surface of what is possible; how about creating different *shades* of colors, using functions such as `darken()`, `tint()` or `lightness()`? Such functions already exist in most preprocessors, such as SASS; let's explore how we can achieve the same results using PostCSS plugins.

Creating color functions with PostCSS

In our journey through manipulating colors using PostCSS, we've so far seen how to define colors using palettes — this may work in some instances, but there will be occasions when we need to specify a color that doesn't feature in a palette.

We can always try to specify the value manually, but what happens if we need to alter it? Do we try to find every instance of it, and risk the possibility of missing an instance?

The answer is no. Instead, we can use the `postcss-color-function` plugin to create our colors dynamically; we can then assign the resulting value to a variable if we find ourselves frequently using this color. We can use this route to produce some nice shades of colors, so let's get stuck in and explore using this plugin in more detail.

Adjusting colors using functions

A useful facility within most CSS preprocessors is the ability to create new colors dynamically, we can do this either by adjusting a color channel, or applying a filter effect to the color, such as making it darker:

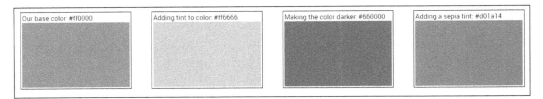

The benefit of this is simple, it allows us to reduce the number of base colors we assign by default; the remaining colors can be created automatically. If we need to change one of our base colors, then any colors created dynamically should still work.

Thankfully, we can achieve the same effects within PostCSS, to do this, we need to make use of the `postcss-color-function` plugin, available from `https://github.com/postcss/postcss-color-function`. We'll also be using the `css-color-converter` plugin, to help manage conversion between different color formats.

Let's explore this in more detail with a simple demo:

1. We start by extracting a copy of the `Tutorial25` folder from within the code download that accompanies this book—go ahead and save this to our project area.

2. If the project area already has a `package.json` and/or a `gulpfile.js` present, then remove them; replace them with the files from within the `Tutorial25` folder.

3. Although we have the right configuration files in place, we still need to install the plugin—go ahead and fire up a Node.js command prompt session, then change the working folder to our project area.

4. At the prompt, enter these commands, pressing *Enter* after each:

   ```
   npm install postcss-color-function --save-dev
   npm install css-color-converter --save-dev
   ```

5. At this point, we can now go ahead and compile our style sheet—look for `styles - pre-compile.css` from within the `css - completed version` subfolder, and save it to the `src` folder within our project area as `style.css`.

6. Switch to the Node.js command prompt from earlier, then enter `gulp` at the prompt and press *Enter*.

7. If all is well, we should see the by now compiled style sheets appear (both uncompressed and minified), along with the source map in the `dest` folder. Copy the contents of this folder to the `css` folder within the `Tutorial25` folder.

Try previewing the results within a browser, if the compilation was successful, we should see four boxes with different shades of red appear, as shown at the start of this exercise. The question is though, we've seen the results appear, but how does PostCSS know to create these colors?

Dissecting our demo

It's a good question, the conversion process is very simple; the trick to it, though, lies not within compiling, but working out how to achieve the color! Odd as it may seem, choosing the color isn't as easy as it looks; let me explain more:

The compilation process is, like other PostCSS plugins, very easy to configure—we begin of course with creating a variable that defines the `color-function` plugin:

```
var colorfunction = require('postcss-color-function');
```

Next up, we add a reference to our principal gulp task, here we've used both `autoprefixer` and the `color-function` plugin together, but the former isn't strictly needed, as we're not adding any vendor prefixes:

```
gulp.task('autoprefixer', function() {
    return gulp.src('src/*.css')
      .pipe(postcss([ autoprefixer, colorfunction() ]))
      .pipe(gulp.dest('dest/'));
});
```

The real magic, though, is in the colors we assign within our style sheet—our first box is a control, with a standard red color:

```
#box0 { background-color: #ff0000; }
```

Next up, we're adding a `tint` of `60%` to `box1`, which has the effect of turning it a light pink:

```
#box1 { background-color: color(red tint(60%)); }
```

Box2 goes the other way, even though we've used a lightness filter (where you might expect a similar result as box1), the negative number makes it a brown-red color:

```
#box2 { background-color: color(red lightness(-20%)); }
```

The final box, box3, continues the brown theme from box2, but makes it lighter. Note though, that in the comment, this shade is what would be produced if we had applied a sepia tone:

```
#box3 { background-color: sepia(red, 0.7);}
```

The question is, how would we know that this is indeed a sepia filter being applied?

At face value, it looks like we've selected red, then altered each channel by a specific amount to get the final result.

A drawback of using this plugin is that it doesn't have functions to support all of the equivalent CSS3 filters available today; it does mean we have to be resourceful, and calculate what the color should be directly. We will be able to change that in the next demo—there will be occasions when we need to create our own custom filters; a good example is sepia. It does mean more work upfront, but it allows us to then call a sepia() function by name, rather than approximate the final result.

If you struggle to find what a color should be once a filter is applied, take a look at http://jackiebalzer.com/color; this is a great site that allows us to choose a color and see what the results are when filters are applied. It is written for SASS, but the end result will be identical for PostCSS. A site such as ColorHexa.com (http://www.colorhexa.com) is a good help too, we can use it to verify what color values should be when a filter has been applied.

On we go. We discovered during our exercise that the postcss-color-function plugin doesn't cover all of the CSS3 filters that we can use in CSS; for the sepia example, we had to assign a calculated color value, rather than applying a filter effect. Let's fix that now. With a bit of upfront rework to our demo, we can create our own custom functions. It means that if, for example, we want a sepia effect, then we can call sepia(), rather than calculate what the final color should be!

Creating colors with PostCSS filters

In our previous demo, we took a look at programmatically changing colors—this is a function that has been present in most CSS processors (such as SASS or Less) for some time.

There may be occasions where we require a finer degree of control over changing colors, and that simply using existing functions provided by the `postcss-color-function` plugin isn't sufficient, or that the desired filter isn't available. If we're feeling inclined, we can create our own color functions; for this, we can use the `postcss-functions` plugin, available from `https://github.com/andyjansson/postcss-functions`, to expose the use of JavaScript functions in our task file.

It's worth noting, though, that if a CSS3 filter doesn't exist, then most can be created using a combination of different calculations (such as the `sepia` example from the previous demo). This may technically work okay, but it is easier to simply reference a sepia filter by name, rather than work out that `#box3` has a sepia effect applied!

I feel a demo coming on, so without further ado, here's a screenshot of what we're going to create:

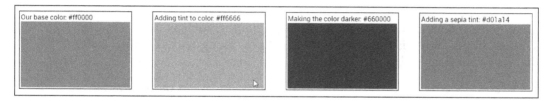

In short, we're using a standard shade of red (`#ff0000`, just to be clear!), and calculating various shades using a tint, darken, or sepia filter.

Let's take a look at how to create these colors in more detail:

1. We'll start by extracting a copy of the `Tutorial26` folder from the code download that accompanies this book; save it to the root of our project area.

2. Next, go ahead and remove any copies of `gulpfile.js` and `package.json` from the root of our project area.

3. From the `Tutorial26` folder, copy both `package.json` and `gulpfile.js` to the root of our project area.

4. With these files in place, we still need to install the plugins. In a Node.js command prompt window, change the working folder to our project, then enter these commands, and press *Enter* after each:

   ```
   npm install postcss-functions --save-dev

   npm install css-color-converter --save-dev
   ```

5. From the `Tutorial26` folder, copy `style - pre-compile.css` to the `src` folder in the project area; rename it to `style.css`.

6. Revert back to the Node.js command prompt window, then at the prompt, enter gulp and press *Enter*.

7. If all is well, we should see a source map and two compiled style sheets appear in the dest folder; copy these to the css folder within the Tutorial26 folder.

8. Try running the demo in a browser. If all is well, we should see four boxes appear, with various shades of red, as shown at the start of this exercise.

If we take a look at the contents of the gulp task file in more detail, it will look larger than previous exercises; it might look like we're doing more, but in reality, a lot of it we've already seen before, in earlier demos. Let's take a look at it in more detail.

Exploring our demo in more detail

If we open up our gulp task file, we can see it contains a number of functions, along with tasks that we've used in previous demos, such as lint-styles. The key in this demo is the three color functions, along with the main part of the autoprefixer task.

Let's start with the color functions, using darkenColor as our example:

```
function darkenColor (value, frac) {
  var darken = 1 - parseFloat(frac);
  var rgba = color(value).toRgbaArray();
  var r = rgba[0] * darken;
  var g = rgba[1] * darken;
  var b = rgba[2] * darken;
  return color([r,g,b]).toHexString();
}
```

We begin by extracting the decimal value, then subtracting it (as frac) from 1. This gives us our adjust value, or the value by how much we will darken our colors. Next up, we convert the color used (in this case, red) to a valid RGBA value, and split it into the RGBA array. We then multiply each array value from rgba by the darken value, and reform it as a valid color, before converting it to a HEX value.

Once each function has been created, we can then reference it from our gulp task, as shown:

```
gulp.task('autoprefixer', function() {
  return gulp.src('src/*.css')
  .pipe(postcss([ autoprefixer, functions({
    functions: {
```

```
      tint: tintColor,
      darken: darkenColor,
      sepia: sepiaColor
    }
  })
  ]))
  .pipe(gulp.dest('dest/'));
});
```

All of the functions use a similar process, but the main calculations that use the values from the `rgba[]` array, such as adding a tint (`tintColor`), or working in a sepia effect (`sepiaColor`), will be different.

The question you may ask though, is where do we get the calculations from? Well, there are plenty of sources available on the Internet, such as this link on Stack Overflow: `http://stackoverflow.com/questions/6615002/given-an-rgb-value-how-do-i-create-a-tint-or-shade`. Another alternative that may be worth a look is on Chris Coyier's CSS Tricks site, at `https://css-tricks.com/snippets/javascript/lighten-darken-color/`. In reality though, the best site I've seen so far is in the CamanJS library, at `http://www.camanjs.com`; the examples in this demo are based on the functions available from this library at `http://camanjs.com/docs/filters.html`.

> A useful little tip, if you want to check what color values should be displayed for a particular tint or shade, is to check out `http://highintegritydesign.com/tools/tinter-shader/`.

Comparing with CSS3 filters

A key question we must ask at this stage is "why should we go through the effort of creating individual functions, when we could easily use a library such as CamanJS?"

Well, there are some key reasons for taking the route that we used in our demo:

- CamanJS is a great library, and produces some wonderful effects, but it is an external dependency; we run the risk that development may be discontinued in the future, which might have an impact on our code.

- Using PostCSS means that we can remove the dependency on external libraries, we are in control over which effects should be included, and which are surplus to requirements. If we use a library such as `CamanJS`, then we may be forced to include lots of extra baggage that unnecessarily inflates our code.

- Not every browser will support standard CSS3 filters — using PostCSS gives us an opportunity to design our own filters that can apply similar effects.

- We can always use existing processors, such as SASS, but again we have a dependency on an external library; using PostCSS means we can still apply the same principles, but without the dependency.

The key here, though, is that filter support in browsers is very good, save for IE — we should always consider using CSS3 filters first, but can look to create an IE-specific style sheet that allows us to use our own versions from within PostCSS.

Adding Instagram effects to your images

Creating filters with PostCSS shouldn't be all boring though, we can absolutely have some fun with filters! A quick and easy way to apply some additional style to an image is through the use of Instagram filters — thankfully there is a pre-built plugin we can use for this purpose.

Enter the `Instagram` plugin, available from `https://github.com/azat-io/postcss-instagram`. Let's get stuck in and create a simple demo:

1. We'll begin, as always, by extracting a copy of the `Tutorial27` folder from the code download that accompanies this book — save this to the project area.

2. Next, extract copies of `gulpfile.js` and `package.json`, replace any that are stored at the root of our project area, with these new copies.

3. We now need to install the `postcss-instagram` plugin, so go ahead and fire up a Node.js command prompt session, then change the working folder to our project area.

4. At the prompt, go ahead and enter this command, then press *Enter*:

   npm install postcss-instagram --save-dev

5. Copy the `style - pre-compile.css` file to the `src` folder at the root of our project area, then rename it as `style.css`.

6. Once the plugin is installed, enter `gulp` at the prompt, then press *Enter*.

7. PostCSS will go away and compile our code, if all is well, we should see the usual files appear in the `dest` folder; copy these to the `css` folder within the `Tutorial27` folder.

At this point, if we try to preview the results in a browser, we should see something akin to this screenshot:

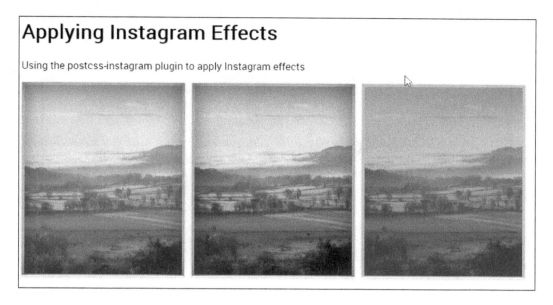

The key to this is in the main CSS style sheet, we can apply the required filter using nothing more than this within the rule:

```
37    .seventies_img_div {
38        filter: 1977;
39    }
```

This applies the 1977 filter (one of the filters available with the plugin). If we take a look at the compiled code, we can see that the plugin has added some additional rules; one to take care of creating the filter, and two to take care of positioning the filter on top of the image.

If we take a look at the compiled code, we can see the changes made by the plugin:

```
37    .seventies_img_div:after {
38      box-shadow: inset 0 0 3em #222;
39      position: absolute;
40      top: 0;
41      right: 0;
42      bottom: 2px;
43      left: 0;
44      z-index: 1;
45      content: '';
46    }
47
48    .seventies_img_div img {
49      -webkit-filter: sepia(0.5) hue-rotate(-35deg) saturate(1.6) contrast(0.9);
50      filter: url('data:image/svg+xml;charset=utf-8,<svg xmlns="http://www.w3.org/
51      -webkit-filter: sepia(0.5) hue-rotate(-35deg) saturate(1.6) contrast(0.9);
52      filter: sepia(0.5) hue-rotate(-35deg) saturate(1.6) contrast(0.9);
53    }
54
55    .seventies_img_div {
56      position: relative;
57      display: inline-block;
58    }
```

If you really want to get into the depths, then it's worth taking a look at the source code for this plugin, at https://github.com/azat-io/postcss-instagram/blob/master/index.js. It is fairly complex, but if you look carefully, you can see signs of the filter code that is used to apply the effect to our images.

Summary

Manipulating images and color can either be very rewarding, or somewhat daunting, depending on how simple or complicated we make our processes! Fortunately, PostCSS can help automate a fair degree of our processes, so let's take a moment to consider what we've covered throughout this chapter.

We kicked off with a look at adding media assets, and using PostCSS to automatically update asset links, this helps remove any risk that we inadvertently use the wrong link!

We then moved on to manipulating images, we started with a look at creating image sprites, first using SASS, before transitioning to using PostCSS. Next up came a more in-depth look at altering images, where we used the Evil Icons SVG library and set up PostCSS to alter the color of each icon at compilation. We then moved on to learn about how we can switch in the WebP image format; while most people might use standard format images, we learned how easy it is to switch-in WebP images, when using a supported browser.

Moving on, we then turned our attention to manipulating colors through the use of specific palettes, we covered how you can use PostCSS to compile in human-readable color names, and then mix or manipulate them within our style sheet. We then amped things up a little, with a look at using PostCSS to apply specific color filters, to alter color levels in a chosen color. We then explored some of the disadvantages of using standard plugins, and why we might need to create our own custom filters, that can be applied during compilation of our code. We then rounded out the chapter with a quick look at using some fun Instagram filters, where we can easily see how multiple filters are put together to manipulate images within our site.

Wow, we've certainly covered a lot of content! But our journey doesn't stop there: in the next chapter, we'll take a look at creating grids, which we can then use to construct layouts within our projects.

6
Creating Grids

There are several different routes to take when creating basic site layouts, and in many cases, developers may decide to use CSS grids.

A classic example for those using CSS pre-processors, is of course, the SASS grid system, **Bourbon Neat** — a great package, spoiled by the need to install Ruby. We can easily fix this in PostCSS, by using one of several plugins available, without the need for extra dependencies. In this chapter, we'll take a look at what's available, and work through some examples, using a plugin for creating grids within PostCSS.

We will cover a number of topics throughout this chapter, which will include:

- Introducing the basic principles of using CSS grids
- Exploring the grid plugins available for use within PostCSS
- Working through some simple examples using Bourbon Neat
- Replicating pure SCSS examples using the PostCSS plugin, PostCSS-Neat
- Adding responsive capabilities using the PostCSS-media-minmax plugin

Let's get cracking...!

Introducing grid design

The principles of using grids in design are not new, they date from the Second World War, with a number of graphic designers questioning the design of conventional page layouts, in favor of designing a system that provided a flexible, yet coherent, layout.

The same principles have been transferred to the web, starting with plain HTML, and CSS-based designs, before newer frameworks took over and helped to make construction easier.

It doesn't matter how the design is constructed, we can of course use HTML and CSS, or we might favor the image template approach (using packages such as PhotoShop), particularly if responsibility for designing the front end falls with a different team.

These are perfectly acceptable methods, but require a lot of manual effort — in this age of web design, time is critical; we can instead make use of newer frameworks (such as SASS, Bourbon Neat, or Bootstrap) to create our grids, as shown in this example (which uses plain SASS):

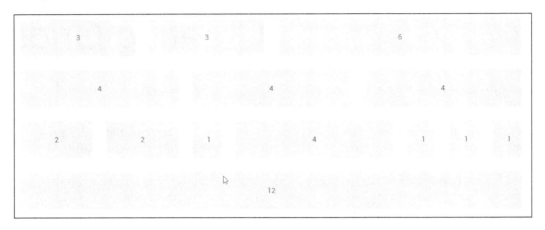

We can see this type of layout in action, if we go ahead and extract the Tutorial28 folder from the code download that accompanies this book, then review it using a browser. We will see this grid appear, the style.css file used by this demo was created using the online SASS playground, Sassmeister at: http://www. sassmeister.com.

Much of the code used in this demo centers around each column width and the overall .wrapper container; if you take a look at the code, you will notice that there are no static values for column widths. There are a couple of static values, but their sizes are not critical to the overall effect.

The key to our demo working centers around this block of CSS styling:

```
32    @media #{$breakpoint-medium} {
33      .wrapper {
34        width: 95%;
35        max-width: $grid-max-width;
36      }
37      @for $i from 1 through $grid-columns {
38        .column-#{$i} {
39          width: 100% / $grid-columns * $i;
40        }
41      }
42    }
43
```

Here, we're using SASS's interpolation to first build our media query (to make it responsive), followed by styles for a series of columns that form our grid. When compiled, it creates a number of styles that apply to each part of our grid:

```
53    @media only screen and (min-width: 30rem) {
54      .wrapper { width: 95%; max-width: 72rem; }
55
56      .col-1 { width: 8.33333%; }
57
58      .col-2 { width: 16.66667%; }
59
60      .col-3 { width: 25%; }
```

It's a simple matter of matching up the style with the number shown on the grid. If we want to change the widths, we simply need to increase the number of columns, and our `for` statement will automatically calculate a new set of values at the next compilation.

Okay, enough chitchat: time, I think, for a demo! Throughout this chapter, we will work through the principles of migrating from some basic examples using SASS, through to using Bourbon Neat, before converting to using PostCSS plugins. We always have to start somewhere, so let's begin with automating our compilation process using SASS.

Automating the compilation process

"Installing SASS?" I hear you ask Why, when this book is about PostCSS?

I hear you, it's a good question: there is logic, though, in this madness — let me explain all:

While we are installing SASS, we're not going to use the standard route to installing it; instead, we're going to use the `gulp-sass` plugin. This allows us to make the initial switch to using a `gulp` file; this puts us one step further on down the route to converting our processes to use PostCSS. The use of a `gulp` file provides a convenient framework where we can switch components in, or out, while we transition to using PostCSS.

 In *Chapter 12, Mixing Preprocessors*, we will see how PostCSS works well with other preprocessors, as a basis for adopting a consistent approach to compiling code.

So, without further ado, let's make a start on installing the `gulp-sass` plugin, before putting it to work:

1. We'll start by firing up a Node.js command prompt session, then changing the working folder to our project area.

2. At the prompt, go ahead and enter this command, then press *Enter*:

   ```
   npm install gulp-sass --save-dev
   ```

   Don't close the window, we will need it shortly!

3. Node will go away and install `gulp-sass`; it returns to the prompt when the installation is completed.

4. With the plugin installed, we now need to compile our code — go ahead and extract a copy of the `Tutorial29` folder to our project area.

5. Copy the contents of the `sass - pre-compile` folder to the `src` folder at the root of our project area.

6. We also need to add the `gulpfile.js` and `package.json` files from the `Tutorial29` folder to the root of our project area.

7. Revert back to the Node.js window we had earlier, then at the prompt, enter `gulp` and press *Enter*.

8. The files will now compile — once completed, copy them into the `css` folder within the `Tutorial29` folder.

9. Try previewing the results of our work in a browser; if all is well, we should see something akin to this screenshot:

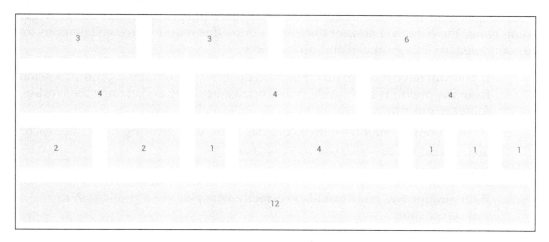

Right, we now have automatic support for compiling in place; "What next?" I hear you ask. We're one step closer, in that our code can now be compiled automatically:

```
1    'use strict';
2
3    var gulp = require('gulp');
4    var sass = require('gulp-sass');
5
6    gulp.task('sass', function () {
7      gulp.src('src/*.scss')
8        .pipe(sass.sync().on('error', sass.logError))
9        .pipe(gulp.dest('dest/'));
10   });
11
12   gulp.task('default', ['sass']);
13
14   var watcher = gulp.watch('src/*.scss', ['sass']);
15   watcher.on('change', function(event) {
16     console.log('File ' + event.path + ' was ' + event.type + ', running tasks...');
17   });
```

However, manual effort is still required to construct our grid! Let's start to change that now, there are several frameworks available that we can use, but in my view, one of the cleanest is SASS's Bourbon Neat. We'll use this as the basis for our next few exercises, before migrating to use the PostCSS version of this framework.

Adding support for Bourbon Neat

For the uninitiated, SASS's grid capability is provided by the Bourbon Neat add-on (available from `http://neat.bourbon.io/`). For the purposes of our exercise, we're going to use the Node versions of the framework — this requires two installations to be completed, so let's go ahead and do that now:

1. If you still have it open, revert back to the Node.js command prompt session from the previous demo; otherwise, open a new one and change the working folder to our project area.

2. At the prompt, enter these two commands in turn, pressing *Enter* after each:

    ```
    npm install node-bourbon --save-dev

    npm install node-neat --save-dev
    ```

3. Both plugins will have installed correctly when we see a result akin to this screenshot:

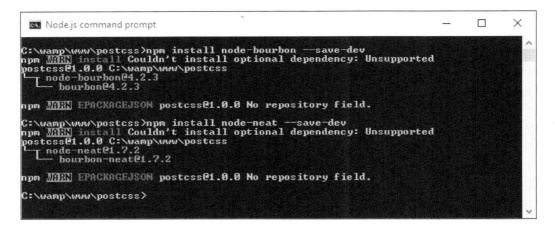

4. With the plugins now installed, we need to modify our `gulp` file — go ahead and add this at line 5:

    ```
    var neat = require('node-neat').includePaths;
    ```

5. Next, leave a line, then add the code as shown, at line 7:

    ```
    var paths = {
      scss: 'src/*.scss'
    };
    ```

6. The original SASS task can be replaced with this new task:

```
gulp.task('styles', function () {
  return gulp.src(paths.scss)
  .pipe(sass({
    includePaths: require('node-neat').includePaths
  }))
  .pipe(gulp.dest('dest/'));
});
```

7. The reference to SASS in the default task is now incorrect — go ahead and change it to: `gulp.task('default', ['styles']);`

8. Finally, change this line as indicated:

```
var watcher = gulp.watch('src/*.scss', ['styles']);
```

9. We're now ready to test our compilation process — go ahead and extract a copy of the contents of `style - pre-compile.scss` from the code download and save it to the `src` folder.

10. At this point, we can run `gulp` from a Node.js command prompt. If this works okay, we should get a `style.css` file appear in the `dest` folder. If we open it up, we should see some compiled styles, as follows, that prove Neat is installed and working:

```
@media only screen and (min-width: 30rem) {
  .wrapper {
    width: 95%;
    max-width: 72rem; }
  .col-1 {
    width: 8.33333%; }
```

At this point, we now have a working compilation process, and we're good to go with building a working site! For now, don't worry too much about the individual styles in the compiled `test.css` file, we will cover this in more detail over the next few pages. Let's put our new compilation process into practice and assemble a working example, so that we can see the grid facility in action.

Creating an example with Bourbon Neat

Constructing a site using Bourbon Neat is a simple process, it does not require any special markup on our web page; the effort is all within the compiled style sheet.

To prove this, we'll construct a simple web page that could easily be part of any website—I've used a Japanese theme as the basis for my page, but the principles we will use can apply to any site. You'll see that (with the exception of the standard SASS style of code used) there are only three instances where we have used Bourbon Neat-specific code.

Let's make a start:

1. From the code download that accompanies this book, go ahead and extract a copy of `Tutorial30`, and save it to the root of our project area.

2. Copy the contents of the `sample site - pre-compile` from within the `Tutorial30` folder to the `src` folder within our project area. Go ahead and rename it as `sample.scss`.

3. Next, fire up a Node.js command prompt, then change the working folder to our project area.

4. At the prompt, enter `gulp`, then press *Enter*—Node.js will compile the code; if all is well, we should see two compiled style sheets and a source map in the `dest` folder.

5. Go ahead and copy the contents of the `dest` folder into the `css` folder at the root of the `Tutorial30` folder.

If we try previewing the results of our work, we should see a stylish page appear, with our Japanese theme:

The demo covers a couple of key points and useful tricks, so let's dive in and work through them in more detail.

Exploring our demo in more detail

At this point, be surprised to hear that, our first tip is not directly related to SASS or even Bourbon Neat, but to the color scheme!

"Why", I hear you ask, "are we talking about the color scheme first?" There is a good reason for this: we've used variables to reference our colors, but could equally have used SASS functions to create the values. We've already covered this back in *Chapter 5, Managing Colors, Images and Fonts*, where we covered the use of the `postcss-color-function` plugin to build these values; we will use it again later in this chapter.

The real tip here, though, is using a nifty applet by Lokesh Dhakar, called **Color Thief** (hosted at `http://lokeshdhakar.com/projects/color-thief/`). We can simply drag and drop our header image in and get a full swatch of suitable colors:

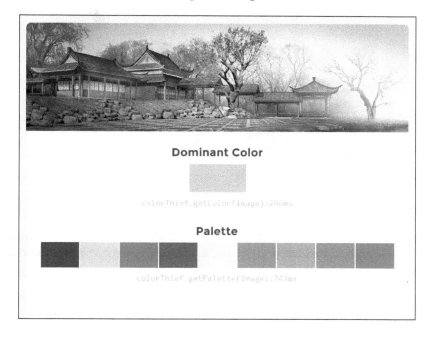

The only downside is that it doesn't provide the color values; we can get these from the page's source instead.

 If your preference is to use RGB(A) colors instead, then a site such as **Color Hexa** (`http://colorhexa.com`) will be a great help.

The key to our demo is at lines 33, 63 and 69-these are Bourbon Neat mixins that control the format of the outer container (line 33):

```
32    section {
33        @include outer-container(72%);
34        text-align: center;
35        margin-bottom: 3rem;
```

They also control the format of each of the two content areas within (lines 63 and 69):

```
62    #alpha {
63        @include span-columns(3);
64        margin-left: 1.5%;
65        background: linear-gradient(to bottom, rgba(
66    }
67
68    #beta {
69        @include span-columns(8.5);
70        h2 {
71            border-bottom: 1px solid $textdarkorange;
72            display: block;
73            margin-bottom: 0.5rem;
74        }
75    }
```

When compiled, the `outer-container` mixin adds a `max-width` of 72% to the `.wrapper` class controlling the main section, while the `span-columns()` mixins add `float`, `display`, `width`, and `margin-right` attributes to each element, like this:

```
#alpha    {                                          sample.css:212
    float: left;
    display: block;
    margin-right: 2.35765%;
    width: 23.2318%;
    margin-left: 1.5%;
  ▶ background:   transparent linear-gradient(to bottom,   #E2CC8C 25%,
    #E2C08C 25%,    rgba(246, 245, 194, 0.63) 100%) repeat scroll 0% 0%;
}
```

In addition to the `outer-container()` and `span-columns()` mixins, the demo uses percentage values as much as possible, where `rem` or `pixel` values have been specified, then maintaining a cohesive design when resizing these elements is less critical.

We will, however, make some improvements later in this chapter, when we improve the responsive capabilities of our demo. For now, let's continue with our transition, and introduce the use of PostCSS plugins into our process.

Exploring the grid plugins in PostCSS

Throughout this chapter we've used SASS with Bourbon Neat to produce our grids. It's a perfectly valid option to use, but is not the only one available. We might have preferred to work with something like Bootstrap or the Semantic Grid System instead; it's ultimately down to our personal choice as to which grid system we use, based on our preferences and requirements.

Up until now, we've focused on using Neat. This is largely due to familiarity and ease of use. There will come a point, though, when we need to make the transition to using PostCSS — the beauty is that there is a dedicated plugin available for using Neat within PostCSS, at `https://github.com/jo-asakura/postcss-neat`. It's not the only grid system plugin available for PostCSS, so let's take a moment to cover the others that can be used:

- `Grid`: Downloadable from https://github.com/andyjansson/postcss-grid, this plugin splits some of the configuration between PostCSS and the stylesheet, which helps to simplify the calculations required for formatting each column.

- `Lost`: Available from `https://github.com/corysimmons/lost`, it describes itself as the Autoprefixer for grid systems; it provides support for most preprocessors, such as Less, SASS, or Stylus.

- `Simple-grid`: From `https://github.com/admdh/postcss-simple-grid`, this plugin takes a different route: all of the configuration is done in CSS, not within the task configuration.

Without further ado, it's time for us to make the transition — let's make a start by getting the plugin installed and configured for use.

Transitioning to using PostCSS-Neat

Making the transition to PostCSS is relatively straightforward. We need, of course, to update our compilation process to remove links to SASS, and introduce our PostCSS plugin.

 The transition process will be completed over this and the next two sections.

In terms of changing the CSS, it's a little more complicated, as we have to work out how many columns are required for each grid block. Fortunately, our example is relatively straightforward, as we numbered the original blocks with the appropriate column count, so we can use that as a basis for changing our CSS.

Let's make a start with updating our compilation process:

1. We'll start by extracting a copy of the `Tutorial31` folder from the code download that accompanies this book. Save it to the root of our project area.

2. From the `Tutorial31` folder, go ahead and extract copies of `package.json` and `gulpfile.js` files. Save these to the root of our project area.

3. Next, we need to install the `postcss-neat` plugin. For this, fire up a Node.js command prompt, then change the working folder to our project area.

4. At the prompt, go ahead and enter this command, then press *Enter*:

    ```
    npm install postcss-neat --save-dev
    ```

5. Node will go away and install our plugin—the plugin is installed, when we see this confirmation:

```
Node.js command prompt                                  —    □    ×

C:\wamp\www\postcss>npm install postcss-neat --save-dev
npm WARN install Couldn't install optional dependency: Unsupported
postcss@1.0.0 C:\wamp\www\postcss
├─┬ autoprefixer@6.1.1
│ └── postcss@5.0.12
└─┬ postcss-neat@2.4.2
  └── postcss@5.0.12

npm WARN EPACKAGEJSON postcss@1.0.0 No repository field.

C:\wamp\www\postcss>_
```

We now have a plugin installed and configured for use. Before we create a test to confirm it works OK, let's take a quick look at our gulp file, at the root of our project area.

If you were expecting a complex configuration, then I'm sorry to disappoint you — it's even easier than installing Bourbon and Neat using the normal method outlined on their site! Our gulp file contains the requisite variable calls to each plugin at the start, with a watch facility at the end of the file. The section of interest to us is this:

```
gulp.task('neat', function () {
  var processors = [
    require('autoprefixer-core')({ browsers: ['last 1 version']
    }),
    require('postcss-neat')(/* { options } */)
  ];
  return gulp.src('src/*.css')
    .pipe(require('gulp-postcss')(processors))
    .pipe(gulp.dest('dest/'));
});
```

This setup should satisfy most scenarios, with a default of 12 columns; if there is a need to override it, we can do so by specifying the appropriate option in our configuration object:

```
postcss([
  ...
  require('postcss-neat')({
    neatMaxWidth: '128em'
  })
  ...
])
```

We will use this option later in this chapter in the *Testing our configuration section*, when we build our test example.

 For a full list of the attributes that can be modified, head over to https://github.com/jo-asakura/postcss-neat#custom-settings.

We have a basic configuration now in place, but hold on...it looks a little short! The sharp-eyed among you should notice that we've included additional options in the gulp files in previous exercises, such as creating source maps or minifying our CSS files. Let's fix that now, by amending our gulp file to include these missing options. Everything will then be in place, ready for when we create our example site.

Refining our task list

Our `gulp` file, as it stands, is perfectly usable, but isn't really as useful as it could be — there are a handful of tasks we've built into previous exercises, but which of these are missing here.

A perfect example is the addition of source maps, but how about minifying our code too? Let's take a moment to refine our task list, and add in the missing tasks:

1. The first task is to add in some variables that will act as references for the various plugins we will use — this goes in immediately after the last `var` statement, at the top of our `gulp` file:

   ```
   var cssnano = require('cssnano');
   var sourcemaps = require('gulp-sourcemaps');
   var rename = require('gulp-rename');
   var stylelint = require('stylelint');
   var reporter = require('postcss-reporter');
   ```

2. The first task to add in is a facility to lint our styles:

   ```
   gulp.task("lint-styles", ['neat'], function() {
     return gulp.src("dest/css/*.css")
       .pipe(postcss([ stylelint({
         "rules": {
           "color-no-invalid-hex": 2,
           "declaration-colon-space-before": [2, "never"],
           "indentation": [2, 2],
           "number-leading-zero": [2, "always"]
         }
       }),
       reporter({
         clearMessages: true,
       })
     ]))
   });
   ```

3. With our styles checked for accuracy and consistency, we can now minify our code. Add the following block:

   ```
   gulp.task('rename', ['lint-styles'], function () {
     return gulp.src('dest/css/*.css')
       .pipe(postcss([ cssnano() ]))
       .pipe(rename('style.css'))
       .pipe(gulp.dest("dest/css"));
   });
   ```

4. The next step is to add a source map option:

```
gulp.task('sourcemap', ['rename'], function () {
  return gulp.src('dest/css/*.css')
    .pipe(sourcemaps.init())
    .pipe(sourcemaps.write('maps/'))
    .pipe(gulp.dest("dest/css"));
});
```

5. With the additions to our `gulp` file, we need to adjust the main default task to call these additional tasks:

```
gulp.task('default', ['neat', 'lint-styles', 'rename',
'sourcemap']);
```

6. We have a watch facility in place, but it knows nothing about these extra tasks; let's add them in now:

```
var watcher = gulp.watch('src/*.css', ['default',  'lint-
styles', 'rename', 'sourcemap']);
```

We now have a working `gulp` file, that includes all of the configuration tasks required for our exercise—let's put it to the test by compiling some example code, to confirm it all works as expected.

Testing our configuration

A key part of our process is testing our `gulp` file to ensure it works; not only should it run all of the required tasks, but in the correct order, and produce the expected results. Although we've reused existing code for our gulp file, we've made some major changes to our `gulp` file—let's take a moment to test it is working, using the code from our previous demo.

To get our demo working under PostCSS, we need to make some changes to our code:

1. We'll start by resaving the `style.scss` file (from within the `css` folder in the `Tutorial31` folder) as a plain CSS file, and not a SASS stylesheet, we've removed the use of SASS from our previous demo, making the use of the `.scss` extension redundant.

2. Next, we used a `.wrapper` class in our previous demo. This needs to be modified as indicated:

```
.wrapper {
  @neat-outer-container;
  margin: 0 auto;
}
```

3. Our `col-*` class rules need to change too. In place of the static percentages from the old demo, we're going to replace them with this:

```
.col-1 { @neat-span-columns 1; }
.col-2 { @neat-span-columns 2; }
.col-3 { @neat-span-columns 3; }
.col-4 { @neat-span-columns 4; }
.col-5 { @neat-span-columns 5; }
.col-6 { @neat-span-columns 6; }
.col-7 { @neat-span-columns 7; }
.col-8 { @neat-span-columns 8; }
.col-9 { @neat-span-columns 9; }
.col-10 { @neat-span-columns 10;}
.col-11 { @neat-span-columns 11; }
.col-12 { @neat-span-columns 12; }
```

4. Our code is now ready, so go ahead and copy the `style.css` file into the `src` folder at the root of our project area.

5. Next, fire up a Node.js command prompt, then change the working folder to our project area.

6. At the command prompt, enter `gulp` then press *Enter*.

7. If all is well, we should see a compiled `style.css` file appear in the `dest` folder. If we open it up, we should see a number of styles displayed that relate to each column, such as is shown in this screenshot:

```
70  .col-1 { display: block; float: left; margin-right: 2.35765160%; width: 6.17215270%; }
71
72  .col-1:last-child {
73      margin-right: 0;
74  }
75  .col-2 { display: block; float: left; margin-right: 2.35765160%; width: 14.70195700%; }
76  .col-2:last-child {
77      margin-right: 0;
78  }
```

8. If we try previewing the demo in a browser, we should see something akin to this screenshot. Notice how similar it is to the original version, which we built in SASS:

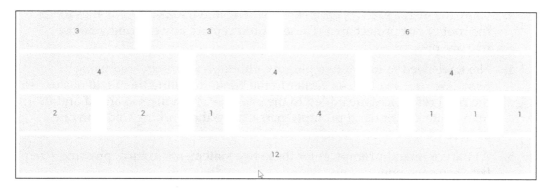

The demo that we've constructed is nearly identical to the original version. This proves that we have a working capability, which we can use to build our sites. The changes we made to our code are very simple, we added a `@neat-outer-container` to define how wide our site should be, followed by multiple instances of `@neat-span-columns`, to define how many columns each element should span.

Let's put some of this new knowledge to constructing something a little more useful, in the form of an example site with content. We'll reuse the example site page we created earlier in the chapter, and work through converting it for use with PostCSS plugins.

Creating a site using Neat and PostCSS

Remember our demo with a Japanese theme from earlier, in *Creating an example with Bourbon Neat?* It's a simple demo, using Bourbon Neat to help create our grid. The downside, though, is, of course, the dependency on SASS!

Well, we can fix that: PostCSS has a plugin available that mimics Bourbon Neat, but is written entirely in JavaScript, so there is no dependency on SASS. It's easy to install and use, over the next few pages, we'll work through the changes required to switch to this plugin.

First though, let's get it set up:

1. We'll begin by extracting a copy of the `Tutorial32` folder from the code download that accompanies this book. Save this to the root of our project area.

2. Copy the `sample pre-compile.css` file to the `src` folder at the root of our project area.

3. Copy the `gulpfile.js`, `samplesite.html` and `package.json` files to the root of our project area. These should replace any existing versions that are present.

4. Next, we need to install two plugins, although we've covered using `postcss-css-variables` earlier in the book, installing them will ensure the right references are added to the `package.json` file. Go ahead and fire up a Node.js command prompt, then change the working folder to our project area.

5. At the command prompt, enter these two statements in turn, pressing *Enter* between each one:

```
npm install postcss-css-variables --save-dev
npm install postcss-nested
```

6. When both plugins are installed, go ahead and enter `gulp`, then press *Enter* to fire off a compilation of our style sheet.

7. If all is well, we should see two style sheets and a source `map` folder appear in the `dest` folder. Copy these to the `css` folder at the root of our project area.

8. If we fire up a copy of `samplesite.html`, we should see our demo appear as before, but this time without the dependency on SASS:

Do you notice any difference to our SASS-only version of this demo, from earlier? Hopefully not; while it may not be pixel-identical to the original, it is not far from it! However, it does show that with a little ingenuity, it is possible to make the transition to using PostCSS and still maintain the same results. It will require a few changes to your code and processes, so let's take a look at these in more detail, starting with the style sheet.

Making the change to PostCSS

Making the switch requires changes in both the `gulp` task file and style sheet. These are not to change how the page will look, but to maintain the same theme from the original demo. The key changes made to the style sheet are:

- The `_reset.scss` partial style sheet that we import will no longer work, as we are removing the reliance on SASS. To maintain its use, a compiled version was created using the online playground at Sassmeister (`http://www.sassmeister.com`); we can then link to it from our markup page.

- If you take a peek at the source version of `sample.css`, you will see a `:root` block at the top of the file; this replaces the `import` statements we used. This block can be used to store any variables used, and we will cover this in more detail when we explore the changes made to our `gulp` task file.

- We no longer needed the following three statements; they are used to debug the SASS version of Bourbon Neat, and were then removed:

```
$visual-grid: true;
$visual-grid-color: #E6F6FF;
$visual-grid-opacity: 0.4;
```

- We're using PostCSS equivalents for all of the variable statements. The SASS versions were modified using search and replace from `$...` to `var(--....)`, where the ... represents the variable name.

- Our original code had a number of references to `Bourbon` mixins which had to be updated. We used the same search and replace principle, this time changing `@include outer...` to `@neat-outer...` throughout the code.

- To keep things simple, we manually calculated any instance where `$body-line-height` was referenced, and replaced the calculation with the result. We could have stayed with using calculations, but it would have required the use of another plugin which would have been overkill for their limited use in our code.

- We also adjusted the width of the main area in our page; it's a minor quirk, but required to ensure we had two areas side by side, and not one above the other!

In addition to altering our style sheet, we also had to make some changes to the `gulp` task file. They center around replacing the main compilation task and adding in additional tasks to manage production and minification of our source files:

- We added in the rename, lint-styles, and sourcemap tasks covered in earlier demos. These already worked well, and required no modification.

- We stripped out the original styles task, and replaced it with this:

```
16  gulp.task('styles', function () {
17    return gulp.src('src/*.css')
18      .pipe(postcss([ nested(), cssvariables(), neat({neatMaxWidth: '64rem'}) ]))
19      .pipe(gulp.dest('dest/'));
20  });
```

This time, we're calling them `nested()`, `cssvariables()` and Neat plugins. These are referenced used variables and are added in at the top of our `gulp` file.

- Our final change is at the end of the `gulp` file, where we had to adjust the default and watcher tasks to include the additional tasks that we added to our `gulp` file.

At this stage, do we have a working demo ready for use? Well, not quite, but let's try resizing our demo:

Hmm, what's happened to our content? It doesn't look great, does it? We can easily fix it though; it just requires the addition of some media queries to reorganize how our content is displayed on the screen. Let's dive in and take a look at what is needed to get our demo looking better at smaller sizes.

Adding responsive capabilities

Although Bourbon does add a degree of responsivity to our code, it's not quite enough for our needs. If we try resizing our demo, it soon becomes apparent that the elements don't quite go where we would want them, to say the least!

The quickest way to see just how the design looks when resized for smaller devices is to use Google Chrome. Press *Shift* + *Ctrl* + *I* to enable Chrome's developer tools:

The design works well when viewed at 1280px x 1024px, but this soon changes if we change the available viewing estate to suit an Apple iPhone 6 at 375px by 627px:

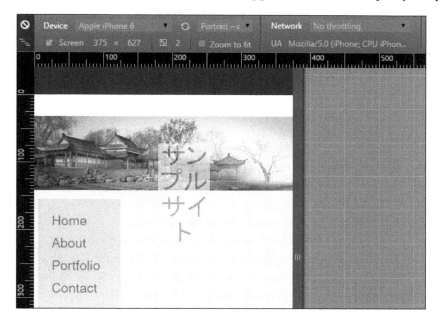

See what I mean? It just doesn't look right, does it? Fortunately, it's easy to fix using PostCSS, so let's dive in and see what is required to get our design working again.

Correcting the design

Getting our design to work properly for smaller devices such as iPhones is easy when working with PostCSS: we can use the `postcss-media-minmax` plugin available from `https://github.com/postcss/postcss-media-minmax`.

"How can PostCSS help us though?", I hear you ask. Easy, the point at which most people trip up when working with media queries is in setting the breakpoints, or determining where our designs break at specific sizes. The `postcss-media-minmax` plugin helps to make the text a little more human; after all, if a design works when the size is greater than or equal to an amount, why not say that in our code?

To see what I mean, let's get stuck into fixing our code. For simplicity, we will focus entirely on resizing our content for an iPhone 6, using 375px by 627px as our breakpoint (as determined by using Google Chrome's Responsive Design view). We will continue exactly where we left off from the previous demo:

1. We first need to install the `postcss-media-minmax` plugin—to do this, fire up a Node.js command prompt session, then at the prompt add this command and press *Enter*:

   ```
   npm install postcss-media-minmax --save-dev
   ```

2. Next, open up a copy of the `sample.css` file from within the `src` folder in our project area. We'll add the media query first, adjusted to ensure we catch the right breakpoint:

   ```
   /* media queries */
   @media screen and (width >= 370px) and (width <= 630px) {

   }
   ```

3. Immediately inside the query, go ahead and add this rule. We don't want to resize below `375px` as a minimum:

   ```
   body {
     min-width: 375px;
   }
   ```

4. The header image text needs to be resized to a smaller space, and we can also reduce it in size and move it over to the left a little:

```
header {
    width: 50%;
    font-size: 2rem;
    margin-left: 45%;
}
```

5. The #alpha content area (or menu) has automatically resized itself, but the main content area (#beta) is too wide; let's resize it down to fit. Our area won't cope with all of the text, so we'll add an overflow attribute, and set it to hide text outside the viewable area:

```
#beta {
    margin-right: 2.35765160%;
    width: 55.1748%;
    overflow: auto;
}
```

6. At this point, we need to install the postcss-media-minmax plugin, so fire up a Node,js command prompt and change the working folder to our project area.

7. At the prompt, enter this command, then press *Enter*:

```
npm install postcss-media-minmax --save-dev
```

8. When the plugin is installed, enter gulp at the command prompt, and press *Enter*.

9. PostCSS will now compile the code, and if all is well, we should see updated style sheet and source map files appear in the dest folder.

10. Go ahead and copy these into the css folder in the Tutorial32 folder, then try previewing the results in a browser.

If all is well, we should see something akin to the following screenshot, when enabling Chrome's Responsive Design view, and switching the Device setting to Apple iPhone 6:

The changes we've made to our code are simple, and limited to supporting iPhones. This is just the tip of the iceberg, though: there is so much more we can do!

For example, instead of specifying an exact width value as our `min-width` attribute (or for the width of #beta, for that matter), we could consider using `@neat-span-columns` to provide this value for us. Of course, we can't limit ourselves to one media query, we need to ensure we have enough media queries to cater for the devices we need to support.

This does not mean that we need to have a 1:1 relationship between a query and a device. Provided we design our queries carefully, we can set existing ones to cover several devices. Ultimately, though, the principle is still the same, but instead of using the standard colon notation, we can use the easier to read `>=` or `<=` symbols to define the breakpoint range when working with queries using PostCSS.

Summary

For many developers or designers, using grid-based development forms a key part of their working process. Many will be familiar with the likes of Bootstrap or Bourbon Neat; we can easily replicate the same functionality within PostCSS. Let's take a moment to review what we've covered throughout this chapter.

We kicked off with a brief introduction to using grid-based development, before swiftly moving on to beginning the transition process to using PostCSS. Our first stop was a look at automating the compilation process so we can make the switch to using Gulp.

Next up, we then took a look at making the switch from using pure SASS to using the SASS-based grid system, Bourbon Neat; we covered how easy it is for Bourbon to build the structure of our grid system with minimal effort.

We then moved on to exploring the plugin options available from within PostCSS, before making the transition to using the `postcss-neat` plugin. We then explored how easy it is to refine our Gulp task process, by adding in tasks that we introduced from earlier in the book, to help build up a process that more closely represents real-world development. To confirm the process works, we performed a test using an adapted version of the original demo from Bourbon Neat, before moving on to converting our Japanese-themed demo to using PostCSS equivalent plugins. We then rounded out the chapter with a brief look at refining the responsive capabilities within our design, to ensure it works better on smaller devices.

Phew, it may not seem like much, but we certainly covered a lot over the last few pages! But, as always, we continue apace: in the next chapter, we'll really get animated (sorry, pun intended!), with a look at how PostCSS can help with animating content.

7

Animating Elements

A question: if you had the choice of three websites: one static, one with badly done animation, and one which has been enhanced with subtle use of animation, which would you choose? Well, my hope is the answer to that question should be number three: animation can really make a site stand out if done well, or fail miserably if done badly!

So far, our content has been relatively static, save for the use of media queries. It's time, though, to take a look at how PostCSS can help make animating content a little easier. We'll begin with a quick recap on the basics of animation, before exploring the route to moving away from pure animation, through to SASS, and finally, across to PostCSS. We will cover a number of topics throughout this chapter, which will include:

A recap on the use of jQuery to animate content:

- Switching to CSS-based animation
- Exploring the use of pre-built libraries such as `Animate.css`
- Exploring the options available when making the change to using PostCSS
- Working through creating an animation-based demo, using PostCSS
- Learning how to optimize animations using PostCSS

Let's make a start…!

Revisiting basic animations

Animation is quickly becoming king in web development, more and more websites are using animations to help bring life and keep content fresh. If done correctly, they add an extra layer of experience for the end user; done badly, and the website will soon lose more custom than water through a sieve!

Throughout the course of the chapter, we'll take a look at making the change from writing standard animation, through to using processors such as SASS, and finally, switching to using PostCSS. I can't promise you that we'll be creating complex JavaScript-based demos such as the *Caaaat* animation (`http://roxik.com/cat/` — try resizing the window!), but we will see that using PostCSS is really easy when creating animations for the browser.

To kick off our journey, we'll start with a quick look at the traditional animation — how many times have you had to use `.animate()` in jQuery, over the years? Thankfully, we have the power of CSS3 to help with simple animations, but there was a time when we had to animate content using jQuery.

As a quick reminder, try running `animate.html` from the `T34 - Basic animation using jQuery animate()` folder. It's not going to set the world on fire, but is a nice reminder of times gone by, when we didn't know any better:

If we take a look at a profile of this animation from within a DOM inspector from within a browser such as Firefox, it would look something like this screenshot:

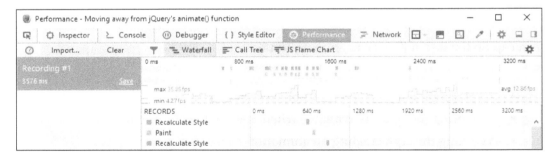

Whilst the numbers aren't critical, the key point here is the two dotted green lines, and that the results show a high degree of inconsistent activity. This is a good indicator that activity is erratic, with a low frame count, resulting in animations that are jumpy and less than 100% smooth.

The great thing, though, is that there are options available to help provide smoother animations; we'll take a brief look at some of the options available, before making the change to using PostCSS. For now though, let's make that first step to moving away from using jQuery, beginning with a look at the options available for reducing dependency on the use of `.animate()` or jQuery.

Moving away from jQuery

Animating content can be a contentious subject, particularly if jQuery or JavaScript is used — if we were to take a straw poll of 100 people and ask which they used, it is very likely that we would get mixed answers! A key answer of *it depends* is likely to feature at or near the top of the list of responses; many will argue that animating content should be done using CSS, while others will affirm that JavaScript-based solutions still have value.

Leaving aside that…shall we say…lively debate, if we're looking to move away from using jQuery, and in particular `.animate()`, then we have some options available to us:

- Upgrade your version of jQuery! Yes — this might sound at odds with the theme of this chapter, but the most recent versions of jQuery introduced the use of `requestAnimationFrame`, which improved performance, particularly on mobile devices.

- A quick and dirty route is to use the jQuery Animate Enhanced plugin, available from `http://playground.benbarnett.net/jquery-animate-enhanced/`; although a little old, it still serves a useful purpose. It will (where possible) convert `.animate()` calls into CSS3 equivalents; it isn't able to convert all, so any that are not converted will remain as `.animate()` calls.

- Using the same principle, we can even take advantage of the JavaScript animation library, GSAP — the Greensock team have made available a plugin (from `https://greensock.com/jquery-gsap-plugin`), that replaces `jQuery.animate()` with their own GSAP library. The latter is reputed to be 20 times faster than standard jQuery! With a little effort, we can look to rework our existing code — in place of using `.animate()`, we can add the equivalent CSS3 style(s) into our stylesheet and replace existing calls to `.animate()` with either `.removeClass()` or `.addClass()`, as appropriate.

- We can switch to using libraries such as Transit (`http://ricostacruz.com/jquery.transit/`), it still requires the use of jQuery, but gives better performance than using the standard `.animate()` command.

- Another alternative is Velocity JS by Jonathan Shapiro, available from `http://julian.com/research/velocity/`; this has the benefit of not having jQuery as a dependency. There is even talk of incorporating all or part of the library into jQuery, as a replacement for `.animate()` — for more details, check out the issue log at `https://github.com/jquery/jquery/issues/2053`.

Many people automatically assume that CSS animations are faster than JavaScript (or even jQuery). After all, we don't need to call an external library (jQuery); we can use styles that are already baked into the browser, right? The truth is not as straightforward as this—in short, the right use of either will depend on your requirements and the limits of each method. For example, CSS animations are great for simple state changes, but if sequencing is required, then you *may* have to resort to using the JavaScript route.

The key, however, is less in the method used, and more in how many frames per second are displayed on screen. Most people cannot distinguish above 60FPS—this produces a very smooth experience. Anything less than around 25FPS will produce blur and occasionally appear jerky—it's up to us to select the best method available, that produces the most effective solution.

 To see the difference in frame rate, take a look at `https://frames-per-second.appspot.com/`—the animations on this page can be controlled; it's easy to see why 60FPS produces a superior experience!

So, which route should we take? Well, over the next few pages, we'll take a brief look at each of these options. At this point, you may well be asking, "How is this relevant to PostCSS though, given that this is the subject of this book?"

In a nutshell, they are all methods that either improve how animations run, or allow us to remove the dependency on `.animate()`, which we know is not very efficient! True, some of these alternatives still use jQuery, but the key here is that your existing code could be using any or a mix of these methods. Later in this chapter, we'll take a look at how we can begin to remove jQuery, and focus more on using CSS3 animations, using the PostCSS plugin system.

 A small word of note, all of the demos over the next few pages were run at the same time as a YouTube video was being run; this was to help simulate a little load and get a more realistic comparison. Running animations under load means less graphics processing power is available, which results in a lower FPS count.

Let's kick off with a look at our first option, the `Transit.js` library.

Animating content with Transit.js

In an ideal world, any project we build will have as few dependencies as possible; this applies equally to JavaScript or jQuery-based content as it does to CSS styling.

To help with reducing dependencies, we can use libraries such as TransitJS or Velocity to construct our animations. The key here is to make use of the animations that these libraries create, as a basis for applying styles we can then manipulate using `.addClass()` or `.removeClass()`. To see what I mean, let's explore this concept with a simple demo:

1. We'll start by opening up a copy of `animate.html` — to make it easier, we need to change the reference to `square-small` from a class to a selector:

   ```
   <div id="square-small"></div>
   ```

2. Next, go ahead and add in a reference to the Transit library, immediately before the closing `</head>` tag:

   ```
   <script src="js/jquery.transit.min.js"></script>
   ```

3. The Transit library uses a slightly different syntax, so go ahead and update the call to `.animate()` as indicated:

   ```
   smallsquare.transition({x: 280}, 'slow');
   ```

Save the file, then try previewing the results in a browser — if all is well, we should see no material change in the demo:

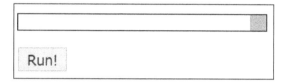

However, the animation will be significantly smoother — the frame count is higher, at 44.28FPS, with fewer dips:

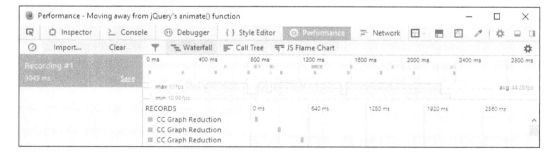

Let's compare this with the same profile screenshot taken for the *Revisiting basic animations* section, earlier in this chapter — notice anything?

Profiling browser activity can be complex, but there are only two things we need to concern ourselves with here: the FPS value and the state of the green line. The FPS value, or Frames Per Second, is over three times higher, and for a large part, the green line is more consistent, with fewer, more short-lived dips.

This means that we have a smoother, more consistent performance; at approximately 44FPS, the average frame rate is significantly better than using standard jQuery — but we're still using jQuery!

There is a difference, though — libraries such as Transit or Velocity convert animations, where possible, to CSS3 equivalents — if we take a peek under the covers, we can see this in the flesh:

```
<!DOCTYPE html>                          Filter Styles
<html>
  <head></head>                  element {
  <body>                             transition: transform 600ms   ease 0s;
    <div class="rectangle">              transform: translate(280px, 0px);
      <div id="square-small"       }
      style="transition: transform
      600ms ease 0s; transform:    #square-small   {
      translate(280px, 0px);"          display: block;
      ></div>                          width: 1.25rem;
    </div>                             height: 1.25rem;
                                       position: absolute;
```

We can use this to our advantage, by removing the need to use `.animate()` and simply use `.addClass()` or `.removeClass()` — we'll see this in action later in this chapter, in the *Switching classes using jQuery* section.

 If you would like to compare our simple animation when using Transit or Velocity, there are examples available in the code download, as demos T35A and T35B, respectively.

To take it to the next step, we can use the Velocity library to create a version of our demo using plain JavaScript — we'll see how as part of the next demo. Beware though — this isn't an excuse to still use JavaScript; as we'll see, there is little difference in the frame count!

Animating with plain JavaScript

Many developers are used to working with jQuery — after all, it makes it a cinch to reference just about any element on a page! Sometimes though, it is preferable to work in native JavaScript; this could be for speed. If we only need to support newer browsers (such as IE11 or Edge, and recent versions of Chrome or Firefox), then adding jQuery as a dependency isn't always necessary.

The beauty about libraries such as Transit (or Velocity) means that we don't always have to use jQuery to still achieve the same effect; as we'll see shortly, removing jQuery can help improve matters! Let's put this to the test, and adapt our earlier demo to work without using jQuery:

1. We'll start by extracting a copy of the T35B folder from the code download that accompanies this book. Save this to the root of our project area.

2. Next, we need to edit a copy of `animate.html` within this folder—go ahead and remove the link to jQuery, then remove the link to `velocity.ui.min.js`; we should be left with this in the `<head>` of our file:

```
<link rel="stylesheet" type="text/css" href="css/style.css">
<script src="js/velocity.min.js"></script>
</head>
```

3. A little further down, alter the `<script>` block as shown:

```
<script>
  var smallsquare =
    document.getElementById('square-small');
  var animbutton =
    document.getElementById('animation-button');
  animbutton.addEventListener("click", function() {
    Velocity(document.getElementById('square-small'),
      {left: 280}, {duration: 'slow'});
  });
</script>
```

4. Save the file, then preview the results in a browser—if we monitor the performance of our demo using a DOM Inspector, we can see a similar frame rate being recorded in our demo:

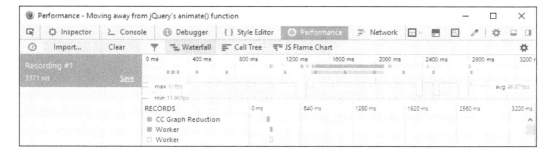

With jQuery as a dependency no longer in the picture, we can clearly see that the frame rate has improved; the downside, though, is that support is reduced for some browsers, such as IE8 or 9. This may not be an issue for your site—both Microsoft and the jQuery Core Team have announced changes to drop support for IE8 - 10 and IE8 respectively, which will help encourage users to upgrade to newer browsers.

It has to be said though, that while using CSS3 is preferable for speed and keeping our pages as lightweight as possible, using Velocity does provide a raft of extra opportunities that may be of use to your projects. The key here, though, is to carefully consider if you really do need them, or whether CSS3 will suffice, and allow you to use PostCSS.

Switching classes using jQuery

At this point, there is one question that comes to mind: what about using class-based animation? By this, I mean dropping any dependency on external animation libraries, and switching to using plain jQuery with either .addClass() or .removeClass() methods.

In theory, it sounds like a great idea—we can remove the need to use .animate(), and simply swap classes as needed, right? Well, it's an improvement, but it is still lower than using a combination of pure JavaScript and switching classes. It all boils down to a trade-off between using the ease of jQuery to reference elements, against pure JavaScript for speed:

1. We'll start by opening a copy of animate.html from the previous exercise—first, go ahead and replace the call to Velocity.JS with this line, within the `<head>` of our document:

   ```
   <script src="js/jquery.min.js"></script>
   ```

2. Next, remove the code between the `<script>` tags, and replace it with this:

   ```
   var smallsquare = $('.rectangle').find('.square-small');
   $('#animation-button').on("click", function() {
       smallsquare.addClass("move");

       smallsquare.one('transitionend', function(e) {
         $('.rectangle').find('.square-small')
         .removeClass("move");
       });
   });
   ```

3. Save the file—if we preview the results in a browser, we should see no apparent change in how the demo appears, but the transition is marginally more performant than using a combination of jQuery and Transit:

The real change in our code, though, will be apparent if we take a peek under the covers using a DOM Inspector:

```
element {
    ▶ transition: transform 600ms ease 0s;
      transform: translate(280px, 0px);
}
```

Instead of using `.animate()`, we are using CSS3 animation styles to move our square-small `<div>`. Most browsers will accept the use of transition and transform, but it is worth running our code through a process such as Autocomplete, to ensure we apply the right vendor prefixes to our code.

The beauty of using CSS3 here is that, while it might not suit large, complex animations, we can at least begin to incorporate the use of external stylesheets such as `Animate.css`, or even use a preprocessor such as SASS to create our styles.

It's an easy change to make, so without further ado, and as the next step on our journey to using PostCSS, let's take a look at this in more detail.

> If you would like to create custom keyframe-based animations, then take a look at http://cssanimate.com/, which provides a GUI-based interface for designing them, and will pipe out the appropriate code when requested.

Making use of pre-built libraries

Up to this point, all of our animations have had one thing in common—they are individually created, and stored within the same stylesheet as other styles for each project.

This will work perfectly well, but we can do better—after all, it's possible that we may well create animations that others have already built! Over time, we may also build up a series of animations that can form the basis of a library that can be reused for future projects.

A number of developers have already done this. One example of note is the Animate.css library, created by Dan Eden. It's worth getting to know this library, as we will use it later in this book in the guise of the postcss-animation plugin for PostCSS. In the meantime, let's run through a quick demo of how it works, as a precursor to working with it in PostCSS.

 The images used in this demo are referenced directly from the LoremPixem site, as placeholder images.

Let's make a start:

1. We'll start by extracting a copy of the T37 folder from the code download that accompanies this book—save the folder to our project area.

2. Next, open a new file and add the following code:

```
body { background: #eee; }

#gallery {
   width: 745px;
   height: 500px;
   margin-left: auto;
   margin-right: auto;
}

#gallery img {
   border: 0.25rem solid #fff;
   margin: 20px;
   box-shadow: 0.25rem 0.25rem 0.3125rem #999;
   float: left;
}

.animated {
   animation-duration: 1s;
   animation-fill-mode: both;
}

.animated:hover {
   animation-duration: 1s;
   animation-fill-mode: both;
}
```

3.   Save this as `style.css` in the `css` subfolder within the `T37` folder.

4.   Go ahead and preview the results in a browser — if all is well, then we should see something akin to this screenshot:

If we run the demo, we should see images run through different types of animation — there is nothing special or complicated here; the question is, though, how does it all fit in with PostCSS?

Well, there's a good reason for this — there will be some developers who have used `Animate.css` in the past, and will be familiar with how it works; we will also be using the `postcss-animation` plugin later, in *Updating code to use PostCSS*, which is based on the `Animate.css` stylesheet library. For those of you who are not familiar with the stylesheet library though, let's quickly run through how it works, within the context of our demo.

Dissecting the code for our demo

The effects used in our demo are quite striking — indeed, one might be forgiven for thinking that they required a lot of complex JavaScript!

This, however, could not be further from the truth — the `Animate.css` file contains a number of `@keyframe` based animations, similar to this:

```
@keyframes bounce {
    0%, 20%, 50%, 80%, 100% {transform: translateY(0);}
    40% {transform: translateY(-1.875rem);}
```

```
    60% {transform: translateY(-0.9375rem);}
}
```

We pull in the animations using the usual call to the library, within the `<head>` section of our code. We can then call any animation by name from within our code:

```
<div id="gallery">
  <a href="#"><img class="animated bounce"
src="http://lorempixum.com/200/200/city/1" alt="" /></a>
...
  </div>
  </body>
```

You will notice the addition of the `.animated` class in our code—this controls the duration and timing of the animation, and is set according to which animation name has been added to the code.

The downside of not using JavaScript (or jQuery for that matter) means that the animation will only run once when the demo is loaded; we can set it to run continuously by adding the `.infinite` class to the element being animated (this is part of the Animate library). We can fake a click option in CSS, but it is an experimental hack, which is not supported across all browsers—to effect any form of control, we really need to use JavaScript (or even jQuery)!

 If you are interested in the details of the hack, then take a look at this response on Stack Overflow, at `http://stackoverflow.com/questions/13630229/can-i-have-an-onclick-effect-in-css/32721572#32721572`.

Okay, onwards we go: we've covered the basic use of pre-built libraries, such as Animate. It's time to step up a gear, and make the transition to PostCSS. As a start, we will use Gulp as our task runner of choice, with SASS. The latter is a perfect choice, as it fits in with the plugin we will use later in this chapter. Let's take a look at what is involved in laying the groundwork for our conversion to PostCSS.

Switching to using SASS

As a developer or designer, if our development workflow includes the use of SASS, then the temptation is to use mixins such as this to construct our styles:

```
@mixin transition ($value...) {
  @if length($value) >= 1 { // If we set value
    @include prefixer($property: transition, $value: $value);
  } @else { // If value is not set, return default value
```

```
    @include prefixer($property: transition, $value: all 0.15s
      ease-in 0.05s);
  }
}
```

There's nothing wrong with this, but it will take effort to manage our mixins if we need to use more than just a small handful! The easier option is to explore using a pre-built animation library, as a way of reducing our development effort.

There are a number of developers who have created mixin libraries to handle animations; a perfect example is the SASS port of Animate, by Geoff Graham, which is available for download at https://github.com/geoffgraham/animate.scss.

There is something, though, that we have to be mindful of when working with mixins—it's all too easy to use them to manage vendor prefixes, such as this:

```
@mixin prefixer($property, $value) {
  -webkit-#{$property}: $value; // Attach webkit prefix
    (Chrome, Safary, Some Android native browsers)
  -moz-#{$property}: $value; // Attach moz prefix (FireFox)
  -o-#{$property}: $value; // Attach o prefix (Opera)
  #{$property}: $value; // no prefix (modern browsers
    and latest IE versions)
}
```

Although it will add the relevant vendor prefixes when the code is compiled, it's **not** considered best practice.

The onus is on us to ensure that each animation includes all of the relevant vendor prefixes—with the best will in the world, it's a challenge to keep up! There is also the issue of adding rules that won't have any effect—for example, there is no point in adding –o as a prefix for transition; this prefix is no longer needed.

Fortunately, there is a better way to handle prefixes—we can use Autoprefixer (from https://twitter.com/autoprefixer) to automatically handle vendor prefixes for us. The great thing about Autoprefixer is that it uses the Can I Use (http://www.caniuse.com) database to keep details up to date.

There are various plugins available that allow us to use task runners such as Grunt or Gulp. We can of course use a standalone GUI-based compiler for this purpose, but why run something like this when we can tie in much more functionality when using a task runner? We can even use any one of several plugins to remove vendor prefixes, prior to running a new compilation—this will ensure any redundant prefixes are removed.

With this in mind, let's get practical. For our next demo, we're going to construct a simple gallery effect, which showcases the same animations we saw earlier, but this time using the SASS version of `Animate.css`. We'll use Gulp as our task runner to compile the SASS code, before adding a source map, checking our code for consistency, adding vendor prefixes, and so on. You get the idea!

Suffice to say that we can do a lot using a task runner, so without further ado, let's get started with constructing our gallery.

Creating an animated gallery

Animating content can be a double-edged sword. Added with care, it can really lift a site to the next level. If it is done badly, then patronage of the site is likely to drop like a stone!

In our last demo, we constructed a simple gallery effect—this was more to show off the different types of animated effects we can add, rather than produce something that would win awards. Over the next few pages, we'll continue with our demo, but this time reconfigure it to use the SASS version of `Animate.css`. We will also introduce the use of a task runner to compile our code—as this is a requirement for using PostCSS, it seems a perfect point to start using it, as the final part of our transition to working with animation and PostCSS.

 The files for this tutorial are available in the `T38` folder in the accompanying code download.

Without further ado, let's add the changes to our previous demo:

1. We need to download the SASS version of Animate—it's available from `https://github.com/geoffgraham/animate.scss/archive/master.zip`. Go ahead and extract the contents of `Animate.scss-master` into the `src` folder at the root of our project area.

2. In the `src` folder, rename the `Animate.scss` file to `_animate.scss`—this is to indicate that it is a **partial**, which prevents it being compiled as a separate file by the SASS compiler.

3. In the `src` folder, go ahead and rename it as `style.scss`—this changes it to a SASS file, which is required for compilation later in the exercise. We should have something akin to this screenshot in our `src` folder:

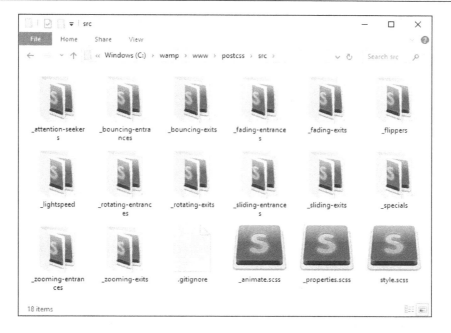

4. Go ahead and open up the `style.scss` file. At the bottom, add this line at the top of the stylesheet:

    ```
    @import "_animate.scss";
    ```

5. Next, add the following additional lines at the end of the stylesheet—these pull in the animations from the SASS version of `Animate.css`; the timing has also been extended to five seconds, as the original example was too quick:

    ```
    .bounce { @include bounce(); }
    .flip { @include flip(); }
    .hinge { @include hinge(); }
    .flash { @include flash(); }
    .shake { @include shake(); }
    .swing { @include swing(); }

    .animated:hover {
      animation-duration: 5s;
      animation-fill-mode: both;
    }
    ```

6. Save the file, then copy the contents of the `src` folder under `T38` to the `src` folder at the root of our project area—we will be compiling this file shortly.

7. In a new file, go ahead and add the following code, then save it as `gulpfile.js` to the root of our project area—this will form our gulp file, which we will use to compile our code:

```
'use strict';

var gulp = require('gulp');
var postcss = require('gulp-postcss');
var sass = require('gulp-sass');

gulp.task('sass', function () {
  return gulp.src('src/*.scss')
    .pipe(sass().on('error', sass.logError))
    .pipe(gulp.dest('dest/'));
});

gulp.task('default', ['sass']);

var watcher = gulp.watch('src/*.scss', ['sass']);
watcher.on('change', function(event) {
  console.log('File ' + event.path + ' was ' +
    event.type + ', running tasks...');
});
```

8. We also need a `package.json` file—this will store details of the plugins we will be using. For now, we will limit ourselves to using `gulp-sass`, but this will soon change! Go ahead and add the following lines to a new file, saving it as `package.json` in the root of our project area:

```
{
  "name": "postcss",
  "version": "1.0.0",
  "description": "Configuration file for PostCSS",
  "main": "index.js",
  "scripts": {
    "test": "echo \"Error: no test specified\" && exit 1"
  },
  "author": "Alex Libby",
  "license": "ISC",
  "dependencies": {
    "postcss": "^5.0.8"
  },
  "devDependencies": {
    "gulp": "^3.9.0",
    "gulp-postcss": "^6.0.0",
    "gulp-sass": "^2.1.1"
  }
}
```

9. The keen-eyed among you should spot that we've not installed the gulp-sass plugin. Let's fix that now by firing up a Node.js command prompt, then changing the working directory to the project area. Go ahead and run this command from the prompt:

```
npm install gulp-sass --save-dev
```

10. At the prompt, enter `gulp` then press Enter—Gulp will now go away and compile our file; if all is well, we should see a compiled style sheet appear in the `dest` folder of our project area.

11. At this point, try running `animate.html` in a browser—if all is well, we should see no change to our gallery effect, but can be safe in the knowledge that we're now using the SASS version of `Animate.css`.

Our demo has now been converted to using `Animate.scss`—we could easily have chosen to use any one of several compilers (such as Koala—http://www.koala-app.com), but instead chose to use Gulp. It acts as a perfect route into making the transition to using PostCSS—as we've seen in earlier demos, we've already used a task runner in the form of Gulp for this purpose. This allows us to make that gradual transition—when all of the SASS elements have been converted, we simply drop the task from within our gulp file to complete the transition.

Adding the finishing touches

So, what next? We've created a basic gulp task file, which we used to compile our SASS code to valid styles.

But this is just a small part of the story; we need to add a lot more to make our compilation process useful and ready for conversion to using PostCSS.

Let's get started:

1. The first change we need to make is in the `package.json` file—go ahead and add the lines as highlighted:

```
"cssnano": "^3.2.0",
"gulp": "^3.9.0",
"gulp-postcss": "^6.0.0",
"gulp-rename": "^1.2.2",
"gulp-sass": "^2.1.1",
"gulp-sourcemaps": "^1.5.2",
"postcss-reporter": "^1.3.0",
"stylelint": "^2.3.7"
    }
}
```

2. Next, we need to configure our gulp file with some additional tasks — the first task is to add references to some additional plugins that we've already used from earlier in the book. Go ahead and add the following highlighted lines:

```
var sass = require('gulp-sass');
var autoprefixer = require('autoprefixer');
var cssnano = require('cssnano');
var sourcemaps = require('gulp-sourcemaps');
var rename = require('gulp-rename');
var stylelint = require('stylelint');
var reporter = require('postcss-reporter');
```

3. With the additional plugin references added, we now need to add in our extra tasks — immediately below the SASS task, add in this task; this manages the linting of our code, for consistency:

```
gulp.task("lint-styles", ['sass'], function() {
  return gulp.src("dest/*.css")
    .pipe(postcss([ stylelint({
      "rules": {
        "color-no-invalid-hex": 2,
        "declaration-colon-space-before": [2, "never"],
        "indentation": [2, 2],
        "number-leading-zero": [2, "always"]
      }
    }),
    reporter({
      clearMessages: true,
    })
  ]))
});
```

4. Add this next task immediately below the previous step — this renames the files as part of the minification process:

```
gulp.task('rename', ['lint-styles'], function () {
  return gulp.src('dest/*.css')
    .pipe(postcss([ cssnano() ]))
    .pipe(rename('style.min.css'))
    .pipe(gulp.dest("dest/"));
});
```

5. Our next gulp task manages the generation of source maps — this can be done within SASS automatically, but using a separate plugin allows flexibility during compilation. Go ahead and add this task immediately below the previous one:

```
gulp.task('sourcemap', ['rename'], function () {
  return gulp.src('dest/*.css')
    .pipe(sourcemaps.init())
    .pipe(sourcemaps.write('maps/'))
    .pipe(gulp.dest("dest/"));
});
```

6. We're almost at the end — go ahead and alter these lines as indicated:

```
gulp.task('default', ['sass', 'lint-styles', 'rename',
'sourcemap']);

var watcher = gulp.watch('src/*.scss', ['sass', 'lint-styles',
'rename', 'sourcemap']);
watcher.on('change', function(event) {
  console.log('File ' + event.path + ' was ' +
    event.type + ', running tasks...');
});
```

7. Save the file. Go ahead and fire up a Node.js command prompt, then change the working folder to our project area.

8. At the prompt, type in `gulp` then press *Enter* — Gulp will go away and compile our file.

9. If we take a look in the `dest` folder, we should see the same compiled `style.css` file, but this time with accompanying minified versions of the source map and style sheet:

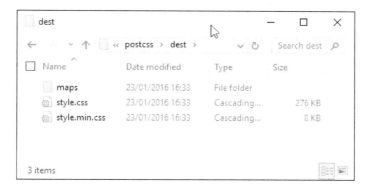

If we preview the results of our work, we should see no change in functionality within the demo, but can be safe in the knowledge that we now have minified versions of our files available for use — after all, it is always better to use minified files in a production environment!

We've now laid the groundwork for our conversion to using PostCSS — the keen-eyed among you should spot that the plugin reference for PostCSS has already been added to our gulp file, ready for the next stage in our conversion process. Everything is now in place in our gulp file, save for the SASS task – at the appropriate point we will remove the SASS task and replace it with a PostCSS equivalent; this will take place in our next exercise. Before we do so, it's worth taking a little time to explore what is available within the PostCSS ecosystem — although there isn't a great deal on offer, we can still produce usable code for compilation within PostCSS.

Making the switch to PostCSS

Okay…it's time to make that change to PostCSS!

Before we get stuck into exploring what is available, there is a key question that I am sure you will be asking — how come we've been exploring animation using JavaScript, when this book is clearly about PostCSS?

There is a very good answer for this — not only are we exploring the different routes we might take to transition to PostCSS, but at a more basic level, whether we can make the change. This might sound contradictory, so let me explain all:

A key limitation of animation is the FPS count, or Frames Per Second — jQuery's standard `.animate()` method is notoriously slow, and has not been optimized for speed. The FPS count on our animation at the start of this chapter was significantly lower than that of Velocity. The same applies for the alternative Transit library that we also covered earlier in this chapter.

Making the switch to using CSS will improve the frame rate, but CSS-based animation is not yet sufficiently powerful to manage complex animations. It means that we as developers have to assess any requirements for a project, and weigh up whether CSS-based animation will work, or if we have to fall back to using JavaScript-based libraries.

This translates through to using PostCSS — it may be tempting to use CSS-based animation for a project, but this will only work if our animation requirements are such that it is not going to result in an overly complex, difficult to manage, solution.

Exploring plugin options within PostCSS

Assuming the use of CSS3 animations will be suitable for our project, it's at this point that we can begin to make the transition to using PostCSS.

If you're expecting to see an array of plugins, then I'm sorry to disappoint — at present, there are only four plugins for use with animations:

- **Animation**: Available at `https://github.com/zhouwenbin/postcss-animation`, this adds `@keyframes` from `Animate.css`. This plugin uses `https://github.com/zhouwenbin/postcss-animation-data`, which hosts the converted animations.

- **PostCSS Easings**: Downloadable from `https://github.com/postcss/postcss-easings`, this plugin converts easing names from `http://www.easings.net` to `cubic-bezier()` equivalent values.

- **PostCSS Transform Shortcuts**: This plugin allows us to specify individual values when creating transform statements — the source for this plugin is available from `https://github.com/jonathantneal/postcss-transform-shortcut`.

- **PostCSS MQ Keyframes**: This plugin will move any keyframes from inside media queries to the bottom of our CSS file.

One could be forgiven for wondering what is possible with such a small range of plugins! We will add to the list a little later on though. Toward the end of the chapter, we will create a version of the `postcss-animation-data` plugin that allows us to use the Magic animations from `http://www.minimamente.com/example/magic_animations/`.

Okay, let's put some of these to use: time for a demo!

Updating code to use PostCSS

Although the PostCSS ecosystem doesn't yet have a plentiful selection of animation-based plugins, this should not stop us from using it to compile our animation styles. To prove this, we're going to modify the jQuery and .add/remove class version of our previous demo — we'll use PostCSS to add an animation easing from the `Animate.css` library created by Dan Eden.

The plugin we require is the `postcss-animation` plugin, which is available from `https://github.com/zhouwenbin/postcss-animation` and uses the `postcss-animation-data` plugin from `https://github.com/zhouwenbin/postcss-animation-data`. It's a cinch to install the plugin, which uses the same method as all of the other plugins we've installed to date.

Let's get started on the demo:

1. We'll start by installing the `postcss-animation` plugin — for this, go ahead and open a Node.js session, then change the working directory to our project area.

2. At the prompt, enter this command and press Enter:

```
npm install postcss-animation --save-dev
```

If all is well, we should see the plugin install:

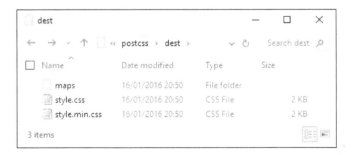

3. From the code download that accompanies this book, extract and save a copy of the contents of the T39 folder to our project area — we'll use this as a basis for converting to PostCSS.

4. Open `style.css` from the `css` sub-folder of the tutorial folder, then at the bottom, modify the `.move` rule as indicated:

```
.move {
  animation-name: bounce;
  transform: translate(17.5rem, 0rem);
  transition-duration: 3.5s;
}
```

5. Save this file into the `src` folder, then fire up a Node.js command prompt and change the working folder to our project area.

6. At the prompt, enter `gulp` then press Enter — if all is well, we should see these files appear in the `dest` folder:

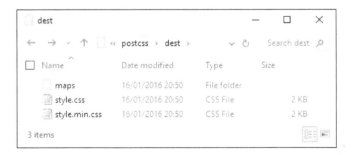

7. The last step is to copy the contents of this folder into the `css` folder within the T39 folder.

At this point we're good to test our demo—if we try previewing the results of our work, we should see no change in appearance of our demo, but can be safe in the knowledge that we're now compiling our code using PostCSS.

Testing our altered code

Although we may not see any change in the appearance of our demo, there will clearly be a difference in how it behaves. To view this, we need to take a look under the covers of our demo, at the code.

For this demo, we added an animation-name property, and assigned it the name bounce; when compiled, PostCSS adds in the appropriate @keyframes rules to the code:

```
37   .move {
38      animation-name: bounce;
39      transform: translate(17.5rem, 0rem);
40      transition-duration: 3.5s;
41   }
42
43   @keyframes bounce {
44
45      from, 20%, 53%, 80%, to {
46         animation-timing-function: cubic-bezier(0.215, 0.610, 0.355, 1.000);
47         transform: translate3d(0,0,0);
48      }
49
50      40%, 43% {
51         animation-timing-function: cubic-bezier(0.755, 0.050, 0.855, 0.060);
52         transform: translate3d(0, -30px, 0);
53      }
54
55      70% {
56         animation-timing-function: cubic-bezier(0.755, 0.050, 0.855, 0.060);
57         transform: translate3d(0, -15px, 0);
58      }
59
60      90% {
61         transform: translate3d(0,-4px,0);
62      }
63   }
64   /*# sourceMappingURL=maps/style.css.map */
```

So, if we were to take a look at the performance, how does it compare? Even with the extra animation property assigned, it still pulls a respectable frame rate of 48.29FPS, when compared to using standard `.animate()`:

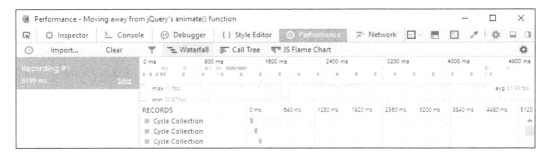

This helps reinforce that where possible, we can improve performance by removing any dependency on using `.animate()` in our code. The use of CSS styling to animate content isn't quite ready to replace JavaScript, but it is slowly getting there!

Okay, onwards we go: we've briefly looked at the various ways to animate content; it's time to make that final transition to using PostCSS. How many times have you seen forms that display the label above, or to the left of, each field? Sure, it gets boring after a while, seeing the same old design! It's easy to change, so there is no excuse for not doing so. To prove this, we're going to use PostCSS to slide each label up when that field has focus. Yes, you heard me right...*slide up*. Let's take a look at how we can provide a new take on that venerable piece of functionality for any site.

Creating a demo in PostCSS

As an afterthought to the previous exercise, I posed the question, "How many times have you seen forms that display labels above, or to the right of, fields?" If I were to collect a dime for each answer, I suspect I would be off on some exotic island, rich, and without a care in the world — I've lost count of the number of times I've seen such forms, let alone anyone else who uses the Internet!

There is no excuse for plain, boring forms. To prove this, we're going to create a simple demo using the `postcss-transform-shortcut` plugin by Jonathan Neal, available from `https://github.com/jonathantneal/postcss-transform-shortcut`. It's a straightforward plugin that allows us to specify single properties, which the plugin combines into a single line of code within our style sheet. Let's quickly install it:

1. First, go ahead and fire up a Node.js command prompt session, then change the working folder to our project area.

2. At the prompt, enter this command, then press Enter:

    ```
    npm install postcss-transform-shortcut --save-dev
    ```

3. Node will now install the plugin—it will return back to a flashing prompt when this is complete.

There is no need to configure it, although there is a small task we have to complete before we can use it.

Updating the plugin

While researching for this book, I came across an issue in the current release (1.0.0), whereby style sheets weren't compiling properly if they had multiple rules within; there are occasions when plugins may or may not work for your environment, and this is one of them!

Thankfully, this is an easy fix—if we take a look within the postcss-transform-shortcut folder within the node_modules folder in our project area, we should see this:

Simply copy the contents of the file at https://raw.githubusercontent.com/pc035860/postcss-transform-shortcut/07af8a78d1fb5e7fdeebc8c7f56c0c9ecdd83efb/index.js and paste straight over the top of index.js; this should resolve the issue.

    This has been logged as an issue in the developer's GitHub site, at https://github.com/jonathantneal/postcss-transform-shortcut/issues/4, if you would like to see more details about the issue.

Building our demo

Now that we have our updated plugin in place, we can get on with building our demo! The next exercise will take the form of a simple credit card form—*I don't* suggest you use it in a production environment, as it is purely designed to show the animation effects *only*, and does not have any security attached to the form!

That aside, here's a screenshot of what we're going to produce, using PostCSS:

It's a simple demo, based on a codepen created by Michael Arestad, which you can view at http://codepen.io/MichaelArestad/pen/ohLIa—I've simplified and reworked the demo to illustrate how we can use PostCSS to compile the code into valid CSS styles.

Okay, let's make a start with setting up our demo:

1. We'll start by extracting a copy of the T40 - Creating a demo in PostCSS folder from the code download that accompanies this book; save it to our project area.

2. From within the folder, move the package.json and gulpfile.js files up a level to the root of our project area.

3. In the `css - completed versions` folder, copy `style - pre-compile version.css` to the `src` folder, and rename as `style.css`.

4. Next, fire up a Node.js command prompt session, then change the working folder to our project area.

5. At the prompt, enter gulp, then press Enter—PostCSS will go away and compile our code; if all is well, we should see our compiled style sheet files and `source maps` appear in the `dest` folder.

6. Copy the contents of the `dest` folder to the `css` folder within the original `T40 - Creating a demo in PostCSS` folder.

7. Go ahead and preview the results—if all is well, we should see something akin to the screenshot shown at the start of our exercise.

It's a simple demo, but it shows off how we can use animations perfectly—it adds a subtle effect to the label, and doesn't spoil the overall use of our form. The use of the plugin does raise a couple of useful points, so let's take a moment to explore what we've just created in more detail.

Dissecting our demo in more detail

The key to a successful plugin in PostCSS is one that follows the *1:1* principle—one plugin for one task. The `postcss-transform-shortcut` plugin is no exception: it takes the various elements that make up a transition rule, and puts them together in the right order. To see what we mean, take a look at these lines from within our style sheet before it is compiled:

```css
76  .slide-up + label {
77      display: inline-block;
78      position: absolute;
79      transform: translateX(0);
80      top: 0;
81      left: -2px;
82      padding: 10px 15px;
83      text-shadow: 0 1px 0 rgba(19, 74, 70, 0.4);
84      transition: all .3s ease-in-out;
85      border-top-left-radius: 3px;
86      border-bottom-left-radius: 3px;
87      overflow: hidden;
88  }
```

Where's our `transform:` statement? Well, when using this plugin, it's not needed — instead, we can simply specify the various attributes, thus:

```
.transform {
  transform: skewX(25deg);
  rotate: 180deg;
  scale: 2 2;
  translate: 10px 10px;
}
```

The plugin is set to recognize these four attributes and compile them into one single rule, as shown in this code excerpt:

```
.transform {
  transform: skewX(25deg) rotate3d(180deg,0,1)
    scale3d(2,2,1) translate3d(10px,10px,0px);
}
```

Any gaps in the attributes will be automatically filled in with default values from within the plugin. We can even use this plugin as the basis for an equivalent for transitions — we will do this toward the end of the next chapter.

Optimizing our animations

When working with animations, there may be occasions when we need to use custom effects; one way to achieve this is through the use of `@keyframes`. Trouble is, some browsers don't support their use within media queries (yes, I'm looking at you, `IE10` and `IE11`!).

How does this affect us, I hear you ask? Well, if you're building any responsive sites, then this is absolutely something we need to bear in mind; media queries form the basic structure for any responsive functionality.

It's an easy fix though — the developer, Andy Walpole, has created a simple PostCSS plugin called `mq-keyframes`, which is available at `https://github.com/TCotton/postcss-mq-keyframes`.

Imagine we have code such as this in our style sheet:

```
@media only screen and (min-width: 375px) {
  .custom-bounce {
    animation: side-bounce 5s;
  }

  @keyframes side-bounce {
    100% {
```

```
      opacity: 0;
    }
  }
}
```

All the plugin does is move the code to the bottom of our style sheets, which makes it easier to read, and allows IE to continue working correctly:

```
@media only screen and (min-width: 375px) {
  .pace {
    animation: pace-anim 5s;
  }
}

@keyframes pace-anim {
  100% {
    opacity: 0;
  }
}
```

This is probably one of the simplest plugins to use in PostCSS, particularly where animating content is concerned; it's worth using if you have to support these versions of Internet Explorer! The plugin can be installed in the same way as most other plugins for PostCSS, and does not require any additional attributes as part of the configuration process.

 As a challenge, how about trying out the demo available at `http://urbaninfluence.com/2015/05/make-a-background-image-slider-with-css-keyframes/?`

Using our own animation plugin

Throughout the course of this chapter, we've used the small number of animation-based plugins that are available for PostCSS, and demonstrated some of the effects possible. This is all well and good, but one can't help but feel that this is a little limiting—and can we do something about it?

Absolutely, the beauty of PostCSS is that if there is a need for a plugin, then we can create something to fill that gap. A perfect example of this is the lack of CSS-based animation plugins available; at present, all we have is `postcss-animations`, which inserts animations from the `Animate.css` style sheet created by Dan Eden. I've used this as a basis for a new plugin—we'll use the same framework, but convert it to use the Magic set of animations, available from `http://www.minimamente.com/example/magic_animations/`.

We will cover the construction of plugins in more detail in *Chapter 8, Creating PostCSS Plugins.* Let's make a start:

1. From the code download that accompanies this book, go ahead and extract a copy of the T41 folder, and save the contents to the root of our project area.

2. Copy the `postcss-animation` and `postcss-animation-data` folders to the `node_modules` folder within our project area.

3. Copy the `gulpfile.js` and `package.json` files to the root of our project area—if any are already present, replace them (or take copies for safekeeping).

4. Crack open your text editor and add the following code, saving it as `style.css` in the `src` folder of our project area:

```
.foo {
    animation-name: openDownLeft;
}
```

5. Fire up a Node.js folder, then change the working folder to our project area.

6. At the prompt, enter `gulp`, then press Enter—PostCSS will go away and compile the code; if all is well, we should see the `@keyframes` code added to our compiled style sheet (in the `dest` folder), as shown in this screenshot:

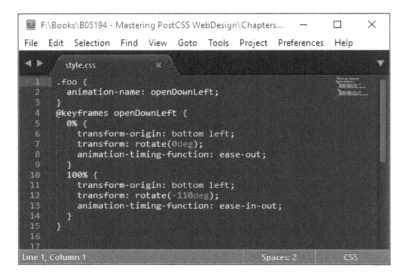

Although our example only shows the single style, this doesn't matter—any style sheet that uses animation-name can be used, provided the animation-name value used matches one in the `postcss-animation-data` plugin. There are a few key points, though, that we should cover, so let's take a moment to explore these in more detail.

Exploring the plugin in more detail

Our new plugin is a perfect example of how we can adapt an existing framework to use different values — there are a few key points we should note when using this plugin:

- A key point to consider when constructing any plugin: don't worry about adding vendor prefixes. These should be added as part of the compilation stage when the plugin is used within your projects; this will take care of any vendor prefixes that are required.

- At present, the plugin only lists two animation types from the Magic Animations library as examples — the full list of original animations is available from the Magic Animations GitHub repository at `https://github.com/miniMAC/magic/blob/master/magic.css`. We can easily add in any that we need, using the format of `"<name of animation>" : "<keyframe to use>"`, as shown in this screenshot:

```
1  module.exports = {
2    "openDownLeft": "@keyframes openDownLeft { 0% {transform-origin: bottom left; transform: rotate(0deg);
3    "openDownRight": "@-webkit-keyframes openDownRight { 0% {transform-origin: bottom right; transform: rot
4  }
```

As an experiment, how about trying to convert the animations from the Motion UI library at `http://zurb.com/playground/motion-ui`, for example? Or we can try the animations for AngularJS at `http://www.justinaguilar.com/animations/#` - it's entirely up to you!

- Alternatively, it's worth applying the same principles to the `postcss-easings` plugin available from `https://github.com/postcss/postcss-easings`; this has some well-known easings built in, but they can easily be replaced. A great tool for this purpose is the site at `http://www.cubic-bezier.com`. For example, if we take the `easeInExpo` easing, we create a Bezier curve that looks something like this:

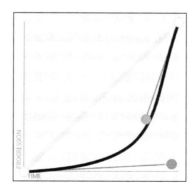

This translates to a value of `cubic-bezier(.95,.05,.79,.35)`, which we can use in our code. It's worth noting that some sites will show this easing as `(0.05, 0.795, 0.035)`—`http://cubic-bezier.com/` only shows values to two decimal places.

There are plenty of ways we can extend, modify, or create new plugins—the key to any should be that they are kept simple, limited to one task only, and that where possible, you should use the PostCSS plugin boilerplate as the basis for creating the plugins. The plugin we used in this exercise was created manually—this isn't an issue if you are creating it for your own needs, and don't intend to publish the plugin. In the next chapter, we will explore how easy it is to create something using the boilerplate code—it avoids a lot of issues at a later date!

Summary

Animating content is an almost de facto part of building modern sites – this can be something as simple as providing subtle effects on form labels, right through to providing a complex background slider. We've covered a lot of useful tips and tricks throughout this chapter, so let's take a moment to review what we've learned.

The theme for this chapter has been about making the transition (sorry, pun intended!) from using vanilla CSS or SASS to PostCSS; we kicked off with a quick recap of the types of animation available.

This was swiftly followed by a look at some of the methods available for starting to make the transition away from standard CSS, such as using prebuilt animation libraries, or using CSS3 transitions. We then switched to covering how similar animations would look within SASS, so we can compare use of libraries such as `Animate.css`, before starting the switch to using PostCSS.

We started this part of the journey by exploring the various plugins available, before converting our code to use PostCSS equivalent styles. We then took things up a step, by creating a simple demo using PostCSS, before rounding out the chapter with a look at a simple animation plugin created for PostCSS, which is based on the Magic Animation set of animations.

Phew - we've certainly covered a lot! But our journey doesn't stop there. In the next chapter, we'll explore some of the tips and tricks we can use to create plugins within PostCSS. No longer are we limited to what is available from others; we can now begin to create our own plugins instead...

8
Creating PostCSS Plugins

Plugins, plugins…we can't escape them; by now, you will have seen that they are an essential part of developing within PostCSS. Its modular nature is built entirely around plugins, and is how we can streamline our processing through selective use of these plugins.

In this chapter, we'll cover the anatomy of a PostCSS plugin and take a look at some pre-built examples, before embarking on the construction of a simple plugin that we can then test and submit for inclusion in the PostCSS system.

We will cover a number of topics throughout this chapter, which will include the following:

- Discovering how plugins can be used to extend PostCSS
- Examining the architecture of a standard plugin
- Creating a PostCSS plugin using the plugin boilerplate
- Building some example plugins
- Testing and submitting your plugin for inclusion in the PostCSS plugin library
- Exploring some examples of existing plugins available for PostCSS

Let's make a start…!

Extending PostCSS with plugins

A question, how many times have you worked with plugins that by themselves don't actually achieve anything?

I'll bet the answer won't be a high figure—and no, I'm not including those plugins that claim to perform an operation, yet don't seem to work for some reason! The power of PostCSS lies not in the core system, but the plugins that we use to manipulate our CSS style sheets.

At the time of writing, there are more than 200 plugins available for use within PostCSS—these range from extending PostCSS (such as postcss-nested or postcss-mixins), to manipulating colors (such as postcss-color-hcl or postcss-rgba-hex), to plugins that cater for future CSS syntax (such as adding @extend support).

 The full list is available at https://github.com/postcss/postcss/blob/master/docs/plugins.md, or via the searchable catalogue hosted at http://www.postcss.parts.

To date, we've used a fair number of plugins throughout our examples—we've configured them for use, but there is still an element of *black box* about them, where we don't always know how the insides work. It's time to change that. As a first step, let's briefly meet the toolset that helps make plugins possible, the PostCSS API.

Any plugin created for PostCSS will have been constructed using the API. The key to this API will be the Node and Container methods, which can be used to manipulate content once the postcss object has been initialized in the plugin. We will explore these in more detail throughout this chapter, but before doing so, it makes sense to explore the architecture of a PostCSS plugin first, so let's have a look and see what makes one tick.

Dissecting the architecture of a standard plugin

Creating a PostCSS plugin is a straightforward process—the beauty of PostCSS is that we as developers are free to design and construct any plugin we desire; it does mean that not every plugin will be of the same quality as others!

This aside, the recommended way to construct any PostCSS plugin is to use the boilerplate code, which is available from https://github.com/postcss/postcss-plugin-boilerplate; we can see an example of it in this screenshot:

If we explore the source code for any PostCSS plugin hosted in GitHub, there will be a host of different files present; not all of them will be the same for each different plugin!

Nonetheless, if we delve in deeper, there are some files we would expect to see as part of the architecture of any plugin; they are as follows:

- `index.js`: This contains the main functionality for each plugin
- `package.json`: This is used to configure and manage locally installed NPM packages
- `test.js`: This contains the tests required to ensure the plugin works as expected

Let's explore these in more detail, beginning with `index.js`.

Exploring index.js

The crux of any plugin centers around `index.js` — we start with a reference to PostCSS (as a dependency for our plugin); this is followed by the exports function, which exposes functionality to anyone using the plugin:

```
var postcss = require('postcss');

module.exports = postcss.plugin('myplugin', function(options) {
```

```
    return function (css) {
      options = options || {};

      // Processing code will be added here
    }
  });
```

Discovering package.json

Next up, we have `package.json` — this is used to configure and manage locally installed Node packages; given that PostCSS is based on Node.js, we will see something akin to this for any plugin installed as part of the PostCSS ecosystem:

```
{
  "name": "PLUGIN_NAME",
  "version": "0.0.0",
  "description": "PostCSS plugin PLUGIN_DESC",
  "keywords": [
    "postcss",
    "css",
    "postcss-plugin"KEYWORDS
  ],
```

The first section contains some basic details about the plugin name, description, and version. If we look through the `package.json` file, it's not difficult to spot a number of keywords in capitals — at first glance, one might be mistaken for thinking that it renders as invalid JSON.

There is a reason for this — one of the steps for using this boilerplate plugin is to run a script that will replace these keywords with information; the script will transform this into valid JSON. This is something we will cover in more detail later, in the *Creating a transition plugin* section. For now, assume that this file will be converted to valid JSON during the build process.

Moving on, we then store the name of the author, the plugin's license, and where we can get the source or file bugs relating to the plugin:

```
    "author": "AUTHOR_NAME <AUTHOR_EMAIL>",
    "license": "MIT",
    "repository": "GITHUB_NAME/PLUGIN_NAME",
    "bugs": {
      "url": "https://github.com/GITHUB_NAME/PLUGIN_NAME/issues"
    },
    "homepage": "https://github.com/GITHUB_NAME/PLUGIN_NAME",
```

This section is the most critical—the dependencies section stores details of any dependencies, when used in production; the `devDependencies` section takes care of dependencies when working in a development environment:

```
"dependencies": {
  "postcss": "^5.0.10"
},
"devDependencies": {
  "ava": "^0.7.0",
  "eslint": "^1.10.2"
},
"scripts": {
  "test": "ava && eslint *.js"
}
}
```

A key guideline given by the PostCSS team is that every plugin should be tested — this should always be a given, to help ensure we are creating something that is solid and not likely to cause issues for our users. A part of the boilerplate code contains a suitable test script for this purpose, so let's take a quick look at it now.

Exploring test.js

The third element that is key to any plugin is the test—this should be stored in `test.js`, and will look similar to this:

```
import postcss from 'postcss';
import test from 'ava';

import plugin from './';

function run(t, input, output, opts = { }) {
  return postcss([ plugin(opts) ]).process(input)
    .then( result => {
      t.same(result.css, output);
      t.same(result.warnings().length, 0);
    });
}

/* Write tests here
test('does something', t => {
  return run(t, 'a{ }', 'a{ }', { });
});
*/
```

We will cover this part in more detail later in this chapter, in the *Testing and submitting a plugin* section—for now, let's get stuck in to creating a PostCSS-based plugin. We'll start with a quick look at the API, before diving into creating a plugin that applies a specific font stack based on a chosen font, and adds updated declarations if one of those fonts needs to be imported into our site.

With the framework in place, we can then build up our plugin using the PostCSS API; this contains a number of classes, modules, and methods that we can use. The key function in the API is of course `postcss`—this is the main entry point for PostCSS and is required for all plugins:

```
var postcss = require('postcss');
```

Let's take a quick look through what else is available in the API, beginning with the Vendor module.

The Vendor module

This module contains helpers for working with vendor prefixes—we can initiate it using this object:

```
var vendor = postcss.vendor;
```

The module contains two methods, as shown in the table:

Module	Format	Value returned

vendor.prefix	String	The vendor prefix extracted from an input string:
		`// prefix extracted = '-webkit-'`
		`var vp = postcss.vendor;`
		`vp.prefix('-webkit-clip-path')`

vendor.unprefixed	String	The input string stripped of its vendor prefix:
		`// value extracted = 'tab-size'`
		`var vp = postcss.vendor;`
		`vp.unprefixed('-moz-tab-size')`

The List module

This module contains helpers to safely split lists of CSS values, whilst preserving parentheses and quotes. We can initiate it using this object:

```
var list = postcss.list;
```

The module contains two methods, as shown in the table:

Module	Format	Designed to split

`list.space`	String	Space-separated values (such as those for background, border-radius, and other shorthand properties):
		
		`// expected result:`
		`// ['1px', 'calc(10% + 1px)']`
		`var ls = postcss.list;`
		`ls.space('1px calc(10% + 1px)')`

`list.comma`	String	Comma-separated values (such as those for transition-* and background properties):
		
		`// Expected result:`
		`// ['black', 'linear-gradient(white, black)']`
		`var ls = postcss.list;`
		`ls.comma('black, linear-gradient(white, black)')`

Classes available in the API

Once the PostCSS object has been defined as a dependency in our plugin, we can begin to manipulate its contents—for this purpose, there are a number of classes available to assist, as shown in this table:

Name of class	Role within plugin
`Processor`	Creates a Processor instance, initializes any plugins, then uses this instance on CSS files as specified in the configuration.
`LazyResult`	Acts as a promise proxy for the result of PostCSS transformations. Promises are a key part of working with Node.js—if you are not familiar with this concept, take a look at `https://www.promisejs.org/` for a detailed explanation.
`Result`	Provides the result of any PostCSS transformations.
`Warning`	Allows a user to manage a warning within the plugin.
`CssSyntaxError`	Allows a user to retrieve any errors for broken CSS, generated by the CSS parser.
`Input`	Represents the source CSS being manipulated by PostCSS plugins.

Nodes available in the API

Of course, we cannot manipulate content from within a PostCSS plugin without having access to each CSS node — the API contains a group of useful nodes to help with parsing and manipulating content:

Node	Represents

Root	A CSS file and its parsed nodes:
	
	```var root = postcss.parse('a{color: darkred}');```
	```root.type //=> 'root'```
	```root.nodes.length //=> 1```

AtRule	An @-based rule in CSS, such as @media print {...}

Rule	A CSS rule, containing a selector and declaration block:
	
	```var root = postcss.parse('h1{}');```
	```var rule = root.first;```
	```rule.type //=> 'rule'```
	```rule.toString() //=> 'h1{}'```

Declaration	A CSS declaration:
	
	```var root = postcss.parse('a{color: darkred}');```
	```var decl = root.first.first;```
	```decl.type //=> 'decl'```
	```decl.toString() //=> 'color: darkred'```

Comment	A comment between declarations or statements (in both rules and @-rules):
	
	```var root = postcss.parse('a { color: /* inner */ darkred; /* outer */ }');```
	```var decl = root.first.first;```
	```var comment = root.first.last;```
	
	```comment.type //=> 'comment'```
	```decl.between //=> ': /* inner */'```

Methods available in the API

A key role of a plugin is to navigate through each node to help determine if it should perform some action; the API contains a number of methods to assist with parsing nodes:

Method group	Purpose
Nodes	These methods are for working with each CSS node – this includes methods such as the following: • `node.type`: returns a string representing the node type • `node.parent`: returns the parent node as a string • `node.next()` or `node.prev()`: returns the next or previous child of a node's parent. More details are available at `https://github.com/postcss/postcss/blob/master/docs/api.md#nodes-common-methods`
Containers	These methods contain methods for working with children in a container node – this includes methods such as the following: • `container.nodes`: returns an array containing the container's children. • `container.first`: return the container's first child node. • `container.last`: return the container's last child node. More details are available at `https://github.com/postcss/postcss/blob/master/docs/api.md#containers-common-methods`

The main site contains details and examples of all of the methods and classes available within the API – it is worth taking time to familiarize yourself with the options available.

 Details for each method or class are available on the PostCSS API page at `https://github.com/postcss/postcss/blob/master/docs/api.md`

Okay, enough with theory: on we go! Let's change tack and put some of what we've just learnt to good use by constructing a couple of plugins for PostCSS. These will use a real mix of the API commands that we've briefly looked at earlier in this chapter; our first demo centers around a shorthand plugin for creating transition statements within CSS rules in a style sheet, so let's get stuck in and see how it works.

Creating an transition plugin

The idea for this plugin is not new; it's loosely based on the `postcss-transform-shortcut` plugin by Jonathan Neal, available from `https://github.com/jonathantneal/postcss-transform-shortcut`. The concept is not necessarily a shorter means to create transition statements, but it makes it easier by allowing authors to specify values independently. These are then automatically inserted into the correct order within the transition declaration.

> The source code for this plugin is also available on GitHub, at `https://github.com/alexlibby/postcss-transition-shortcut`; the NPM package is also available at `https://www.npmjs.com/package/postcss-transition-shortcut`.

Let's dive in and take a look at how it is put together, in more detail:

1. We'll start by installing Git—this is required for installing the plugin boilerplate. To do this, browse to `https://git-scm.com/book/en/v2/Getting-Started-Installing-Git`, and follow the instructions for your platform.

2. Open a Node.js command prompt, then change the working folder to our project directory.

3. In the prompt, enter this command then press *Enter*:

   ```
   git clone https://github.com/postcss/postcss-plugin-boilerplate.git
   ```

4. Git will clone the `postcss-plugin-boilerplate` repository to our project area, as shown in this screenshot:

   ```
   Node.js command prompt                                    —   □   ×

   C:\wamp\www\postcss>git clone https://github.com/postcss/postcss-plugin-boilerpl
   ate.git
   Cloning into 'postcss-plugin-boilerplate'...
   remote: Counting objects: 235, done.
   remote: Compressing objects: 100% (6/6), done.
   Receivingemote: Total 235 (delta 1), reused 0 (delta 0), pack-reused 229
   Receiving objects:  77% (181/235)
   Receiving objects: 100% (235/235), 36.14 KiB | 0 bytes/s, done.
   Resolving deltas: 100% (120/120), done.
   Checking connectivity... done.

   C:\wamp\www\postcss>
   ```

5. The plugin boilerplate includes a script to automatically generate the skeleton for our plugin—go ahead and run this command in the prompt:

   ```
   node ./postcss-plugin-boilerplate/start
   ```

6. It will show a series of prompts for various bits of information. Go ahead and fill in appropriate responses, similar to that shown in this screenshot. Note that it is not obligatory to have a GitHub account, as the information is simply added to the `package.json` file; if you spend any time developing plugins in the future, then it is recommended that you go ahead and create one:

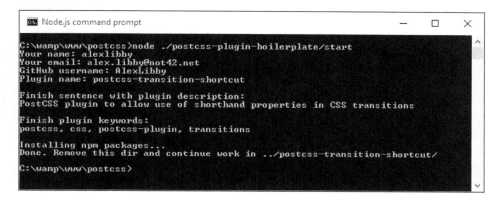

7. Once the plugin folder has been created, we can remove the `postcss-plugin-boilerplate` folder from the project root folder, as this is no longer needed.

8. If all is well, we should see something akin to this screenshot, when browsing the contents of our plugin folder:

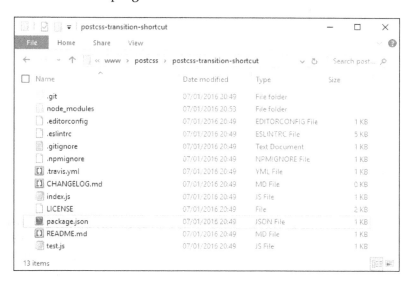

9. At this point, we can now add the code for our plugin into `index.js` — to do this, open up a copy of the file from within the `postcss-transition-shortcut` plugin from within our project area, and alter the code as shown:

```
var postcss = require('postcss');

module.exports = postcss.plugin('postcss-transition-shortcut',
function (opts) {
  opts = opts || {};

  var defaults = {
    property: 'all',
    duration: '1s',
    timing: 'ease-in-out',
    delay: '1s'
  };

  return function (css, result) {
    css.walkRules(function (rule) {
      var transitionRule;
      var transitionValues = [];
      var index = -1, node;
      var attributes = /^ (property|duration|timing|delay)$/;

      while (node = rule.nodes[++index]) {
        if (attributes.test(node.prop)) {
          transitionRule = transitionRule ||
            node.cloneBefore({ prop: 'transition' });
          var transValues = postcss.list.space(node.value);
          transitionValues.push(transValues.join(','));
          node.remove();
          --index;
        }
      }
      transitionRule.value =
        transitionValues.join(' ');
    });
  };
});
```

At this stage we will have a working plugin — the proof, though (to quote an old English saying), is in the pudding: does the plugin work as we expect? Well, there's no better way to find out than by trying it out, so let's set up a quick demo to confirm it works as expected. Before we do so, though, there is one important point I need to make, which concerns the generation of PostCSS plugins.

Creating a test for our plugin

The sharp-eyed amongst you will notice though that if we don't specify one of the four values for our transition plugin, then the code at present won't use the default; hopefully an update will come in a future version of the plugin.

This aside, the process for testing our plugin uses the AVA test runner, available from `https://github.com/sindresorhus/ava`. The framework for the test is already created within the plugin boilerplate, which leaves us to add the test code to test.js file. Let's take a peek at what's required:

1. We'll start by installing the AVA test runner — for this, fire up a Node.js command prompt, and change the working folder to the root of our plugin folder.

2. In the prompt, enter these commands, pressing *Enter* after each — the first installs AVA, with the second adding it to our `package.json` file:

   ```
   npm install --global ava

   ava --init
   ```

3. Open a new file in your text editor of choice — go ahead and add the following highlighted lines to `test.js`, within the plugin folder we created in the previous exercise:

   ```
           t.same(result.warnings().length, 0);
       });
   }


   test('transitionShtct', t => {
     return run( t, 'div { property: all; duration: 1s;
       timing: ease-in-out; delay: 1s; }',
         'div { transition: all 1s ease-in-out 1s; }', { });
   });
   ```

4. Next, fire up a Node.js command prompt, then change the working directory to our plugin project folder.

5. At the prompt, enter `npm test` and press *Enter*.

6. AVA will perform the test, which is then linted using ESLint. If all is well, we should see the results shown in this screenshot—assuming nothing was amiss with the test:

All good so far, right—at this point, we're OK to create a simple demo to prove plugin works…or are we? Well, the test shows a pass, so the code should be OK. But further down there are a ton of errors displayed, similar to this screenshot—what gives?

The test has passed, yet the tests would seem to indicate otherwise; a look further down reveals yet more errors:

This raises some important points about testing, so let's cover these before continuing with our demo.

Correcting the errors

The main error, or `Exported linebreaks to be 'LF'`..., is a simple one to fix — it's being caused by Sublime Text being set to use Windows as the default line endings setting. Assuming we're using Sublime Text, let's go ahead and deal with that error:

1. Open up Sublime Text, then open `index.js` from our plugin folder.
2. Click on View | Line Endings.
3. Change the selected option to **Unix**, and save the file.
4. Repeat steps 1 to 3 for `test.js` — once done, close both files.

If we re-run the test, we should see a significant drop in listed errors — there will be some left for us to fix in `index.js` and `test.js`, similar to this screenshot:

```
C:\wamp\www\postcss\postcss-transition-shortcut\test.js
    7:3     error   Expected indentation of 4 space characters but found 2   indent
    9:7     error   Expected indentation of 8 space characters but found 6   indent
   10:7     error   Expected indentation of 8 space characters but found 6   indent
   11:3     error   Expected indentation of 4 space characters but found 2   indent
   14:31    error   Trailing spaces not allowed                             no-trai
ling-spaces
   15:1     error   Line 15 exceeds the maximum line length of 80           max-len

   15:3     error   Expected indentation of 4 space characters but found 2   indent
   15:141   error   Trailing spaces not allowed                             no-trai
ling-spaces

? 16 problems (16 errors, 0 warnings)

npm ERR! Test failed.  See above for more details.

C:\wamp\www\postcss\postcss-transition-shortcut>_
```

Most of the errors are self-explanatory — the two that are less obvious are `Expected indentation of X spaces...` and `Line X exceeds the maximum line length`.... We can fix the first by replacing all instances of tabs with four individual spaces per tab. The second error is simple to fix — simply split the line of code into two lines.

We need to work through all of the remaining errors, as far as possible — these won't entirely be the same for your version of the plugin, but some will be similar.

 If you come across any errors where you want to understand the reason behind the error, take a look at `https://jslinterrors.com/` — it's a great source for defining what an error means!

Assuming we've cleared most of the errors, we should be left with just one:

```
Node.js command prompt                                    —    □    ×

C:\wamp\www\postcss\postcss-transition-shortcut>npm test
> postcss-transition-shortcut@0.0.0 test C:\wamp\www\postcss\postcss-transition-
shortcut
> ava && eslint *.js

 1 passed

C:\wamp\www\postcss\postcss-transition-shortcut\index.js
  14:20  error  Expected a conditional expression and instead saw an assignment
  no-cond-assign

? 1 problem (1 error, 0 warnings)

npm ERR! Test failed.  See above for more details.

C:\wamp\www\postcss\postcss-transition-shortcut>_
```

Is this an error we should fix, and therefore can clear from the report? The simple answer is that it depends — it highlights an important point about using linting for code, so let's take a moment to cover this in more detail.

Clearing the final error

The last error shown in the report presents some challenges — the code is valid, yet ESLint flags the error. The reason for this is that it has found an assignment expression within a while statement initializer; it is treated as a possible mistake in the code and *may* have unintended effects on the code.

In some respects, it can be treated as a warning, and not necessarily as an error. Prior to July 2013 we could have configured our test to ignore this, but changes made to ESLint since that date mean that this error cannot be cleared without reworking the code.

 If you would like to understand more about the causes of this error, then please refer to http://jslinterrors.com/unexpected-assignment-expression/.

In our instance, the code is valid and will not cause any errors — it leaves us with several options as to what we can do going forward:

- We can simply ignore the error and carry on — it's not great that the test fails, but in this case it won't cause any harm to our code
- We can switch off the test for it, so that while this condition is not tested, the test will at least show a 100% pass

- We can look to alter the code to design out the error/warning—this is the ideal solution, but it may be a longer term route, depending on the nature of the changes we need to make

For now, we're going to switch off the test for this error—we can do this by editing the `.eslintrc` file from within our plugin, and set the value in square brackets to `0`:

```
52      "space-unary-ops":      [2],
53      "no-cond-assign":       [0],
54      "no-func-assign":       [2],
```

This will work in the short term, but with a view to revisiting the code to design out the ambiguity at some point in the future.

Performing a test using the plugin

With our plugin in place, let's test it out—for this, we need a couple of files from the code download that accompanies this book; the files are available in the `T43 - building a transition shortcut plugin` folder:

1. Go ahead and extract copies of `gulpfile.js` and `package.json`, then save them to the root of our project area.

2. In a new file, add the following CSS styles, saving it as `style.css` in the `src` folder in our project area:

```
div {
    property: all;
    duration: 1s;
    timing: ease-in-out;
    delay: 1s;
}
```

3. Fire up a Node.js command prompt, then change the working directory to our project area.

4. At the prompt, enter `gulp` then press *Enter*—PostCSS will go away and compile the source style sheet. If all is well, we should see the compiled results of our style sheet in the `dest` folder of our project area:

At this stage, we've run the test for our plugin—we go one step further, and add our plugin to a test runner service such as Travis CI (at https://travis-ci.org). Although this is a mandatory part of the process for creating any PostCSS plugin, there is a fairly steep learning curve, and anyone working on Windows may run into difficulties! If you are a Windows user, you will have to make test.js executable via the command line—this requires prior knowledge of using Git, which is beyond the scope of this book.

For now, we'll skip past the Travis CI part of the process—the plugin is sufficiently straightforward that the local testing with test.js will suffice. Let's change tack— our plugin contains a number of useful concepts in PostCSS, so let's explore how it is put together in more detail.

Dissecting our plugin in detail

The inspiration for this plugin is twofold—at the time of writing, PostCSS doesn't have a great number of animation-based plugins, and it borrows the same concept used in the postcss-transform-shortcut plugin.

We start with the ubiquitous call to initialize PostCSS as a dependency for our plugin:

```
var postcss = require('postcss');
```

Next up, we initialize postcss.plugin, to expose functionality within our plugin to the ecosystem:

```
module.exports = postcss.plugin('postcss-transition-shortcut',
   function (options) {
```

At present, our plugin doesn't contain any options, so it will be set as blank; if we had had some options set, then these will be stored in the options array:

```
options = options || {};
```

A key part of our plugin is to set some default options—we need to have some default values set, if we don't specify one or more values:

```
var defaults = {
  property: 'all',
  duration: '1s',
  timing: 'ease-in-out',
  delay: '1s'
};
```

Up next comes the crux of our plugin—it returns the result of this function:

```
return function (css) {
```

```
css.walkRules(function (rule) {
  var transitionRule;
  var transitionValues = [];
  var index = -1, node;
  var attributes = /^(property|duration|timing|delay)$/;
```

We walk through each rule using `css.walkRules`—it sets up a number of variables and an array; we also set a search string that will be used to find any instance of our transition properties.

If we find a suitable instance of our property, we then clone it, adding the property name `transition` before it. We then work through each of up to four properties that may be set, joining them together into the final transition declaration:

```
  while (node = rule.nodes[++index]) {
    if (attributes.test(node.prop)) {
      transitionRule = transitionRule ||
        node.cloneBefore({ prop: 'transition' });
      var transValues = postcss.list.space(node.value);
      transitionValues.push(transValues.join(','));
      node.remove();
      --index;
    }
  }
  transitionRule.value = transitionValues.join(' ');
});
};
});
```

Let's move on. Our first example was a straightforward plugin; although it does need some further development (as indicated in *Testing our plugin*), it still serves a useful purpose. In our next example, we'll take a different approach: we will use an existing plugin as a basis for our new version. This plugin, unlike the first one, will not see the light of day in GitHub, though—we'll explore the reasons for this, and more, as part of our next exercise.

Building a custom font plugin

For our next demo, we're not going to build something original, but start with adapting an existing plugin that is already available for PostCSS. The plugin we will use is `postcss-fontpath` by Seane King (available from `https://github.com/seaneking/postcss-fontpath`); we're going to incorporate an autocomplete facility that automatically adds the relevant font stack, based on the name provided, and using the lists available at `http://www.cssfontstacks.com`.

"Why do this", I hear you ask? To prove a point—it isn't always necessary to re-invent the wheel; sometimes it is preferable to simply adapt something that exists, which doesn't quite fit our requirements. In this instance, the code we're adding will make it more useful; it will need some further development to allow for error-checking, but nonetheless still serves a purpose.

 A point of note—recommended practice is to use the plugin boilerplate we covered in the previous section. For this next exercise, we will build it manually—this is to show you something of the process, even though it is not one we would release into the wild.

Okay, that aside, let's get stuck in and start developing our plugin:

1. We'll start by creating a folder within the root of our project area—go ahead and name this folder `postcss-custom-fonts`.

2. Next, we need to set up the folder as a Node module, so fire up a Node.js command prompt and change the working folder to our plugin folder.

   At the prompt, enter `npm init` to start the process of creating a `package.json` file—use the details shown in this screenshot, at the appropriate prompt:

```
version: (1.0.0)
description: A PostCSS plugin to autocomplete font statements using font stacks
entry point: (index.js)
test command:
git repository: https://github/alexlibby/postcss-custom-fonts
keywords:
author: Alex Libby
license: (ISC)
About to write to C:\wamp\www\postcss\postcss-custom-fonts\package.json:

{
  "name": "postcss-custom-fonts",
  "version": "1.0.0",
  "description": "A PostCSS plugin to autocomplete font statements using font stacks",
  "main": "index.js",
  "scripts": {
    "test": "echo \"Error: no test specified\" && exit 1"
  },
  "repository": {
    "type": "git",
    "url": "https://github/alexlibby/postcss-custom-fonts"
  },
  "author": "Alex Libby",
  "license": "ISC"
}
```

3. With the prompt still open, go ahead and enter these commands, then press *Enter*—the first one is needed to install PostCSS as a dependency for our plugin, with the second installing `underscore.js`, as a second dependency (it's used for the extend method):

   ```
   npm install postcss --save
   npm install underscore --save
   ```

Keep the session open—we will need it towards the end of this exercise.

4. From the code download that accompanies this book, we need to extract a copy of `index.js`—copy this to the plugin folder.

5. If all is well, we should see something akin to this screenshot when browsing the contents of our plugin folder:

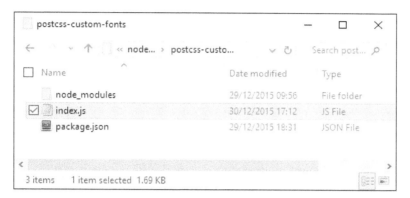

6. With our plugin in place, let's test it out. For this, we need a couple of files from the code download that accompanies this book. Go ahead and extract copies of `gulpfile.js` and `package.json` from the `T42 - Building a custom font` plugin folder (and *not* the plugin one!), then save them to the root of our project area.

7. In a new file, add the following CSS styles, saving it as `style.css` in the `src` folder in our project area:

```
@font-face {
    font-family: 'robotoregular';
    font-path: '/fonts/Roboto-Regular-webfont';
    font-weight: normal;
    font-style: normal;
}

h1 { font-family: robotoregular,  fontstack("Extra Stack");  }
```

8. Revert back to the Node.js command prompt session we had open at the start of this exercise. Make sure the working folder is set to our project area before continuing.

9. At the prompt, enter `gulp` then press *Enter*—PostCSS will go away and compile the source style sheet. If all is well, we should see the compiled results of our style sheet in the `dest` folder of our project area:

At this stage, we now have a working plugin—even though this is not an original creation, it still highlights a number of key concepts around construction of PostCSS plugins. Let's take a moment to explore the functionality of our plugin in more detail.

Dissecting the functionality of our plugin

At first glance, the code for our plugin may look complex, but in reality it is relatively straightforward to follow—let's go through it in sections, beginning with defining instances of the `postcss` object and a `fontstacks_config` object we will use in the plugin:

```
var postcss = require('postcss');
var _ = require('underscore');

// Font stacks from http://www.cssfontstack.com/
var fontstacks_config = {
  'Arial': 'Arial, "Helvetica Neue", Helvetica, sans-serif',
  'Times New Roman': 'TimesNewRoman, "Times New Roman", Times,
  Baskerville, Georgia, serif'
}
```

Next up, we add a simple helper function—this is used to convert font names into title case; the names listed in `fontstacks_config` are case sensitive, and will fail if they don't match:

```
// Credit for this function: http://stackoverflow.com/a/196991
function toTitleCase(str) {
  return str.replace(/\w\S*/g, function(txt){
    return txt.charAt(0).toUpperCase() + txt.substr(1).toLowerCase();
  });
}
```

This is the start of the plugin—the first two lines are the obligatory initialization to make the plugin available for use, followed by defining an options object. We then use `_.extend` to extend the predefined values in our chosen font stack with those added to the configuration object when running the plugin:

```
module.exports = postcss.plugin('customfonts', function (options) {
  return function (css) {

    options = options || {};
    fontstacks_config = _.extend(fontstacks_config,
      options.fontstacks);
```

We then walk through each rule and node, working out if they first contain a font declaration, then if they contain a font name that matches one in the predefined font stacks. If there is a match, then the font name is converted to the appropriate font stack and inserted with any additional fonts specified, but which don't match our font stacks:

```
css.walkRules(function (rule) {
  rule.walkDecls(function (decl, i) {
    var value = decl.value;
    if (value.indexOf( 'fontstack(' ) !== -1) {
      var fontstack_requested = value.match(/\(((['^)]+)\)/)[1].
      replace(/["']/g, "");
      fontstack_requested = toTitleCase(fontstack_requested);

      var fontstack = fontstacks_config[fontstack_requested];
      var first_font =  value.substr(0, value.
      indexOf('fontstack('));

      var new_value = first_font + fontstack;
      decl.value = first_font + fontstack;
    }
  });
});
```

In the second half of the plugin, we perform a simpler task—we work our way through each rule and declaration, looking for any instances of @font-face in the code. We then define a `fontpath` variable that removes any quotes from the supplied values, and a `format` array to manage the different font formats available for use:

```
css.walkAtRules('font-face', function(rule) {
  rule.walkDecls('font-path', function(decl) {
    var fontPath = decl.value.replace(/'/g, ''),
    src = '',
    formats = [
```

```
                    { type: 'woff', ext: '.woff' },
                    { type: 'truetype', ext: '.ttf' },
                    { type: 'svg', ext: '.svg' }
                ];
```

We then build up the relevant statement for each font type, before assembling the custom font declaration and inserting it back into the appropriate point in our style sheet:

```
                formats.forEach(function(format, index, array) {
                    if (index === array.length - 1){
                        src += 'url("' + fontPath + format.ext + '")
                format(\'' + format.type + '\')';
                    } else {
                        src += 'url("' + fontPath + format.ext + '")
                format(\'' + format.type + '\'),\n ';
                    }
                });

                decl.cloneBefore({ prop: 'src', value: src });
                decl.remove();
            });
        });
    }
});
```

Our plugin has exposed some key concepts in PostCSS plugin design—the main ones are the use of `.WalkDecls` and `.WalkRules` (or `.WalkAtRules`). I would strongly recommend familiarizing yourself with the API documentation at `https://github.com/postcss/postcss/blob/master/docs/api.md`, which outlines all of the commands available within the API, and gives a brief description of their purpose.

Despite creating what should be a useful plugin, it isn't one that I would recommend releasing into the wild. At this point you may think I have completely lost the plot, but as I always say, "there's method in the madness"—there are good reasons for not publishing this plugin, so let's take a moment to explore why it might not be a sensible move to release this plugin in its current format.

Exploring the dangers of publishing this plugin

Over the last few pages, we've created what should be a useful plugin to manipulate custom fonts — it automatically builds up the right font stack based on pre-defined settings, and will fill in the appropriate `@font-face` code for us. At this point we should have a plugin that can be released into the wild, for anyone to use...surely?

Well yes, and no — even though this plugin serves a purpose, it is not one that I would recommend making available...at least not yet! There are a few reasons why, which also help to illustrate the benefits of using the boilerplate code we covered earlier in this chapter:

- The plugin doesn't have a `test.js` file or configuration associated with it — one of the requirements for releasing plugins is that each be tested, using a `test.js` file. Ideally we might use a service such as Travis CI to help with this, but this really only works if you use a Unix-based environment for development.

- The plugin itself performs two different roles, which is not recommended — best practice for PostCSS plugins is to try where possible to limit the role to one task only. The benefits of this can be seen when using a task runner — we can pick and choose which plugins to use, without introducing too much extra unwanted functionality.

- The architecture of our code is not optimal — this is primarily due to the use of `css.WalkRules` (line 16), and `css.WalkAtRules` (line 28). These two commands parse each node within the container, and call the callback function for each rule node and at-rule node. The difference here is that `css.WalkRules` works on every rule; `css.WalkAtRules` will only work on `@`-rules (such as `@font-face`). They are not interchangeable, which makes it very inefficient at compilation.

- If we don't use the plugin boilerplate, then most of the files required for publishing code will not be present — these either have to be created by hand, or created as part of submitting to GitHub. If we use the boilerplate, then this will be done for us automatically, along with configuring the `package.json` file for us — all we need to do is add a suitable task runner such as Gulp or Grunt.

One might ask why we would even consider this route, if it is likely to throw up issues during development — the simple answer is that it helps us understand something of how plugins should be built. If we're building a plugin for personal use only, then there is no need for some of the files or processes that we have to use when releasing plugins for general use.

Simplifying the development process

Leaving aside the intended audience for our plugins, throughout our development process we've used a mix of different techniques, but with one thing in common— our plugins have very few dependencies! This is not to be sniffed at, as clearly any dependencies that change may have a resulting knock-on effect for our plugin.

This aside, there will be times when the lack of any dependencies may require more development effort than is sensible (or practical) — it is at this point where we may need to consider using additional plugins to handle some of the processing. A perfect example of this is to parse a font: statement so that we can work on the constituent elements; there are a few others that are worthy of note:

Type of parser or helper	URL of plugin source	Purpose of plugin
Selector	`https://github.com/ postcss/postcss- selector-parser`	Manages selector strings.
Value	`https://github.com/ TrySound/postcss-value- parser`	Transforms CSS values and `@-rule` parameters into a tree of nodes for easy traversal.
Property	`https://github.com/ jedmao/postcss-resolve- prop`	Resolves a rule's property value — this is particularly useful if multiple values are specified for the same property.
Font	`https://github.com/ jedmao/parse-css-font`	Parses a `font` property, and returns values for each element, such as `font-size`, `family`, `style`, or `lineHeight`.
Dimension	`https://github.com/ jedmao/parse-css- dimension`	Parses a CSS dimension such as `number`, `length`, or `percentage`, to return a JavaScript object.
Sides	`https://github.com/ jedmao/parse-css-sides`	Parses an element's side attributes (such as `margin`, `padding`, or `border` properties), and returns values for all four sides as strings.
Font helpers	`https://github.com/ jedmao/postcss-font- helpers`	Used to manipulate font statements in CSS — it either returns individual elements or a combined font object, as required.
Margin helpers	`https://github.com/ jedmao/postcss-margin- helpers`	Used to manipulate margin values for any specified element.

So, should we use them? It's not obligatory by any means, but they may help remove some of the effort required to create our plugin. If any are used, then it pays to keep a close note of any changes being made to the plugins, so that we can correct any issues that occur promptly; after all, no-one likes a plugin that isn't maintained properly by the developer!

Let's move on, a key part of plugin construction is consistency; the power of PostCSS allows any plugin to be created, so keeping a sense of uniformity is essential. To help with this, the developer of PostCSS has released a set of guidelines: let's dive in and take a look at these in more detail.

Guidelines for plugin building

One of the key benefits of the PostCSS ecosystem is its flexibility — it allows any developer to create any plugin, or adapt existing ones, as long as the license allows for further development!

To help retain a sense of consistency, the developer has issued a series of mandatory guidelines, which should be followed where practical:

- The name of your plugin should clearly indicate the purpose of that plugin — for example, if you built one to mimic the CSS4 `:hover` pseudo-class, then `postcss-hover` would be a good example.

- It is better to create a plugin that does one thing well, and not one that tries to perform multiple tasks at the same time.

- Always use the `postcss.plugin` method when creating plugins — you are then hooking into a common plugin API.

- Where possible, try to use asynchronous methods — you should also set a `node.source` for each node, so that PostCSS can generate an accurate source map.

- Do not use the console when displaying errors — some PostCSS runners do not allow console output. Use `result.warn` instead to manage errors.

- Any plugin created and published must be tested, with documented examples (where possible) and a change log in English.

- If you are writing a plugin for Node, then the postcss-plugin keyword must feature in the `package.json` file — this is used for feedback about the PostCSS ecosystem.

 More details on these guidelines are available at `https://github.com/postcss/postcss/blob/master/docs/guidelines/plugin.md`.

In addition, it is likely that we will use a task runner of some description, such as Broccoli, Grunt, or Brunch, or as in our case, Gulp. To help retain that consistency, the developer has issued a series of guidelines that should be followed where appropriate:

- If your plugin uses a `config` file, then it must always be written in JavaScript, and set to support functions in parameters.

- When using runners, always set the to and from options, even if your runner doesn't handle writing to disk — this is to ensure that PostCSS generates accurate source maps and displays better syntax errors.

- PostCSS runners must only use the publicly available asynchronous API — runners should not rely on undocumented methods or properties that may be removed in a future release.

- Don't simply display the full JavaScript stack when handling `CssSyntaxError` messages — not every developer is familiar with JavaScript! Instead, make sure any errors are handled gracefully.

- Any warnings that appear from `result.warnings()` should be displayed by PostCSS runners; this can be facilitated by using the `postcss-logs-warnings` or `postcss-messages` plugins if needed.

- If your plugin uses the source map option, then by default this will be generated as an inline map by PostCSS. Runners must provide an option to save the map to a separate file, if required.

 More details on these guidelines are available at `https://github.com/postcss/postcss/blob/master/docs/guidelines/runner.md`.

The guidelines provided for plugins are mandatory, but in some cases can be seen as a start point — for example, a change log should always be maintained, but it is up to the developer as to whether this is a `HISTORY.md`, `CHANGELOG.md`, or a GitHub Releases document. The trick here is careful planning, and to keep it simple — focus on the basics first, before moving onto more complex projects. We can then get accustomed to what must be provided as a minimum for each plugin, before extending it to cover task runner use.

Okay, let's change tack at this point: one of the guidelines we've covered states that every plugin should be tested as part of normal practice; now is a perfect opportunity to explore what this means in more detail.

Making the plugin available for use

A key part of creating any plugin is testing—once tested, we can then decide if we want to release it for general use on GitHub and Node's package manager directory. It's not obligatory, but if we have created something that could be useful to others, then it is only fair that we make it available!

There are a few steps involved in the process—they can be split into three groups: testing the plugin, adding the final details (in GitHub), and submitting it for inclusion on the PostCSS plugin directory. We'll be using the `postcss-transition-shortcut` plugin that we've just created, as a basis for releasing it for general use.

We've already covered the requirements for testing our plugin, so let's explore the remaining steps needed to make our plugin available for general use by developers. The first step is to publish our plugin to a suitable repository on GitHub. This process falls outside of the scope of this book, but in a nutshell, the process for making the plugin available is as follows:

- Add examples of code to the `README.md` file—this should show an example of a source file, and what we would expect to see when that file has been processed.

- In the `CHANGELOG.md` file, add the initial version number for the plugin.

- All of the changes need to be committed to GitHub—my preferred choice is GitHub Desktop, available for Windows or Mac from `https://desktop.github.com/`. For Linux users, there are several options available at `https://git-scm.com/download/gui/linux`.

- At this point, we now need to publish our plugin to Node's package directory, NPM. The process involves adding a new user to NPM, then publishing all files to NPM; the details are outlined in full at `https://docs.npmjs.com/getting-started/publishing-npm-packages`.

Once the plugin has been prepared, tested and published, all that remains is to fork PostCSS, add your plugin to the `Plugins` section in `README.md`, and send a `pull` request. We can then monitor the site's Twitter feed for updates about our plugin.

 If you are interested, then you may like to refer to *GitHub Essentials* by *Achilleas Pipinellis*, available at `https://www.packtpub.com/`.

Summary

Unlike other processors, plugins play a central role in PostCSS—we can pick and choose what functionality we want to use; if it doesn't exist, then we are free to create our own version. Throughout the course of this chapter, we've covered some key concepts around the use of plugins, so let's take a moment to review what we have learnt.

We kicked off with a quick introduction to the use of plugins, which was swiftly followed by exploring the architecture of a standard plugin that included a look at some of the key files that make up a standard plugin. We then moved on to take a look at some of the classes, modules, and methods available as part of the API.

Next up, we began working through the construction of an example plugin, before constructing a suitable test process and correcting the errors generated from linting the code as part of the test. We then rounded off our plugin with a look in more detail, to understand some of the key concepts behind how it works.

Moving on, we then covered the construction of a second plugin, but this time explored the manual process, and examined why this is not a recommended practice. We took a look at some of the issues that can arise from this practice, and why using the plugin boilerplate makes development easier.

We then rounded out the chapter by exploring some of the helper plugins we can use to simplify development, along with the recommended guidelines for development, and the process for making the plugin available for other developers to use in the future.

Okay, onwards we go: so far, we've used a variety of plugins throughout the book. There are three particular groups of plugins that are particularly useful—they are for fallback support, implementing shortcuts to creating CSS, and plugin packs. We'll cover all three (and more) in the next chapter.

9
Working with Shortcuts, Fallbacks, and Packs

If you spend any time working with CSS, then it is likely you will come across instances where you wished there was a quicker way to add a particular block of code to your page, apply vendor prefixes, or perhaps set a predefined border to an element on the page.

We can easily achieve this by using one or more of the many shortcuts, fallbacks, or pack plugins available for use with PostCSS. In this chapter, we'll explore some common scenarios where plugins are required, before learning how to create them in the next chapter. We will cover a number of topics throughout this chapter, which will include the following:

- Exploring some of the PostCSS shortcuts and packs available for use
- Using plugins to lint and optimize your CSS code
- Supplementing the existing shortcuts available in PostCSS
- Applying fallbacks to PostCSS code to maintain support for older browsers

Let's get cracking!

Using shortcut plugins in PostCSS

Building a web-based application or site can be a lengthy process — there are so many elements to consider, and it takes time to create content that is engaging and informative.

Naturally, a smart designer or developer will always look for a shortcut to save time — after all, why take an hour to do something, if a shortcut will take half the time? The great thing about PostCSS is that it has a good selection of shortcut plugins that we can use; these include plugins such as the examples:

- `postcss-focus`: This plugin is available at `https://github.com/postcss/postcss-focus`, this simple plugin adds a `:focus` pseudo-selector to any `:hover` attribute encountered in a style rule.

- `postcss-border`: If specified in a shorthand version, this plugin will add a `border-width` attribute to an existing `border:` attribute. The plugin source is available from `https://github.com/andrepolischuk/postcss-border`.

- `postcss-short-data`: This plugin is available at `https://github.com/jonathantneal/postcss-short-data`, this interesting plugin allows us to write shorthand data attribute selectors, akin to pseudo-selectors, which are compiled into data- attributes.

We've already incorporated or talked about a number of the shortcut plugins that are available within PostCSS — these include `postcss-responsive-type` which we used to build a responsive page earlier in the book, `easings`, and of course, `postcss-transform-shortcut` from *Chapter 7, Animating Content*.

There are a lot more plugins available for use. Throughout the course of this chapter, we're going to explore some of the shortcut plugins available, plus some of the packs that we can use to supplement functionality within our preprocessor. A good place to start is the selection of plugin packs available for use within PostCSS — let's take a moment to explore these in more detail.

Exploring plugin packs for PostCSS

Cast your mind back, if you will, to some advice I gave earlier about plugins — remember how I said that in an ideal world, a plugin should serve a single purpose?

Well, one might be forgiven for thinking that we're ignoring this advice when we talk about plugin packs. In reality, we're not; all of the plugin packs available for PostCSS provide a single interface for multiple single plugins. At present, the list of plugin packs include these examples:

- **Oldie**: Available from `https://github.com/jonathantneal/oldie`, this plugin is an interface for nine separate plugins; it handles support for older versions of IE.

- **Short**: Hosted at `https://github.com/jonathantneal/postcss-short`, this plugin lets us write styles using our own shorthand properties.

- **AtCSS** : This plugin is available at `https://github.com/morishitter/atcss`, this interesting plugin provides a new take on SASS' `@extend` by allowing us to create rules that inherit from base rules.

- **precss**: This plugin, from `https://github.com/jonathantneal/precss`, allows us to use SASS-like markup in our style sheets. We will explore this in more detail in *Chapter 11, Manipulating Custom Syntaxes*.

- **Stylelint**: This plugin pack should form part of any PostCSS developer's toolkit: it allows us to lint our style sheets automatically. The pack is available from `https://github.com/stylelint/stylelint`.

- **Cssnano**: In a similar vein, `cssnano` should be part of any developer's toolkit: this pack is perfect for compressing and optimizing code within our style sheets. You can get the plugin from `https://github.com/ben-eb/cssnano`.

- **Rucksack**: Last, but by no means least, Rucksack (as described by the developer), is a "...little bag of CSS superpowers". This pack adds support for functionality such as `font src` generation, providing fallback support for RGBA values, or the `clearfix` hack.

These packs provide a real mix of functionality — it is naturally up to us to decide which plugins we want to use. At this point, though, one might be tempted to ask "why use a pack — surely this adds unnecessarily redundant functionality that we're trying to avoid adding?"

It's a good question, the simple answer is that it will depend on your requirements. If all we're interested in is adding vendor prefixes, then checking and compressing our code, then we would most likely use `autoprefixer`, `cssnano`, and `stylelint`. But if we wanted to add property aliases, then `autoprefixer` can be dropped in favor of using Rucksack with `cssnano` and `stylelint`. The key here, though, is to carefully assess what you need, and work out the best combination of plugins to use from the selection available for PostCSS.

Okay, time for a change: let's move on! We will be exploring some of these plugin packs over the next few pages: let's make a start with a simple plugin, in the form of `postcss-short`.

Writing styles in shorthand

This plugin, available from `https://github.com/jonathantneal/postcss-short`, is a wrapper for several plugins available for the PostCSS ecosystem; these include Shorthand Border, Shorthand Color, and Shorthand Size. Installing the plugin is a breeze—it uses the same format as most other PostCSS plugins, and can be installed using this command within our project root area, in a Node.js command prompt session:

```
npm install postcss-short --save-dev
```

The great thing about this plugin (and other plugin packs) is that it removes the need to call lots of separate plugins. We must bear in mind though that to make this worthwhile, we need to be calling most of the plugins in some form or other. If we're only calling one or two from `postcss-short`, then we may prefer to call them individually, and not use the `postcss-short` plugin.

Leaving aside any concerns about using the plugin, let's take a look at some examples of it in action. The best way to experience it is to use the online editor at `http://jonathantneal.github.io/postcss-short/`. We can use this to experiment before adding the final result to our style sheet prior to compilation:

In this example (taken from the plugin site), we've used all of the plugins, with the exception of Shorthand Text and Shorthand Data. In our code, we've used the relevant shorthand as specified for the plugin—PostCSS will compile this into valid CSS styles, as outlined within each plugin.

Which plugins we use will of course depend on our requirements—there is every possibility that you will find yourselves using particular plugins more than others. Staying with the theme of shorthand, though, there is one plugin pack that is likely to feature often in your toolkit—Rucksack. No, I don't suggest this is an opportunity to go on holiday (no pun intended), but more an occasion to use what will be a very useful set of plugins within PostCSS.

Adding shortcuts with Rucksack

Mention the word Rucksack, and one might be forgiven for thinking we were about to go on a journey or holiday—whilst the desire might be there, there are more practical matters to attend to first!

This said, working with PostCSS can easily be seen as going on a journey; this is particularly true when working with plugins. One of the plugins (or to be more accurate, packs) that you will very likely come across when working with PostCSS is Rucksack (see the play on words there?). This useful pack, available from `http://simplaio.github.io/rucksack/`, contains a number of plugins that have been linked together to provide additional functionality that we can use when compiling style sheets using Rucksack, such as these examples:

- **Alias**: This is available at `https://github.com/seaneking/postcss-alias`, this plugin allows us to create shorthand CSS properties.

- **Clearfix**: As a developer, I am sure you will be familiar with the clearfix hack: this plugin by Sean King provides the PostCSS equivalent, and is available at `https://github.com/seaneking/postcss-clearfix`.

- **Font src expansion**: How many times have you used custom font declarations in your code? They're a pain to write—another plugin by Sean King (at `https://github.com/seaneking/postcss-fontpath`), makes it a cinch to add to your code.

The irony here, though, is that we've already used Rucksack without realizing it—remember the `postcss-responsive-type` plugin we used back in *Chapter 4, Building Media Queries*? Or the `autoprefixer` plugin we've used in just about every chapter throughout the book? Both of these plugins are available via Rucksack—Rucksack is really an abstract layer that ties in access from multiple plugins into one consistent interface for us to use.

Okay, enough chitchat: let's get stuck into a demo and see some action! For our next demo, we're going to construct a simple slider using some standard HTML markup and CSS3 styles; no JavaScript will be used at all. We'll start with a quick run-through of our slider, before we convert the style sheet to use Rucksack.

Introducing our demo

For this next demo, we're going to break tradition and not install the plugin we're about to use first, before creating our demo. Instead, we'll set up our demo first—we can then ascertain where Rucksack can be used once we've set our baseline solution.

Our demo centers on a simple image slider, which uses pure CSS3 styling to control the animation. This is a screenshot of what we're going to create:

To see the demo in action, go ahead and extract the `T45 - converting to use Rucksack` folder from a copy of the code download that accompanies this book—save it to our project area. Go ahead and preview the results by running `slider.html` in a browser, then click on the numbers in the bottom left to move between different images.

> You will need to rename the style `post-completed.css` file `style.css` for it to operate correctly.

Installing Rucksack as a plugin

With our demo in place, it's time to install Rucksack, and ascertain where we can use it in our demo! Rucksack, like most other PostCSS plugins, can be installed using the same method — we can use NPM:

1. Fire up a Node.js command prompt, then change the working folder to our project area.

2. In the prompt, enter `npm install rucksack-css --save-dev`, then press *Enter*.

3. NPM will go away and install the plugin — if all is well, we should see something akin to this:

```
gulp                                                    —    □    ×

C:\wamp\www\postcss>npm install rucksack-css --save-dev
postcss@1.0.0 C:\wamp\www\postcss
├── cwebp@1.1.0
├─┬ gulp-rucksack@0.1.2
│ └── rucksack-css@0.8.5
├── postcss-transform-shortcut@1.0.0  extraneous
├── postcss-transition-shortcut@1.0.6  extraneous
└── rucksack-css@0.8.5
```

A note of caution — there are several plugins available for Rucksack: make sure you install the right one! There is a Gulp plugin, but this does not appear to work within PostCSS, even though we are using Gulp as our task runner.

This aside, let's move on. Before we go through the process of converting our slider to use Rucksack, let's take a quick look at using it in action with a simple easing demo.

Easing into using Rucksack

Any developer who spends time animating content on a website will no doubt have created rules to control how content eases in or out of the page. Striking the right balance between easing content in and out of the page and the site becoming too overladen with effects takes time to get right!

Leaving aside the awful pun in that last comment, this is where Rucksack can help — one of the simpler plugins that forms part of this package is `postcss-easings`. This plugin, available from `https://github.com/postcss/postcss-easings` and one that we touched on in *Chapter 7, Animating Content*, has but one role in life: convert any recognized easing name into a cubic-bezier equivalent value.

For an example of a Bezier curve, take a look at
`http://cubic-bezier.com/#.17,.67,.83,.67`.

Is there any benefit in doing this, I hear you ask? Well, two that come to mind are consistency and a central point of source. Let me explain what I mean.

A central point of source borrows a principle from CSS preprocessors such as SASS or less, where a single value is defined at the top of the file; any instance found elsewhere in the file will be automatically replaced by its value (in this instance, a `cubic-bezier` easing). This then helps with consistency: we can specify names for any custom easings in the configuration, which will replace any instance found during compilation.

The benefit of this means that we only need to update one central point (that is, point of source), and can avoid mixing different types of easing values in our code—they will be converted to cubic-bezier values at compilation.

Okay, let's move on: time for a demo! Before we get stuck in, let's quickly cover what we're going to construct. Our demo is a simple affair with four squares that we will animate using nothing more than plain HTML and CSS (yes, no JavaScript). We will use a handful of effects, such as `easeOutBack`, which looks something like this:

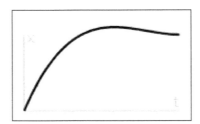

 You can learn more about the details for this particular easing at
`http://easings.net/#easeOutBack`—it translates to `cubic-bezier(0.175, 0.885, 0.32, 1.275)` when used in code.

Let's get on and construct that demo…

Animating content using the plugin

If you're expecting dramatic effects, then I am sorry to disappoint — this exercise has been kept deliberately simple, to show you how easy it is to use Rucksack. We mentioned earlier that the overall result will be four simple squares that we can animate at will — they will look something like this:

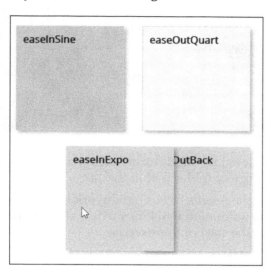

The use of this plugin does raise one important question — we will cover this once we've built our demo:

1. From the code download that accompanies this book, go ahead and extract a copy of the `T44 - postcss-easings` folder, and save it to the root of our project area.

2. Next, copy the `gulpfile.js` and `package.json` files from this `T44 - postcss-easings` folder to the root of our project area — go ahead and replace any that are already present in this location, or save them somewhere for safekeeping.

3. Copy the `style - pre-comile.css` file from the `css - completed versions` folder to the `src` folder within our project area; this sets it ready for compilation. Rename it `style.css`.

4. Go ahead and fire up a Node.js command prompt session, then change the working folder to our project area.

5. In the prompt, enter `Gulp` then press *Enter* — our file will be compiled, like this:

6. Assuming no issues appeared during compilation, copy the contents of the `dest` folder to the `css` folder within the `T44 - postcss-easings` folder.

7. Try previewing the results of our handiwork in a browser — if we hover over each square, the animation will kick in; they should appear similar to the figure shown at the start of this exercise.

Our demo was never meant to be anything more complicated — the aim was to show off how easy it is to get a consistent effect, provided the configuration object is correctly set up! It does, however, raise an important question concerning our choice of plugins, so let's explore that in more detail.

Dissecting our demo in more detail

This is one example of where simplicity pays in spades; the `postcss-easings` plugin requires no configuration for standard use, and will only need configuring if the easing we use are not already part of its core library. The ones we picked for this demo are already defined in the plugin — if we open a copy of the compiled style sheet, we should see something akin to this:

```
28   .box1 {
29       background-color: rgba(106, 112, 89, 0.5);
30       transition: 2s cubic-bezier(0.47, 0, 0.745, 0.715);
31   }
32
33   .box1:hover {
34       transition: 2s cubic-bezier(0.47, 0, 0.745, 0.715);
35       transform: translate(5rem, 0);
36       background-color: rgba(106, 112, 89, 1);
37   }
```

The key to configuring this plugin lies in two lines of code, on or around lines 11 and 16:

```
var rucksack = require('rucksack-css');
  .pipe(postcss([ rucksack() ]))
```

Much of what is present in the Gulp task file that we used in this demo is code that we've already seen before; it frequently pays to think ahead, so that we can build a gulp file that can be reused for future projects. Once configured, then any style recognized by the plugin will be compiled into valid CSS.

If we had decided to use a custom easing style, then we can easily update the configuration object accordingly:

```
14    gulp.task('styles', function () {
15      return gulp.src('src/*.css')
16        .pipe(postcss([ rucksack({ easings: { easeAchieve: 'cubic-bezier(.57,.95,.03,.62)' } }) ]))
17        .pipe(gulp.dest('dest/'));
18    });
```

In case you're wondering about the name given—this effect replicates the motion when punching the air after you've achieved a good result, particularly if it has been a troublesome issue to solve!

Before we move on to our next exercise, we should answer the question that I alluded to earlier: which plugin should we use? But hold on, we're using the postcss-easings plugin, right?

No, I've not completely lost the plot: the postcss-easings plugin is available separately, and is referenced within the Rucksack pack of plugins. The key here, though, is that if we only need to use postcss-easings, then there is no sense in calling in Rucksack's plugins, which will only add an unnecessary burden to our workflow. Instead, we can change line 11 in our gulp task file to the following:

```
var easings = require('postcss-easings');
```

And we can change line 16 to the following:

```
.pipe(postcss([ easings() ]))
```

As long as the plugin is still installed from earlier, then the code will be compiled as before, but without the extra overhead of the other plugins that form Rucksack.

Converting our slider to use Rucksack

If we're working with Rucksack, we've seen that the key to successful use is less about configuring it for use in our Gulp file, and more about deciding which plugins to use. To see what we mean by this, take a look at the original stylesheet from *Introducing our demo* carefully; it should reveal that we can use a number of plugins to improve on existing functionality:

- **Responsive typography**: Our demo is already partially responsive, but the label text isn't resizing if we change the size of our slider. We can fix this by altering our code to trigger Rucksack to make our fonts responsive.

- **Shorthand positioning**: This is a great plugin for adding position attributes; why bother adding top, left, right, and bottom attributes when we do all four in a single line of code? Add this one-liner, and we can get PostCSS to do the heavy lifting for us.

- **Property aliases**: Continuing with the shorthand theme, we can use this plugin to set up shorthand versions of any attribute we care to use; it means we only need to type in one or two letters, which PostCSS will transpile to the full version of that attribute.

- **Font src expansion**: If we look at our source style sheet carefully, we should see a small issue on or around line 6. The code calls for Open Sans as a font, but this is not a standard font! Thankfully, we can easily fix it by telling the browser where to download it from—Rucksack provides a convenient shorthand form for adding this detail to our code.

- **Hex RGBA shortcuts**: We've used a mix of RGBA and HEX codes in our style sheet to represent colors, yet some older browsers don't support the former style. This is becoming less of an issue, but as it is added automatically by Rucksack, then there is no harm in adding the latter values!

- **Easings**: Our slider demo used a single instance of an easing, in the form of ease-in-out-back. In the previous demo, we used `postcss-easings` (that is the basis for this part of Rucksack) to convert the names to `cubic-bezier` values; we should look to continue this theme when updating the slider.

- **Automatic prefixing**: This isn't enabled by default, so it's up to us to decide if we want to use it. It references the same `autoprefixer` plugin we've already used in earlier demos; if we're going to make good use of Rucksack, then it makes sense to enable it and remove any existing reference that is already in our code. We're going to use most of the plugins referenced in Rucksack, so we will enable it for use. If, however, we only need one or two, or we don't need support for older browsers, then it can remain switched off.

- **Legacy fallbacks**: Support for older browsers is provided by the laggard plugin in Rucksack. This provides a mix of fallback mechanisms, such as adding fallback support for rem values, HEX fallbacks for RGBA values, or the 3D transform hack for will-change. We'll be adding rem fallback support, so we will enable this plugin for use.

Now that we've covered the elements we want to use, it's time for us to make the changes. Without further ado, let's make a start:

1. From the code download that accompanies this book, go ahead and extract a copy of the `T45 - converting to use Rucksack` folder, and save it to our project area.

2. From within the `T45 - converting to use Rucksack` folder, copy the `gulpfile.js` and `package.json` files to the root of our project area.

3. Next, copy the contents of the `css-completed` version folder from within the `T45 - converting to use Rucksack` folder to the `src` folder at the root of our project area. Rename pre-compile `version.css` `style.css`, then open up this file in a text editor — we need to make some changes to the styles within the file.

4. Our first change is to make the text in our demo responsive — do a search for `font-size`, and change any instance to `font-size: responsive`. This should cover each of the five number labels, and the `div.slide-content > figcaption` rule.

5. Next up, is adding our shorthand version for the position attribute — in this instance, there is only one we can change, which is on line 42. Comment out the `bottom`, `left`, `right`, and `top` attributes specified on lines 33-36, then replace the `position:` attribute with this:

   ```
   position: 427px 0 0;
   ```

 Note, the other instances of position can't be changed as we've not specified individual placement values in these rules.

6. Our next conversion is to add some aliases — this is just a shortcut to typing in more text! For our demo, go ahead and add this at the top of our style sheet:

   ```
   @alias {
     pb: padding-bottom;
     bs: box-shadow;
     bgc: background-color;
   }
   ```

Next, do a search and replace for each of these three styles—replace the full name with the shortcut names given in the `@alias` block.

1. Remember the small issue I pointed out earlier, about the missing support for the Open Sans font? Well, we can easily fix that—at the top of our style sheet file, go ahead and add this block; this tells the browser where to find the Open Sans font:

```
@font-face {
    font-family: 'open_sansregular';
    font-path: '../fonts/OpenSans-Regular-webfont';
    font-weight: normal;
    font-style: normal;
}
```

2. We touched briefly on Rucksack's ability to convert easing names to cubic-bezier values. The demo uses an easing name—this has already been set to one that is supported within Rucksack, so we don't need to alter our code. The same applies to the RGBA fall-back support—Rucksack will automatically convert any RGBA values it sees to HEX equivalents within our code.

3. The remaining two changes are for legacy support and automatic prefixing—to enable these, we have to modify our gulp file as shown in the screenshot:

```
14  gulp.task('styles', function () {
15      return gulp.src('src/*.css')
16          .pipe(postcss([ rucksack({ fallbacks: true, autoprefixer: true }) ]))
17          .pipe(gulp.dest('dest/'));
18  });
```

4. Save the file, then switch to a Node.js command prompt—at the prompt, make sure the working folder is set to our project area.

5. At the prompt, enter `gulp`, then press *Enter*—PostCSS will go away and compile the code; if all is well, we should see our compiled files in the `dest` folder:

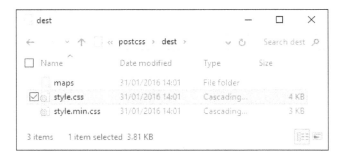

At this stage, we have a compiled set of files. To confirm if the demo works, go ahead and copy them to the `css` folder within the `T45 - converting to use Rucksack` folder; try previewing the results of our work by running `slider.html`. If all is well, we should see the same slider effect:

All should be good, we have a working demo and our code has compiled successfully. At this point we can move on to our next task, right...?

Dissecting our code

Well, it's worth taking a look at our compiled code first: Rucksack has made some additional changes to our code that we may not have expected to see.

For example, Rucksack has provided pixel-based fallback support for the rem units listed throughout our code, along with the HEX fallback support we discussed earlier:

```
body {
    font-family: "open_sansregular";
    line-height: 25.888px;
    line-height: 1.618rem;
    background-color: #ecf0f1;
    background-color: rgba(236, 240, 241, 1.0);
    color: #44466a;
    color: rgba(68, 68, 618, 1.0);
}
```

Next, take a look at line 96 — remember the `font-size: responsive` attribute that we added? This is the compiled result:

```
font-size: calc(12px + 9 * ( (100vw - 420px) / 860));
```

Throughout the bottom two-thirds, there are a number of media queries that have been added; these were added as part of making our font styles responsive. Further down, at around line 226, we have this block:

```
-ms-filter: "progid:DXImageTransform.Microsoft.Alpha(Opacity=0)";
-webkit-transition: opacity 0.35s;
transition: opacity 0.35s;
```

At first glance, you might wonder where this came from, as we didn't specify an `ms-filter` attribute in our code. Well, this is thanks to Rucksack — it has added opacity support for IE automatically.

The key to this little exploration, though, is that choosing plugins should be an iterative process that will only really finish when the site is no longer needed. For example, we could easily add another step to our workflow that reduces `calc()` operations to static values (where allowed — the plugin for this is `postcss-calc`). We should always consider using `postcss-remove-prefixes` periodically to keep our code up to date; there will come a time when we either don't need to add prefixes, or existing prefixes become redundant.

Leaving aside the changes to our style sheet, there is one more to consider — you will note that the Autoprefixer plugin has been commented out in our code:

```
1    'use strict';
2
3    var gulp = require('gulp');
4    var postcss = require('gulp-postcss');
5    //var autoprefixer = require('autoprefixer');
6    var cssnano = require('cssnano');
7    var sourcemaps = require('gulp-sourcemaps');
8    var rename = require('gulp-rename');
9    var stylelint = require('stylelint');
10   var reporter = require('postcss-reporter');
11   var rucksack = require('rucksack');
12
13
14   gulp.task('styles', function () {
15     return gulp.src('/src/*.css')
16       .pipe(postcss([ rucksack({ fallbacks: true, autoprefixer: true }) ]))
17       .pipe(gulp.dest('dest/'));
18   });
```

This is with good reason—Rucksack has built-in support for `autoprefixer`, so there is no need to call it twice; ironically, it simply calls the same plugin that is commented out of our code! It's up to us whether we want to call it from within Rucksack, or separately; this will largely depend on what else is being called from with Rucksack, and whether adding `autoprefixer` will help provide a stronger case for using Rucksack.

Linting and optimizing your code

Bandwidth usage has always been critical to the success of a website; remember the good old days of 56K modems? We've come a long way since then, but this is still no excuse for producing sites that swallow bandwidth like it's going out of fashion!

A part of this comes in the form of linting and minifying our style sheets before deploying into production use—it goes without saying that this should form part of any developer's workflow process by default. We can do this manually, but this manual job is prone to missing opportunities, which can lead to inconsistencies in our code.

Instead, we can use the power of PostCSS to perform the heavy lifting for us; the `stylelint` and `cssnano` plugin packs make for a powerful optimization facility! If we take a careful look at most gulp task files that we've created throughout the course of this book, both processes are taking place; in this example, `stylelint` is used at line 22, and `cssnano` at line 38:

```
20   gulp.task("lint-styles", ['styles'], function() {
21       return gulp.src("dest/*.css")
22       .pipe(postcss([ stylelint({
23           "rules": {
24               "color-no-invalid-hex": 2,
25               "declaration-colon-space-before": [2, "never"],
26               "indentation": [2, 2],
27               "number-leading-zero": [2, "always"]
28           }
29       }),
30       reporter({
31           clearMessages: true,
32       })
33       ]))
34   });
35
36   gulp.task('rename', ['lint-styles'], function () {
37       return gulp.src('dest/*.css')
38       .pipe(postcss([ cssnano() ]))
39       .pipe(rename('style.min.css'))
40       .pipe(gulp.dest("dest/"));
41   });
```

Exploring the use of cssnano

For anyone starting out with PostCSS for the first time, then simply specifying `cssnano()` as one of the processors for PostCSS should be sufficient:

```
36   gulp.task('rename', ['lint-styles'], function () {
37     return gulp.src('dest/*.css')
38       .pipe(postcss([ cssnano() ]))
39       .pipe(rename('style.min.css'))
40       .pipe(gulp.dest("dest/"));
41   });
```

If we take a look at the `T45 - converting to use Rucksack` demo, our original style sheet file weighs in at 4KB when compiled, but which drops to 3KB after compression. Granted, it's only a small file, but a 25% drop in size is still not an insignificant drop!

 At this point, it is worth noting that even though we are using Gulp, the plugin in use is the PostCSS version, and not `gulp-cssnano`.

The `cssnano` plugin is not a single plugin, but a wrapper for a number of plugins, which include examples such as these:

- `postcss-reduce-idents`: This reduces any custom identifier names (such as those used in `@keyframes`) to two letter equivalent codes; this helps with minifying code.

- `postcss-zindex`: This plugin reduces any `z-index` declarations that are unnecessarily higher than they should be.

- `postcss-convert-values`: If our CSS uses any number of different units, then we can reduce the CSS size by expressing the value a different way. For example, `400ms` can be expressed as `.4s` (a reduction by two characters). Some might argue this is a little extreme, but every little helps!

- `postcss-colormin`: In a similar vein, we can reduce the length of color names using this plugin: if `rgba(255, 0, 0, 1)` is used in our code, then we can replace this with `red`. Although the name is indeed shorter, this is at the expense of losing consistency with naming our colors, which may not be so desirable.

Moving on, there are some key points we should be aware of, when using cssnano:

- You will notice the presence of the gulp-rename plugin in use within our Gulp file—cssnano does not have a capability to rename a compressed file to something we would expect to see within our code. We can use gulp-rename to create a version that developers would expect to see in code; it does leave a copy of the original file in place, if needed.

- Most options within cssnano are enabled by default; we can switch off individual ones in the configuration object, as shown in this example:

```
var nano = require('gulp-cssnano');

gulp.task('default', function () {
    return gulp.src('./main.css')
        .pipe(nano({discardComments: {removeAll: true}}))
        .pipe(gulp.dest('./out'));
});
```

> For a full list of the transform options, take a look at http://cssnano.co/options/. Click on the link to view individual configuration options for that plugin.

- This plugin automatically includes autoprefixer. Technically, there is no need to include it separately as we have done in previous exercises, so ideally it should be removed. We will focus on this more as part of optimizing our processor in *Chapter 10, Building a Custom Processor*.

- There are some transforms that are available within cssnano, but which are *not* switched on by default; these are not considered safe and should only be included if you are 100% sure it has not affected your code. The details of unsafe transforms are available on the options page at http://cssnano.co/options/.

Okay, let's move on: the second half of our double act is the stylelint plugin pack; unlike cssnano, stylelint takes the opposite approach and allows you to enable any rule as needed, from a list of over 100 available rules. Let's dive in and take a look in more detail.

Configuring Stylelint as our linter

How does one describe Stylelint, if you've never met it before? Well, to quote its website, "stylelint is a mighty, modern CSS linter".

Whether we agree with such a bold statement, it is certainly worth getting to know Stylelint as a linter. Available from `http://stylelint.io/`, the key to this plugin lies not in the plugin itself, but in the rules that define what we want to check in our code. At present, we can use any one of 100+ rules, or a mix of several; these can be specified in a `.styleintrc` file, within our `package.json` file, or as a `stylelint.config.js` file that exports a JavaScript object.

We've already used `stylelint` in earlier projects; for convenience, our Gulp task for linting styles has a number of rules specified within the object:

```
20   gulp.task("lint-styles", ['styles'], function() {
21       return gulp.src("dest/*.css")
22       .pipe(postcss([ stylelint({
23           "rules": {
24               "color-no-invalid-hex": 2,|
25               "declaration-colon-space-before": [2, "never"],
26               "indentation": [2, 2],
27               "number-leading-zero": [2, "always"]
28           }
29       }),
30       reporter({
31           clearMessages: true,
32       })
33   ]))
34   });
```

I've chosen a number of rules to illustrate how we can use Stylelint; it is, of course, up to each of you as developers to choose which rules you want to test as part of linting your code. Stylelint does not contain a core set of rules that are enabled by default—any checking it does will be dependent on what is specified in the rule configuration.

 A useful source to bookmark is `http://stylelint.io/`—this contains a full set of rules that can be added to our Stylelint configuration prior to compiling code.

For example, if we were building a responsive site that made heavy use of the Golden Rule, we may want to limit any percentage values to no more than three or four places. For this, we would specify the `number-max-precision` rule—this takes an integer value; specifying 3 would flag warnings for these two attributes:

```
.foo { top: 3.2456px; }
.foo { top: 3.245634px; }
```

This is not the case for this one:

```
@media (min-width: 3.234em) {...}
```

I would strongly recommend reading through the list of rules to get a flavor of what is available; it will take time to familiarize yourselves with the contents, but the reward will be code that is optimized and checked prior to it being used in a production environment. There is one small point though—even if we optimize our code ad infinitum, there is always a possibility that we still have to include some support for older browsers.

In an ideal world, we would convince our clients of the merits of limiting such support (or not even covering it). If clients insist on it, however, against our better judgment, then PostCSS can easily help with providing that support. Let's explore what is available—much of this will center around IE (as this is the biggest culprit), but will equally apply to other browsers.

Providing fallback support

A key concern when designing web content is browser support—which browsers do we support? If the only browsers we had to support were the likes of Firefox or Chrome, then our job would be easy. Trouble is, we also have IE, Safari, Edge...not to mention mobile devices! Life would be boring otherwise...

But I digress, back to reality: for those legacy browsers that refuse to conform (yes, I'm looking at you in particular, IE), we have to consider providing some form of support or graceful degradation. Thankfully, there are a number of plugins we can use within the PostCSS ecosystem—we've already used one in the form of Autoprefixer; there are others available, so let's dive in and take a look at a selection of these plugins in more detail. Before we do so, though, there is a useful tip that I want to explore, which can help with checking for, and providing, legacy support in our browsers.

Detecting support for features

A key part of the development process is to ensure that our code works on those browsers we have to support. If we're lucky enough that this range of browsers is limited to newer offerings, then this is less of an issue.

For some developers, there will be a need to have to support older browsers; this is particularly true if the environment contains other browser-based applications that require use of these older browsers, and cannot be replaced.

To help get around this, we could use libraries such as Modernizr (`http://www.modernizr.com`), but a more efficient means is to use the CSS `@supports` directive. In short, this operates in a similar fashion to media queries; we can specify a backup property that is supported by all browsers, and cancel it out if we're using a browser that can support an enhanced property:

```
section {
  float: left;
}

@supports (display: -webkit-flex) or (display: flex) {
  section {
    display: -webkit-flex;
    display: flex;
    float: none;
  }
}
```

In the main, this is more likely to be useful for those who have to provide support for older versions of IE (given that other browsers have offered better support for some time). Ideally, we would look to persuade clients of the merits of not supporting older versions of IE (at least 8, and possibly 9). If we have to support them, this method coupled with the use of autoprefixer could prove very useful.

Providing support for oldie

When it comes to providing support for legacy browsers, the biggest culprit is arguably Microsoft's IE. Whilst it has to be said that support in newer versions is improving, its popularity means that there are still enough old versions to warrant the need to provide support!

To their credit, Microsoft have announced that they no longer support IE8 to 10 — this is a step in the right direction to help encourage users to upgrade, although it will be some time before these versions completely disappear from use.

So, if you still have to support old versions of IE, what can we do? A good solution to try out is the oldie pack of plugins; its name makes a reference to what some term oldIE, or those versions of IE that should have been consigned to history a long time ago!

This plugin, available from `https://github.com/jonathantneal/oldie`, is a wrapper for a host of plugins available within PostCSS; examples include the following:

- `post-calc`: This reduces any instance of `calc()` to single values where possible; instances of `calc()` that use a mix of units may not be replaced

- `postcss-unroot`: If our CSS uses :root selectors, then old versions of IE will fail; this plugin replaces them with HTML to allow our code to compile

- `postcss-unnot`: In a similar vein, if we've specified rules that include elements where `:not` pseudo-elements have been used, then these selectors will be removed

- `postcss-unopacity`: This converts any instance of the opacity property to use `filter: alpha(opacity=XX)`, where XX is the equivalent value for the original opacity property

The pack includes other plugins—to get a feel for what plugins are included, it's worth taking a look at the `index.js` file for the plugin pack; it will look something like this:

```
var processors = [
        {
                plugin:   require('postcss-calc'),
                namespace: 'calc',
                defaults:  {}
        },
        {
                plugin:   require('postcss-unmq'),
                namespace: 'media',
                defaults:  {}
        },
        {
                plugin:   require('postcss-unroot'),
                namespace: 'root',
                defaults:  {}
        },
```

The beauty, though, is that we are not forced to use the oldie plugin in its entirety. If, by some quirk of fate, we've managed to create something that in the main avoids those CSS attributes that are likely to make oldIE choke, then we can opt to simply reference those plugins that we need to use instead.

This will, of course, depend on how much we've used—a more likely scenario is that we will end up needing to use all of the plugins, so it makes better sense to use oldie instead! Of course, we could always encourage our clients to drop oldIE—this might not be as simple as it sounds...

Removing style hacks from code

If we're lucky enough to have understanding clients—and chance would be a fine thing—then there is likely to be a task that we need to perform: remove any style hacks from our code that relate to browsers we no longer support. The removal of these hacks may be trivial if we only have a small style sheet; the reality is that it will likely be a long, manual process for larger sheets, which carries a risk of us missing hacks.

Instead, we can avail ourselves of a plugin, in the form of stylehacks; this works very well with the `stylelint` plugin we've already used in demos throughout this book. Available from `https://github.com/ben-eb/stylehacks`, the plugin uses hacks listed on `http://browserhacks.com`, and is a cinch to install—let's take a look at it in action:

1. We'll start by extracting a copy of the `T47 - using stylehacks` folder from the code download that accompanies this book; save it to the root of our project folder.

2. Copy the `gulpfile.js` and `package.json` files to the root of the project folder.

3. In a text editor, go ahead and add this code, saving it as `style.css` in the `src` folder in our project area (*not* within the `T47 - using stylehacks` folder!):

    ```
    h1 {
      _color: white;
      color: rgba(255, 255, 255, 0.5);
    }
    ```

4. Next, fire up a Node.js command prompt session, then change the working folder to our project area.

5. We now need to install the plugin—in the prompt, enter this command, then press *Enter*:

    ```
    npm install stylehacks --save-dev
    ```

6. When the plugin has installed, go ahead and enter `gulp` in the prompt, then press *Enter*.

7. PostCSS will compile our code—if all is well, we should see this in the `dest` folder at the root of our project area:

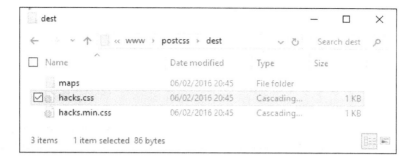

Assuming we have a successful compilation, try opening the `style.css` file in a text editor — we will, of course, have the requisite source map directive at the foot of the code, but otherwise notice how it has removed the color hack:

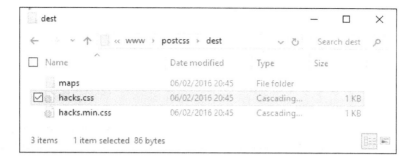

The key to this process lies within this task in our Gulp file:

```
gulp.task('styles', function () {
  return gulp.src('src/*.css')
    .pipe(postcss([ stylehacks({browsers: 'last 1 version, >
      10%'}) ]))
    .pipe(gulp.dest('dest/'));
});
```

In our Gulp file, we've added the browsers attribute — this tells stylehacks to remove any hacks that are *not* required for modern browsers or those that have more than `10%` global usage. This setting is based on the Browserslist query list available from `https://github.com/ai/browserslist` — it's worth noting that this can be used for plugins such as Autoprefixer as well.

If we start to include more plugins that make use of the Browserslist queries, then consider using a variable in place of the query; updating this from a central location will automatically update all plugins that use it accordingly. For more details, please refer to the Browserslist site on GitHub.

Although this is a simple plugin to use, there is one nagging question that kept coming back whilst researching for this book: how useful is this plugin in reality? For some, you may think I need my head examined, but there is a reason behind this—let me explain.

If you've spent any time developing with jQuery, then you should be aware that it has dropped support for IE6-8 from jQuery 2.x, and will only develop support for it within the 1.x branch. Much of the baggage within jQuery within the 1.x branch is based on catering for browser hacks; the biggest culprit for these hacks is IE!

At the time of writing, Microsoft have publicly stated that support for IE10 and below is being dropped (at least for Windows 8)—they will only support IE11 on the Windows 8.1 platform, plus their new browser, MS Edge.

Given that many of the hacks found in CSS are for IE (and that this also applies to jQuery), one can't but wonder if the stylehacks plugin will still remain useful within the not too distant future! We should also be asking ourselves if using hacks is a good design decision. Are we designing a problem for ourselves at a later date, or should we be reconsidering our original design, and perhaps revisiting whether we need to support older browsers with a dedicated style sheet, rather than introducing hacks in amongst code designed for more recent browsers?

Summary

A key part of PostCSS is exploring the ever-increasing array of plugins available for the PostCSS ecosystem; in some respects, it can be likened to a journey of discovery. This is no different for single plugins, or those available within packs—we've already seen that many of these packs are made up of the same plugins that are available individually! Let's take a moment to review what we've learnt.

We kicked off our journey with a look at working with plugins that can help save time with writing—these can either be those that allow us to write in shorthand, or those that add missing styles, based on styles we specify in code. These also included some plugins that help provide fallback support for older browsers.

We then moved onto working with the `postcss-short` plugin, as an example of how we can reduce development time, before moving on to explore the Rucksack suite of plugins that can help add some of the missing elements we may need to use in CSS. To explore how Rucksack works, we started with a simple easing demo, before working our way through a more complex demo of a slider and converting it to use Rucksack, and exploring some of the ways in which this plugin pack can help in our development.

Next up in our journey came a look at what should be a crucial part of any development workflow for a developer — checking our code for consistency, and optimizing it. We covered the use of the `cssnano` and `stylelint` plugins, and how they can be tailored to our needs.

We then rounded out the chapter by revisiting support for older browsers — we supplemented our earlier visit with a more in-depth look at what is available within PostCSS; we explored the fact that many fallbacks are primarily caused by IE, and discussed how we can either help support older versions of this browser, or whether we should consider consigning support for some older browsers to history.

Phew, this was a real whirlwind tour through the plugin packs available for PostCSS! Our journey does not stop here, as we now need to pull all of the last few chapters together and produce a complete custom processor — this will be the subject of the next chapter.

Building a Custom Processor

One of the key benefits of using PostCSS is its modular approach — we're not forced to use a large library, particularly if we only need to make use of a small part of its functionality! In this chapter, we'll pull together some of the themes we've discussed throughout earlier chapters, and create a fully working preprocessor, customized to our needs.

We'll use it to compile code for a simple site, explore using it for CMS systems such as WordPress, then take a look at extending it to work with frameworks such as CSStyle. We will cover a number of topics throughout this chapter, which will include the following:

- Creating our processor
- Optimizing the output
- Adding source map and vendor prefix support
- Testing the final preprocessor on a simple site system
- Extending our preprocessor to use the CSStyle framework

Let's make a start!

Creating your processor

Many developers who work with existing processors such as SASS, less, or Stylus will be accustomed to working with a library that is a necessary dependency, and where it is unlikely that they will be using 100% of the functionality available for their chosen processor.

This is not the case with PostCSS. One of the key attractions is its flexibility; gone are the days when we have excess baggage in our processor that is redundant for our needs! The power of flexibility can also be a shortcoming, where does one start deciding what to include in our processor, I hear you ask?

Throughout the course of this chapter, we will bring together the various elements of the processor we've used in the demos, and work through changes we can make to improve or extend functionality. The key, though, to any processor is that there is no right or wrong answer; each will be different, and they will depend on your requirements.

As time goes by, it is likely that you will find common elements that can be reused between projects, ultimately, it is up to you as the developer to find the combination that meets your requirements. This aside, let's begin with a detailed look at the processor we've used in recent examples, and explore some of the ideas and tips we can use to create our own version.

Exploring our processor

As part of creating the demos we've worked through in this book, we concentrated on ensuring plugins are installed, and that we have the right files in the right place. There is something missing though, and that is—what actually happens in the files? Why do we have tasks in a particular order? What is the reasoning behind choosing some of the plugins that we've used…and so on—you get the idea!

Over the next few pages, we're going to try to answer some of these questions (and more), by exploring the processor that we've used in some of the recent examples; you will see that there isn't a one-answer-fits-all approach, but more a case of working through your requirements, and picking plugins to suit your needs.

Before we go into depth, though, let's just quickly recap the make-up of our processor, starting with the `package.json` file.

Dissecting the package.json file

The `package.json` file tells PostCSS which plugins to use, and may contain some of the key configuration settings to be used during compilation:

```
{
  "name": "postcss",
  "version": "1.0.0",
  "description": "Configuration file for PostCSS",
```

```
    "main": "index.js",
    "scripts": {
      "test": "echo \"Error: no test specified\" && exit 1"
    },
    "author": "Alex Libby",
    "license": "ISC",
    "dependencies": { "postcss": "^5.0.8" },
```

The top half of our processor contains a number of key properties that tell us details such as the version, description, who created it, any dependencies, and the license being used for the project:

```
    "devDependencies": {
      "autoprefixer": "^6.0.3",
      "cssnano": "^3.2.0",
      "gulp": "^3.9.0",
      "gulp-postcss": "^6.0.0",
      "gulp-rename": "^1.2.2",
      "gulp-sourcemaps": "^1.5.2",
      "postcss-reporter": "^1.3.0",
      "stylelint": "^2.3.7"
    }
  }
```

In comparison, the key part for us is in the bottom half; this lists all of the plugins that will be used within our project. In many of our projects, we've installed the plugin — at point of installation, the plugin will add an entry into this file that contains the name and the minimum version required (represented by the ^ symbol).

It is worth noting that we can manually add entries to, or remove entries from this file, or even copy `package.json` files from one project to another if needed. This is particularly useful if we know that a new project has identical (or very similar) requirements to an existing one; plugins will only add an entry into this file at installation, if one does not already exist.

Exploring the Gulp task file

The `gulpfile.js` file is where the real magic happens — this contains all of the tasks that need to be performed on each style sheet within our project. Outside of the style sheet, this is the second of two files that we've simply copied across from the code download to our project area. Now that we've been using it in anger, it's worth taking a moment to explore what happens in more detail.

The `gulpfile.js` file is made up of several sections — in our example, we begin with a list of variables that define references to each of our plugins:

```
'use strict';

var gulp = require('gulp');
var postcss = require('gulp-postcss');
//var autoprefixer = require('autoprefixer');
var cssnano = require('gulp-cssnano');
var sourcemaps = require('gulp-sourcemaps');
var rename = require('gulp-rename');
var stylelint = require('stylelint');
var reporter = require('postcss-reporter');
var rucksack = require('rucksack-css');
```

The first task in our list is the most important one — this picks up and compiles the source code into a valid CSS file and deposits it in the `dest` folder. As part of this, we provide links to any PostCSS plugin that is needed to transform our code — in this example, we're using Rucksack, set to include fallback support but not add vendor prefixes:

```
gulp.task('styles', function () {
  return gulp.src('src/*.css')
    .pipe(postcss([ rucksack({ fallbacks: true,
    autoprefixer: true }) ]))
    .pipe(gulp.dest('dest/'));
});
```

This chunky task is less complicated than it looks — it checks our code for consistency, based on the rules set; it outputs any warnings or errors on screen using the reporter plugin. The key here is the `['styles']` attribute — this tells PostCSS not to perform this task until the styles task has been completed:

```
gulp.task("lint-styles", ['styles'], function() {
    return gulp.src("dest/*.css")
    .pipe(postcss([ stylelint({
        "rules": {
          "color-no-invalid-hex": 2,
          "declaration-colon-space-before": [2, "never"],
          "indentation": [2, 2],
          "number-leading-zero": [2, "always"]
        }
      }),
      reporter({ clearMessages: true, })
    ]))
});
```

In comparison, the next two tasks are relatively straightforward — this one takes care of compressing our compiled code, and renaming it with a `.min.css` extension:

```
gulp.task('rename', ['lint-styles'], function () {
  return gulp.src('dest/*.css')
    .pipe(postcss([ cssnano() ]))
    .pipe(rename('style.min.css'))
    .pipe(gulp.dest("dest/"));
});
```

This task is equally straightforward — it creates a source map of our style sheet, and sets it in a format that PostCSS can release into a file within the dest folder of our project area:

```
gulp.task('sourcemap', ['rename'], function () {
  return gulp.src('dest/*.css')
    .pipe(sourcemaps.init())
    .pipe(sourcemaps.write('maps/'))
    .pipe(gulp.dest("dest/"));
});
```

The last two steps play the most important role in any Gulp task file — the first will fire off calls to each of our tasks if we enter `gulp` in a command line prompt:

```
gulp.task('default', ['styles', 'lint-styles',  'rename',
'sourcemap']);
```

This task, although not obligatory, watches out for any changes to our code and sets off the tasks in our Gulp file automatically. It will respect any constraints set, although for consistency, it is preferable to list the tasks being performed in the same order as they are shown in the file:

```
var watcher = gulp.watch('src/*.css', ['styles',
'lint-styles', 'rename', 'sourcemap']);
watcher.on('change', function(event) {
  console.log('File ' + event.path + ' was ' +
event.type + ', running tasks...');
});
```

There is more to the compilation process than these two files — thought should also be given to how we structure our working environment. A quick look at the Gulp task file should reveal that we've used a simple in-tray/out-tray approach; code is picked up from the `src` folder, and the results placed into the `dest` folder at the end of compilation.

This is an important part of the process—after all, there is no benefit in using PostCSS if we don't give any thought to the structure of our project area! Part of this is to maintain separation between source and compiled files, but also that we may decide to expand our compilation process to include tasks such as shrinking images. There is no right or wrong in how this area should be structured—this will be dictated by our project requirements.

Dissecting issues with our processor

With a Gulp task file and associated `package.json` file in place, we should be good to go, right? Well, not quite—yes, our processor has been used on demos throughout the book to great effect. But there is more that we can do: our Gulp file should never be static; we should always look to review it periodically, to ensure it is working at optimal efficiency.

 To see an updated version of our Gulp file, take a look in the `T49 - fixing issues in Gulpfile` folder within the code download that accompanies this book.

Our Gulp file does have a few issues we need to address, so let's look at these now:

- Some of our tasks are not correctly named—for example, the styles task could be renamed to better reflect that we're using Rucksack in this task.

- There is a question about the use of source maps; so far we've used a dedicated source map plugin to create them. An upcoming change in Gulp 4 will reduce the need for a plugin—support for creating them is being added to Gulp core, so a separate plugin won't be required so often!

- In the rename task, we've hard-coded a `style.min.css` filename as the output; this isn't going to suit all requirements, so we should change this to make it dynamic.

- Staying with the rename task—we're combining two tasks, when they should be split into two separate processes.

- Take a look at the processor list within the styles task at line 16; this isn't too bad now, but over time it could become long and awkward to read! Instead, we need to change it so that at the point of calling PostCSS, we can use an array instead to provide the names.

- When creating source maps, our current setup provides both a full fat and minified version; is this really necessary? The issue comes from `cssnano`, which is compressing every `.css` file it sees; this isn't necessary, so needs to be changed.

- The use of `cssnano` that should be run as a task within PostCSS is causing issues—even though it would make sense to run it this way, it needs to be run independently, to satisfy our needs.

- We should make a decision on whether we use a dedicated plugin for providing vendor prefix support, or rely on the use of other plugins that may have this built in already.

- When compiling source files, our processor is producing two minified files; one is correctly named, but the other is meant to be the uncompressed version for development purposes.

Over the next few pages, we will explore ways of fixing and improving our Gulp task file—it's key to understand that whilst many of these changes are specific to our task file, they are ones that may crop up for your future projects. Above all, it is essential that we should continually review our production process to ensure it is working as needed.

Let's begin the process of fixing and improving our Gulp file before we put it to test on a sample site.

Fixing our Gulp task file

It has to be said that there are a few issues we need to resolve—the key here is that none of them will stop our compilation process; we should consider them more as rough edges on a diamond, which need polishing to make our process sparkle (pun intended!).

 Please note, the line numbers in the next exercise refer to the *unmodified version* of the source code from the T48 - existing processor folder, prior to making any changes. If you want to keep existing copies of files, please move them prior to starting the exercise.

Okay, let's get cracking: there are a few changes to make, so we will start with the key task, which compiles the source file:

1. For this process, we need a copy of the `gulpfile.js` file from the T48 - existing processor folder within the code download that accompanies this book; go ahead and save it as `gulpfile.js` at the root of our project area.

2. The first change we need to make is to enable `autoprefixer` support in the file—you should find it there but commented out on line 5; go ahead and remove the comment.

3. On or around line 16, look for this line:

```
.pipe(postcss([ rucksack({ fallbacks: true, autoprefixer: true }) ]))
```

We're not going to include fallback support, and will take care of `autoprefixer` separately, so for now, alter it as shown:

```
.pipe(postcss([ rucksack(), autoprefixer() ]))
```

4. Our next change is in the lint-styles task—two changes are required here; first, add this block at line 13, below the declaration for Rucksack:

```
var stylerules = {
  "color-no-invalid-hex": 2,
  "declaration-colon-space-before": [2, "never"],
  "indentation": [2, 2],
  "number-leading-zero": [2, "always"]
};
```

5. Next, go ahead and replace the entire lint-styles task with this:

```
gulp.task('lint', ['styles'], function() {
  return gulp.src("dest/*.css")
    .pipe(postcss([ stylelint({ "rules": stylerules }),
    reporter({ clearMessages: true })
  ]))
});
```

6. In the rename task, we have three changes to make—first, remove the `cssnano` line at line 38; we're splitting the task into two, and this will be handled in a new task.

7. This task has a prerequisite, which we've renamed—go ahead and change line 36 to this:

```
gulp.task('rename', ['lint'], function () {
```

8. Next, alter the rename command as indicated—this is on line 39:

```
.pipe(rename(renameFunction))
```

9. In the next task, `sourcemap`, we have one alteration to make—on or around line 47, change this line as shown:

```
gulp.task('sourcemap', ['rename'], function () {
  return gulp.src(sourceMapLocation)
```

10. We've talked about splitting out the minification task—go ahead and add this below the `sourcemap` task:

```
gulp.task('minifyCSS', ['sourcemap'], function () {
  return gulp.src('dest/*.min.css')
```

```
      .pipe(cssnano({ autoprefixer: false }))
      .pipe(gulp.dest("dest/"));
  });
```

11. We've made changes to the task names, so we need to update the default task and watch facility — look for the string of names in square brackets on or around lines 50 and 52. Replace it with this string:

```
['styles', 'lint' , 'rename' , 'sourcemap', 'minifyCSS']
```

12. Our watch task can also be put on a diet — there is no need to specify all of the tasks twice! Instead, go ahead and change the code as indicated — when changes are made, the watch facility will run the default task, which already has the requisite tasks:

```
gulp.task('default', ['styles', 'lint' , 'rename' , 'minifyCSS',
'sourcemap']);

var watcher = gulp.watch('src/*.css', ['default']);
watcher.on('change', function(event) {
```

13. We're almost done — there are some additional declarations we need to add at the top of our file, to ensure everything works as expected. Below the `stylerules` declaration added in step 4, go ahead and add these extra lines:

```
var renameFunction = function (path) {
  path.extname = ".min.css";
  return path;
};

var sourceMapLocation = ['dest/*.css', '!dest/*.min.css'];
```

We now have an updated Gulp task file — we now need to copy the `style.css` from the `src` folder under `T49 - fixing issues in Gulpfile` to the `src` folder at the root of our project area. If all is well, we should have something akin to this in the `dest` folder of our project area when we compile our file, and a file named `style.css.map` in the maps folder:

At this point, I am sure you will have a few questions about some of the changes we've made—the demo highlights a few key points, so it's worth taking time out to explore these in more detail.

 If you come across any issues with changing the gulp file, then check out a completed version in the `T49 - fixing issues in Gulpfile` folder in the code download that accompanies this book.

Understanding the changes made

Throughout the course of our demo, we made a number of changes to our Gulp task file—the key thing to note is that none of them are compulsory. Our task file worked perfectly well prior to making the changes, so if they aren't compulsory, why are we making them?

The answer to this is simple—using a task runner such as Gulp is about automating processes so that you arrive at just the content you need. We had that, but the task runner produced extra files, didn't compress them as expected, and our Gulp file contained tasks that had multiple steps within the same task. The work we completed was about adding polish to the process—although our Gulp task file worked, we explored how we could improve on it by tweaking some of the processes.

We kicked off with changes to how vendor prefixes were added—our existing task completed this as part of compiling using the Rucksack plugin. The Rucksack plugin was to provide fallback support—I'm not a fan of working with older browsers, so we don't need it. This makes it less beneficial to incorporate vendor prefix support from such a large plugin, thus support is not enabled.

 There is another plugin available for PostCSS that handles vendor prefixes—doiuse, available at `https://github.com/anandthakker/doiuse`. Just another option to try!

The lint-styles task worked well—the changes we made focus on making the code easier to read in the task file. We moved the configuration block to the start of the file, and rearranged the format of the task; this means that we should not have to change the task, even though we may change the configuration!

Most of the remaining changes focus on splitting multiple roles into single tasks, and correcting some anomalies in the output. Our compilation process produced a minified file with the right extension, but also minified the original source file. We also had two source map files produced in a similar fashion—this is clearly not ideal! The changes we made now mean that our original source file is not minified, but only one minified file is produced, and that we have a single uncompressed style sheet created during the process.

Perfect, we now have a polished compilation process, which is producing the right files at the appropriate point; what next? Well, we can now add additional functionality to our compilation process. Using a task runner such as Gulp is about automating menial tasks, so let's explore what we might achieve in more detail.

Optimizing the output

The PostCSS system will quite happily play nicely with other plugins, be they Gulp-based, or using another task runner such as Grunt or Broccoli. This opens up a real world of possibilities, limited only by your imagination! There is one small but important point, though—it makes it crucial that we not only optimize our processor output (as we have done), but also fine tune it to ensure that we've added functionality that suits our needs.

So, what can we add? Well, here's a starter for ten: how about compressing images? Another common task relates to adding responsive content—we've already covered this earlier in the book with the `postcss-responsive-type` plugin. We could take that further, by adding a task that resizes images automatically to different sizes; we can then use these as appropriate in a responsive site.

Ultimately, it is up to you—as time goes by and you get more accustomed to using PostCSS, then it is likely that you will find yourself using some plugins more than others. The key here, though, is *not* about simply adding in plugins haphazardly—instead, we're looking for plugins that we would use regularly in our development workflow, and can form the basis of a baseline processor. Any additional functionality that is needed to support a particular project can then be added at the appropriate time.

A great place to look is the PostCSS plugin directory at `http://postcss.parts`—it's worth taking a look to see what is there, and giving them a try! To get us started, we're going to work through a few ideas that are likely to be useful additions to your processor, beginning with improving support for source maps.

Altering our source map support

If we take a look back at our gulp file prior to completing the exercise in *Fixing our gulp task file*, we can see it worked, but it suffered from a major drawback. The compilation process produced an extra source map which was minified by name, but not in reality! This is clearly something we didn't need — the changes made to this task transformed it into what we have now:

```
var sourceMapLocation = ['dest/*.css', '!dest/*.min.css'];
...
gulp.task('sourcemap', ['rename'], function () {
  return gulp.src(sourceMapLocation)
...
});
```

This is a much better version — it only produces one source map file, which is not compressed; compression is not needed. That being said, we can still improve on it; it's simply a matter of working through the documentation to really explore what is available, and see if it can help us. As a starter, try this for size.

There may be instances where we need control over the full URL when compiling our code and creating the source map, for example, if we're transferring from a test environment to a production one. In an ideal world, we would use a relative file structure to avoid this issue, but for those occasions where this isn't possible, a simple change to our Gulp task will suffice:

```
.pipe(sourcemaps.write('maps/', {
  sourceMappingURLPrefix: 'https://www.mydomain.com/'
}))
```

We can see the result in this screenshot:

```
157   div.slide-content > figcaption {
158     position: absolute;
159     background: rgba(0, 0, 0, 0.5) none repeat scroll 0% 0%;
160     color: rgba(255, 255, 255, 1.0);
161     width: 100%;
162     font-size: 14px;
163     padding: 0.6rem;
164     z-index: 96;
165   }
166
167
168   /*# sourceMappingURL=https://www.mydomain.com/maps/style.css.map */
```

Ultimately, the requirements for our projects will determine how source map support needs to be configured — we may even have to go as far as compiling multiple files into one larger master file, if our project requirements dictate.

There's one thing to bear in mind, though — there are plans to include native source map support in Gulp 4; this will likely mean that the need for a separate plugin will become redundant. It pays to keep abreast of changes, particularly if it might affect our processor!

 For a completed version of our Gulp file, which includes these changes, take a look at the `T50 - adjusting source map settings` folder in the code download that accompanies this book.

Let's change tack at this point, changing the source map compilation process was a straightforward alteration. We can take it up a notch with another key area — vendor prefixes. We've already covered the basics, so we'll take a look at how we can improve support.

Taking care of prefixes

Aha, prefixes! The bane of any designer: adding them and keeping them up to date can be a real chore.

The `autoprefixer` task that has already featured throughout these pages goes some way to reducing the burden: it will add the current prefixes and remove any that are no longer needed. This is good…but we can do better! This time around, though, the emphasis is less on code, and more on the kinds of decisions we need to make:

- What browser versions do you need to support? The `autoprefixer` plugin already uses data from `http://caniuse.com/`, which is sufficient for most requirements. However, we can tweak our code to use Browserslist (hosted at `https://github.com/ai/browserslist`) to determine which versions to support. For example, we might add > 5% to limit support to browsers which have over 5% of global use:

  ```
  .pipe(postcss([ rucksack(), autoprefixer({browsers:
  ['last 2 versions']}) ])
  ```

  In an ideal world, I would push that as high as 10%, but that might be taking it too far!

- From a consistency perspective, we should make it clear that `autoprefixer` is `disabled` from within Rucksack — my preference is not to enable it there, as it can get confusing as to which plugin is adding prefixes (given that `cssnano` can add them too). To correct this, all we need to do is to change this line:

  ```
  .pipe(postcss([ rucksack({autoprefixer: false  }),
    autoprefixer({browsers: ['last 2 versions']}) ])
  ```

It's not obligatory, but it at least makes it clear! If we wanted to be real purists, we would split this task into two separate ones, so that we're keeping to the one task: one role mantra:

- Although `autoprefixer` handles the removal of redundant prefixes, there is a useful trick we can use: add support for the `postcss-remove-prefixes` and `postcss-unprefix` plugins. The reason for this is simple—we may well not have a level playing field when running `autoprefixer`, where some vendor prefixes may be missing from our code. Adding these two plugins ensures that our code is as terse as possible prior to running `autoprefixer`.

- If our code is based on using SASS, then there is a good chance that the Compass library is being used—it is worth checking to see if this is being used to add vendor prefixes. If it is, it may be worth switching to using `autoprefixer`, as it is reported to be more efficient at removing code. Don't forget that we can compile SASS code within our Gulp file at the same time as running PostCSS plugins—we will explore more of this later in this book.

It goes without saying that vendor prefixes continually change; with careful planning and the right use of plugins, we can be safe in the knowledge that no matter what happens, our code will be updated at the next compilation.

Now, moving on: I am sure you are familiar with the ubiquitous pseudo-selector, such as hover. This is one area where we need to carefully consider what we might incorporate into our baseline processor; PostCSS has a number of plugins that can facilitate handling pseudo-selectors in our code. Let's take a look at this in more detail.

Adding support for pseudo-selectors

When designing sites, pseudo-selectors are a key part of providing interaction—they can be anything from the simple hover, all the way through to newer elements such as :range or :placeholder. We also have to be mindful of support—thankfully most elements will work in reasonably recent browsers (yes, even IE8!), but not all browsers use the same format of single or double colons when referencing the selector in CSS.

To help with both styling and providing consistency, PostCSS has a number of options we can use; we will explore using the `postcss-pseudo-elements-content` plugin in a moment, but for now, let's take a quick look at some of the options to give you a flavor of what is available:

- Do you often find yourself adding the `focus` pseudo-selector to your code? If the answer is yes, then the `postcss-focus` plugin will be of interest. Available from `https://github.com/postcss/postcss-focus`, this plugin will add a `focus` pseudo-selector automatically, when compiling code. The styles will be the same as the `:hover` element.

- We've just talked about adding a `focus` element automatically — the developer Jonathan Neal had the idea of creating a polyfill to add support for an `:enter pseudo-selector`, which would replace both :hover and :focus within code. When compiled, the code would transpile any instance of `:enter` into `:hover` and `:active` styles in our code. Head over to `https://github.com/jonathantneal/postcss-pseudo-class-enter` for more details on this plugin.

- This next plugin could be euphemistically described as being one for those who have better things to do than write styles for links…. In plain speak, this is a real shortcut of a plugin! It adds styles for *all* of the link-related classes automatically; browse to `https://github.com/jedmao/postcss-all-link-colors` for an example of how to be really lazy…

- For those of you who regularly have to style form buttons (and face it, who doesn't?), then this next plugin from `https://github.com/andrepolischuk/postcss-pseudo-class-any-button` will be of interest: it allows us to use the `:any-button` selector (which isn't an official selector). When compiled, it transpiles this into four different types — plain button and three inputs (reset, submit, and button).

This is just a small selection of the handful of plugins currently available in the PostCSS ecosystem, for handling pseudo-selectors. We can talk about using them, but in reality, the best way to understand their usefulness is to see them in action! With this in mind, let's take a look at one in action: `postcss-pseudo-elements-content`. This little beauty has but one purpose in life: to add a content: attribute to appropriate pseudo-selectors, if one is not present in our code.

Updating our code

There are a few examples of plugins that help handle pseudo-selectors better; our projects will dictate whether we should use them on a per case basis, or can incorporate some or all of them into our baseline processors.

One example that might suit being added to our baseline processor is postcss-pseudo-elements-content, which is available from `https://github.com/omgovich/postcss-pseudo-elements-content`. This simple plugin parses our code and will add a content: " statement to our code, when it sees instances of appropriate pseudo-selectors. It doesn't require any configuration, so without further ado, let's get stuck into using it:

1. We'll start as always with installing the plugin — for this, fire up a Node.js command prompt window and change the working folder to our project area.

2. In the prompt, go ahead and run this command:

    ```
    npm install postcss-pseudo-elements-content --save-dev
    ```

If all is well, we should see something akin to this:

1. From a copy of the code download that accompanies this book, extract a copy of `style.css` and `content.html` from the `T51 - adding before and after content` folder. Save the style sheet to the `src` folder, and the `content.html` to the root of our project area.

2. Open up a copy of `gulpfile.js` that is at the root of our project area, then add this line in at line 11:

    ```
    var pseudoContent = require('postcss-pseudo-elements-
      content');
    ```

3. A little further down, we need to update our first task to allow for the additional plugin; go ahead and alter the line as indicated:

```
gulp.task('styles', function() {
    return gulp.src('src/*.css')
    .pipe(postcss([ autoprefixer(), pseudoContent() ]))
```

4. In the Node.js command prompt, enter `gulp` then press *Enter*—if all is well, we should see our style sheet files and source map appear in the `dest` folder.

5. Copy the contents of this folder to the `css` folder at the root of our project areas; if we preview `content.html`, we should see our menu appear:

In a sense, this could be treated as a shortcut plugin (in a similar fashion to ones we worked with earlier in the book). The magic happens by adding `-c` after our pseudo-selector, as shown in this code extract:

```
.underline a:hover::after-c, .underline a:focus::after-c {
    opacity: 1;
    transform: translateY(0px);
}
```

When compiled, it adds the `content:  ''` attribute, as shown in this screenshot:

```
53   .underline a:hover::after, .underline a:focus::after {
54       opacity: 1;
55       -webkit-transform: translateY(0px);
56         -ms-transform: translateY(0px);
57             transform: translateY(0px);
58             content: '';
59   }
60   /*# sourceMappingURL=maps/style.css.map */
```

Although it is debatable whether it is worth adding a plugin for something this small, it does at least ensure that we keep a consistent code base when compiling our style sheet.

The real decision is whether your code has sufficient instances of pseudo-selectors to warrant installing these plugins as part of a baseline, or if your projects dictate their use on a case-by-case basis.

Let's change tack, most of the improvements we've covered relate to text. Text sites can be very unappealing without images—thankfully, there are some plugins available to help extend our baseline processor, and better manage images. I feel a demo coming on, so let's go explore this in more detail.

Dealing with images

If we were to consider our processor as being solely for compiling PostCSS code, then we are selling ourselves short—we've already covered how the use of a task runner such as Gulp allows us to add additional tasks such as `autoprefixer` and `cssnano`.

A great one to consider adding is the ability to compress our images for optimum size; would you want to do this manually, no matter how much or how little might be saved in size? I thought not. Automating this process means we can get on with tasks that add more value to the process. We can achieve this with the `gulp-imagemin` plugin, available from `https://github.com/sindresorhus/gulp-imagemin`—let's take a look at what might be involved in minifying our images:

1. Fire up a Node.js command prompt window, then change the working directory to our project area.

2. In the prompt, enter both commands, pressing *Enter* after each:

   ```
   npm install gulp-imagemin --save-dev
   npm install imagemin-jpegtran --save-dev
   ```

   Keep the prompt open—we will use it again shortly.

3. From the code download that accompanies this book, go ahead and extract copies of the `gulpfile.js` and `package.json` files from the `T52 - optimizing images` folder; save these to the root of our project area.

4. Create a folder called `img` at the root of our project folder; this will be used as a temporary replacement for the `dest` folder already present.

5. Find some large images—they should be JPEG format, and ideally be several megabytes in size; about four to six images will suffice.

6. Go back to the Node.js prompt, then enter `gulp` and press *Enter* — the screenshot below shows an example I performed with a handful of images:

```
c:\wamp\www\postcss>gulp
[16:38:37] Using gulpfile c:\wamp\www\postcss\gulpfile.js
[16:38:37] Starting 'images'...
[16:38:41] gulp-imagemin: Minified 12 images (saved 1.89 MB - 9.1%)
[16:38:41] Finished 'images' after 3.84 s
[16:38:41] Starting 'default'...
[16:38:41] Finished 'default' after 44 µs
```

If all is well, we should see our newly compressed images in the `img` folder — this is a useful task to have within our processor, so let's go through a few points in more detail.

Exploring the process

Image compression is key to a performant site — users will be turned off if the text appears within a couple of seconds, but images take much longer to appear! There are a few points to consider, though, with this approach:

- It's not particularly fast — minifying a dozen images each around 2 MB in size isn't too bad, but this isn't going to improve if you have to minify large numbers of images.

- We've limited our support to JPEG images — it is possible to optimize SVG and PNG images, but this will require changes to our code. If we look closely at the code used, we can see this:

  ```
  var images = require('gulp-imagemin');
  var jpegtran = require('imagemin-jpegtran');
  ```

The latter plugin is installed automatically by `gulp-imagemin`, and would need to be changed if working with SVG or PNG images:

- Tests performed locally seem to indicate that the size of reduction isn't as good as one might expect; I suspect that this will improve with much larger images. It is worth experimenting with changing the compression level — make sure your source images are as large as possible!

Once our images have been optimized for size, we can then explore further options — here are a couple worth considering:

- In the age of development over multiple devices, we need our images to be responsive; the gulp-responsive plugin available from `https://github.com/azat-io/postcss-responsive-images` can help create these images.

- We might want to use sprites instead. Thankfully, adding sprite support is easy within PostCSS: take a look at the postcss-sprites plugin for this task.

- You may like to consider using an asset manager to resolve URLs — the postcss-assets plugin is a perfect candidate for this task. The source and details for using are available from `https://github.com/assetsjs/postcss-assets`.

There's an important point to note, though — although plugins are available for the purpose, it is not worth considering minifying HTML; it is unlikely that you will get any significant space back, and the code will become hard to read. It is best to reserve minifying files for those external assets that have to be linked to your HTML pages, in order to get the most benefit.

Okay, let's move on: before we test our processor, there is one more idea that may be worth consideration. Adding an automatic reload capability to our code means that we do not need to reload our pages to view updated content. There is a heavy reliance on the use of Chrome to make it work, so it won't be for everyone: let's look at what would be involved in more detail.

Adding reload capabilities

Adding a reload capability reduces the amount of time spent manually reloading our pages after a code change; the latter can be a real pain, especially when working with complex CSS styles!

The downside to this is that it only works in Chrome — if this isn't an issue, then these are the steps you would need to follow to make this work:

1. We'll start by extracting copies of the `gulpfile.js` and `package.json` files from the T53 - adding livereload capabilities folder, from the code download that accompanies this book. Save both copies to the root of our project area.

2. From the same T53 - adding livereload capabilities folder, extract and save a copy of the `style.css` file from the `src` folder within, to the `src` folder at the root of our project area.

3. Fire up a Node.js command prompt, then change the working folder to our project area.

4. In the prompt, enter `npm install gulp-livereload –save-dev` and press *Enter*—let this install.

5. Download and install the Chrome applet for LiveReload from `http://bit.ly/IKI2MY`.

6. Add this line at the end of the `sourcemap` task:

   ```
   .pipe(plugins.livereload());
   ```

7. Remove the semi-colon at the end of line 60.

8. Add this line to our `watch` task:

   ```
   plugins.livereload.listen();
   ```

9. Our task file will look like this, with the changes made at lines 61 and 68:

```
60        .pipe(gulp.dest("dest/"));
61        .pipe(plugins.livereload());
62   });
63
64   gulp.task('default', ['styles', 'lint' , 'rename' , 'minifyCSS', 'sourcemap']);
65
66   var watcher = gulp.watch('src/*.css', ['default']);
67   watcher.on('change', function(event) {
68     plugins.livereload.listen();
69     console.log('File ' + event.path + ' was ' + event.type + ', running tasks...');
70   });
```

At this point, we can test to ensure it works by making a change to our style sheet—if all is well, Gulp will kick in and recompile our code; if we have a site open in a browser that we're developing, then this would be automatically reloaded by the plugin.

> For those of you interested in using this plugin in more detail, please refer to the documentation available on the GitHub site at `https://github.com/vohof/gulp-livereload`. There is a full version of the code used in this example, within the T53 - adding livereload capabilities folder in the code download that accompanies this book.

Right, onwards we go! We're almost at the end of our journey through the art of the possible; before we move onto testing our processor, I thought I would leave you with a few more ideas that you may like to consider using in your processors. All of them should install using the same process that we've seen throughout this book.

Extending our processor further

Over the last few pages, we've explored a number of ways to improve our existing processor, as well as a few ideas for extending functionality. Although we can always keep to PostCSS plugins, we run the risk of limiting the "art of the possible", or what is available for us to use.

Sometimes, we might want to go a little further afield — creating a processor isn't just about the nitty-gritty of compiling code, but also about our working environment and the processes required to support it (at least in part). To prove this, we're going to explore installing the `postcss-stats` plugin as an example of how we can extend both our plugin and working environment.

This plugin helps provide useful statistics about each project as it is compiled — it's based on the CSS Stats system, and is available online at `http://www.cssstats.com`.

 Throughout the demo, you may see a few issues with deprecated warnings — at the time of writing, the plugin needs a little polishing/updating. Don't worry though: the plugin will still work fine for the purposes of our demo.

The source for this plugin is available on GitHub at `https://github.com/cssstats/postcss-cssstats`, and can be installed using the usual route. Let's dive in and take a look:

1. We'll start by firing up a Node.js command prompt session, then changing the working directory to the root of our project area.

2. We need to install the plugin, so in the prompt, enter this command and press *Enter*:

```
npm install postcss-cssstats --save-dev
```

Keep this open — we will need it later in the exercise.

Next, we need to update our `gulpfile.js` and `package.json` files — go ahead and extract copies of both files from the `T54 - using cssstats` folder in the code download that accompanies this book. Save both files to the root of our project area:

1. With our files in place, we can now test that it works — go ahead and save a copy of `style.css` from the same folder into the `src` folder of our project area.

2. Revert to the Node.js command prompt we had open earlier — in the prompt, enter `gulp`, and press *Enter*.

3. PostCSS will compile our code — if all is well, we should see files appear in the now familiar `dest` folder…and we should also see something akin to this screenshot:

If I were a betting man (I'm not, but assume I am for this) — I would bet even odds that you're probably thinking "What on earth does all of that text mean?" Well, let me shed some light on what it all means.

In a nutshell, we've installed what is effectively a reporting system — this details a bunch of statistics about our code. It contains details about all kinds of information, including the number of selectors, colors, the level of CSS specificity, declarations, and so on. It's an easy way to get information about our code, as a means of documenting it for later use. The reason it is so easy to get the information lies in how it is configured — take a look at the `gulpfile.js` file; we will add a call to the plugin at the top:

```
var reporter = require('postcss-reporter');
```

We can then modify the styles single task, by adding this line near the end:

```
        .pipe(postcss([ cssstats( function(stats) {
          console.log(stats);
        })
    ]))
    .pipe(gulp.dest('dest/'));
})
```

The trouble is, whilst it might be easy to get the information, it's not so easy to store it! We can absolutely improve on it; instead of getting the information via our processor, we can go directly to the source. Let's explore how to make this happen:

1. We'll start by firing up a Node.js command prompt, then changing the working folder to the root of our project area.

2. At the prompt, go ahead and enter `npm install gulp-stylestats --save-dev`, then press *Enter*.

3. We now need to edit the `gulpfile.js` and `package.json` files we used in the previous exercise, so open the `gulpfile.js` file in a text editor, and add these lines immediately below the closing bracket of the `sourcemap` task:

```
gulp.task('stylestats', ['minifyCSS'], function () {
  gulp.src('dest/*.css')
    .pipe(stylestats({
      type: 'json',
      outfile: true
    }))
    .pipe(gulp.dest('dest/'));
});
```

4. Next, we need to update the default task—alter it as indicated:

```
gulp.task('default', ['styles', 'lint', 'rename',
  'minifyCSS', 'sourcemap', 'stylestats']);
```

5. Revert to the Node.js command prompt, then enter `gulp` and press *Enter*— assuming we still have the same `style.css` file in the `src` folder, we should see this appear in the `dest` folder at the root of our project area:

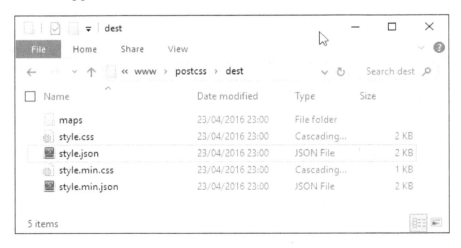

6. Whilst we clearly need to alter the parameters of our Gulp file to prevent it producing minified JSON files, we can at least see the result of the (uncompressed) JSON file. Go ahead and open it up—it will look something like this:

```
C:\wamp\www\postcss\dest\style.json - Sublime Text                    —    □    ×

File  Edit  Selection  Find  View  Goto  Tools  Project  Preferences  Help

     style.json                    ×

  1  {
  2    "published": "2016-04-23T22:00:19.016Z",
  3    "paths": [
  4      "C:\\wamp\\www\\postcss\\dest\\style.css"
  5    ],
  6    "stylesheets": 1,
  7    "styleElements": 0,
  8    "size": 1377,
  9    "dataUriSize": 0,
 10    "ratioOfDataUriSize": 0,
 11    "gzippedSize": 512,
 12    "rules": 6,

  Line 28, Column 30                          Spaces: 2          JSON
```

Although we're still only seeing code, we can now parse the content at will; we could, for instance, use jQuery to explore the contents and render it on screen using an appropriate style and format. I am sure you will agree though that this is a much easier way to view (and store) the information! The plugin needs minimal configuration to get started. We can use it to view any standard CSS file, once it has been through the compilation process.

 There are a number of options we can use with the `gulp-stylestats` plugin—for details, take a look at https://github.com/t32k/stylestats.

Right, we now have a completed processor; hopefully, this will also include a style guide that is running, using one of the plugins we've just discussed in the previous exercise. It's time we moved on—there is one task we should complete, though, before we embark on the next stage of our journey. It's time we put our processor to the test...

Testing the final pre-processor

Throughout this book, we've explored a number of different plugins and concepts to help construct a processor; over the last few pages, we've brought together some of those concepts as the final version of our processor — at least one we can start using in anger.

There is one key step left to complete — we've compiled code for simple exercises, this works well, but doesn't really represent the kind of processes we might go through as developers! For this, we need to construct a real-world example, and put our processor through its paces.

As luck would have it, there is an example web page we can use from the code download that accompanies this book — let's take a look at putting its style sheet code through our processor. We'll begin by running the normal tasks we've done before, but will add a selection of plugins to make for a more realistic example:

1. We'll start by extracting a copy of the T55 - testing our processor folder from the code download that accompanies this book; go ahead and save it to the root of our project area.

2. Copy the gulpfile.js and package.json files from within this sub-folder to the root of our project area.

3. Fire up a Node.js command prompt, then change the working folder to our project area.

4. In the prompt, go ahead and enter these three lines, pressing *Enter* after each:

   ```
   npm install postcss-nesting --save-dev

   npm install postcss-short-color --save-dev

   npm install postcss-pixrem
   ```

5. Copy the site.css file from within the css - completed version folder under T55 - testing our processor, to the src folder at the root of our project area.

6. Revert to the Node.js session, then enter gulp at the prompt and press *Enter* — wait for it to complete compiling.

7. When compilation has finished, copy the contents of the dest folder to the css folder within T55 - testing our processor.

8. Try previewing the results of the compiled file — if all is well, we should see something akin to this screenshot:

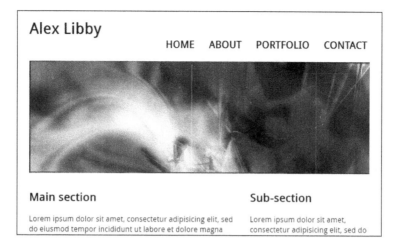

Try resizing the browser window, or enabling Responsive Design mode in your browser (if supported) — we should see that content automatically flows or resizes, according to the size you set for the browser window. Overall, a successful result!

The question is — what happened here? If we take a look at our code, the sharp-eyed should spot the addition of three plugins, plus a lot more code in the compiled version; let's take a moment to digest the results of our exercise.

Digesting the results of our exercise

If we look through our Gulp task file carefully, there should not be much in there that comes as a surprise — many of the tasks used are ones we have used on many occasions throughout the book.

The key here, though, is that whilst we can run the standard processor that we've already used before, it's unlikely to suit all occasions. It's more likely that we can use it as our base (as stated earlier), then add any extra plugins as needed. The great thing about this is that most of the configuration work is done — it keeps a consistent approach to our work. All that remains is to install any plugins that we *don't* already have in place — we of course have most of them, but need to install three additional ones, as highlighted here:

```
gulp.task('styles', function () {
  return gulp.src('src/*.css')
    .pipe(postcss([ rucksack({ fallbacks: true }),
    autoprefixer(), shortcolor, nesting, pixrem ]))
    .pipe(gulp.dest('dest/'));
});
```

These have to be accompanied with the relevant calls at the top of our Gulp task file:

```
var nesting = require('postcss-nesting');
var shortcolor = require('postcss-short-color');
var pixrem = require('pixrem');
```

In turn, these plugins are as follows:

- **Rucksack**: This is to handle responsive/media queries, fallback colors from rgba to hex, and implement `@font-face`.

- **Pixrem**: Available at `https://github.com/robwierzbowski/node-pixrem`, this takes care of providing a fallback mechanism for the rem unit values used throughout our style sheet.

- **Nesting**: Downloadable from `https://github.com/jonathantneal/postcss-nesting` (via Node), this covers an instance of nesting used in our code.

- **Shorthand Color**: In a couple of instances, we combined `background-color` and `color` attributes in a shorthand form that is later transpiled by the plugin. You can see more about this plugin at `https://github.com/jonathantneal/postcss-short-color`.

We can of course add others, and continue converting our code—there are other instances where Nesting can be applied, such as in the rules that control styling for our navigation. The key here, though, is that success is measured in how much we have to change our processor's *default* setup—in this instance, we didn't have to change it at all! We of course added extra plugins that required a change to one line of code in the processor, but none of the other tasks required any changes at all.

It's at this stage that we have effectively completed the journey to create our processor—well, strictly speaking, our journey should always be considered without end; this will help ensure our tool remains up to date. This aside, though, there are some useful tips we can use when creating our processor, so let's take a moment to cover these in more detail.

Getting started with some hints and tips

The time has come when it is over to you as developers to start creating your own processor! It may seem a daunting task at first, depending on the size and nature of your project; I've listed a few tips to help you over the initial hurdle of planning and creating your processor:

- Every processor is unique—do not be afraid to experiment. The processor of course must meet your requirements, but there are several ways to crack a nut, so if the first plugin you try doesn't work, then move on and try another.

- Don't fall into the trap that many do, and consider PostCSS as either a pre-processor or a post-processor; it is neither and yet it is also both. The library itself does nothing; the magic lies in the plugins you add, which determine how it performs.

- Start small—PostCSS was designed to be modular, so if all you need to begin with is a facility to add vendor prefixes, then fine. Over time, you can easily add extra plugins to your processor; it does not matter if this is adding to existing functionality, or replacing an old process that is no longer efficient or works.

- Think iteratively—don't even try to convert something as large as the style sheet for WordPress in one go! You will soon lose patience and momentum, and potentially abandon a project before you get the benefits of using PostCSS.

- The only time a processor should be retired is if there is a fundamental change in the architecture of your project, which makes it incompatible with PostCSS. The versatility of PostCSS is such that this isn't likely to happen—you should always review the functionality periodically to ensure you are getting the best out of your processor. Plugins change, are deprecated, or new ones are added—a check will ensure your solution still works as efficiently as possible.

- Any processor should not be limited to PostCSS plugins only—even though this is what we've focused on, there are thousands of other plugins available for your task runner of choice, which will likely work with PostCSS. The key here is that if it helps automate a mundane task that saves you time as a developer, then consideration should be given to whether it can be included in your processor.

- I personally take the view that if it can be automated reliably, then include a task for it—we live in an age where time is precious; there is no value in manually resizing images, for example, if it can be done automatically!

- Although we've talked about some of the tasks we can complete using a task runner, we must not forget the folder structure too. There is nothing worse than compiling files for different environments, for example, if they land up in badly-organized folders! Gulp can automate a multitude of tasks, so the fewer changes we have to do, or the fewer files we have to copy, the better.

Hopefully, they are a few tips to get you started! The great thing about PostCSS is that no two processors will be the same; whilst some may count that as a shortcoming, it should be noted that there is a wealth of possibilities out there to be explored, and that you can make your processor as simple or as complex as your project requirements dictate.

Before we bow out from our journey through building a custom processor, there is something we should consider. Our processor was constructed entirely using PostCSS plugins; in reality, our processor is more likely to go through a transitional phase, where we convert from the likes of SASS or less to using PostCSS.

To help with this process, we can always make use of a library such as CSStyle — this little interesting gem can work with either SASS or PostCSS, and could be a useful addition to the transition process. Over the course of the next two chapters, we will learn how to create custom syntaxes and explore some of the ways we can process both PostCSS and SASS content through the same process. As a taster for what is coming, let's take a quick tour through CSSStyle and see how it works in action.

Introducing the CSStyle library

Cast your mind back to *Chapter 3*, *Nesting Rules*, where we explored the concepts behind BEM, or the Block, Element, Modifier way of writing CSS. The key benefit of using this method is to help reduce CSS specificity, or where we might otherwise end up using something such as the following to style a simple button:

```
#maincontent .button .red.large:hover
```

Okay, it's a little contrived, but you get the idea: the level of specificity makes it awkward to manage and potentially reuse in future projects.

We took a look at BEM as a possible alternative — it has the benefit of reducing styles down to one or two classes, but can be awkward to remember which conventions to use:

```
.component {
  /* represents a component */
}

.component__element {
  /* represents a small part that is used to make a component */

}
```

```
'.component--modifier {
  /* represents a state modifier for the component */
}
```

Okay, so how can we get around this? Well, here's an option we can consider using: the CSStyle library. There are several reasons why this can help us—let's take a look in more detail.

Exploring the benefits of using CSStyle

The key behind CSStyle (available from `http://csstyle.io/`) is that it is made up of modular blocks, in a similar fashion to BEM. The difference, though, is that instead of having to remember a set of conventions that aren't the most intuitive, we can use a simpler set to create cleaner code.

The real beauty, though, is that we can use either SASS or PostCSS to create our site—we can begin with SASS, but we can also begin to transition over to using PostCSS with minimal changes. Let's put this into practice, and explore a quick demo to see how easy it is to make these changes—before we do so, take a look at `http://codepen.io/alibby251/pen/pgmqjJ`; this is a Pen that illustrates what we're going to create:

It won't win any style awards, but the purpose of this demo is to show you the *process* and not necessarily produce anything that is stunning! With that in mind, let's make a start:

1. We'll begin by extracting a copy of the `T56 - using csstyle with sass` folder from the code download that accompanies this book; save the folder to the root of our project area.

2. Copy the contents of the `src` folder within `T56 - using csstyle with sass` to the `src` folder at the root of our project area.

3. Go ahead and replace the `gulpfile.js` and `package.json` files at the root of our project area with copies from within the `T56 - using csstyle with sass` folder.

4. Fire up a Node.js command prompt session, then change the working folder to the root of our project area.

5. At the prompt, enter gulp and press *Enter* – if all is well, we should see a compiled `style.css` file appear in the `dest` folder in our project area.

6. Copy the contents of the `dest` folder back to the `css` folder within the T56 - using csstyle with sass folder.

At this point, try previewing the results in a browser. If all is well, we will see the three buttons appear, just as they show in the Pen we mentioned at the start of this exercise.

All looks good…we have a working demo, with a compiled style sheet – but hold on…in *SASS*? Yes, if you look carefully, the demo was indeed set to use SASS, but with good reason: we're going to see how easy it is to change to using PostCSS *without* making material changes to our style sheet or our compilation process. Let's make a start:

1. In the `gulpfile.js` that is at the root of our project area, comment out line 5, and uncomment lines 6 and 7; this switches our task file from using SASS to PostCSS.

2. Rename the `[sass]` task `[style]`, on line 9.

3. On line 10, the `gulp.src` call is looking for SASS files; change it to `src/*.css`.

4. Replace line 11 with this line: `.pipe(postcss([nested, csstyle]))` – this removes the dependency on SASS and switches to using PostCSS.

5. On line 15, our default task will call the `[sass]` task; change `[sass]` to `[style]`.

6. Change the watch task on line 17 to monitor CSS files, and not SASS:

```
var watcher = gulp.watch('src/*.css', ['style']);
```

7. Go ahead and open up the SASS style sheet in the `src` folder at the root of our project area – rename the file as `style.css`.

8. In `style.css`, go ahead and remove the `@import 'csstyle'` line at the top of our style sheet.

9. Do a search and replace for `@include` – remove all instances in our style sheet.

That's it for our demo, sorry to disappoint if you were expecting more! All that remains is to replace the `gulpfile.js` and `package.json` files at the root of the project area with copies from the T57 - using csstyle with postcss folder, and compile as normal.

Dissecting our demo

Making the transition from SASS to PostCSS can be as easy or as complex as we make it. Using the CSStyle library can go a long way to easing the transition away from existing processors such as SASS.

Although our demo was just a quick whistle-stop tour through using CSStyle (and we will revisit it in *Chapter 12, Mixing Preprocessors*), it nevertheless illustrates a few important points of interest:

- The library uses the concept of components, options, parts, and tweaks to create the base components, pass styling to override base rules, add extra elements (such as icons), or tweak code. Careful design means that we can reduce or remove the need to alter our HTML as part of the transition to using PostCSS.

- It is perfectly possible to compile the SASS version of our demo using a standard SASS compiler; the reason for choosing to use a task runner version (in this case for Gulp) means that we can centralize the compilation process in one task file, and remove the need to use separate compilers in our process.

- When planning the design or transition of our site to use PostCSS, it pays to choose plugins carefully within PostCSS; this will determine how easy or complex it will be to make the changes in our code and processor.

- Our demo focused on the core compilation process, and didn't include the extra tasks we used in the past, such as adding source maps. This was purely for clarity — there is no reason why we can't add the remaining tasks we've used before, once we've confirmed our compilation process works as expected.

Ultimately though, the use of this library is about helping to ease the process of making the transition to using PostCSS. There are different ways to approach this — using CSSStyle means that we have to completely redesign our HTML, but can easily alter the processor with minimal fuss. The flip side to this is that we can use PostCSS plugins that mimic SASS coding standards, or create our own custom syntax — we will explore these concepts in the next two chapters.

Summary

Creating our own processor can be a satisfying experience—we have total control over what elements should be included, and can add or remove elements at any time. Throughout the course of this book, we've explored a number of elements that make up what might be a typical processor; in this chapter, we pulled together all of these elements to create our final article. Let's take a moment to review what we have learnt.

We began with a look at some of the key elements of our processor, which we've already used previously, but have not really understood in detail how it all fits together. With this in mind, we moved on to examine some of the issues with our processor, before working out ways of correcting those issues and altering our code.

With our updated processor in place, we then took a look at ways of optimizing our output by altering existing functionality, or including new options that may or may not make up a baseline processor or one customized for a specific project. We then took a look at extending our functionality, that includes options we would not normally consider, but will complement our work processes perfectly.

We then rounded out our chapter with a quick test of our processor on a sample site, before exploring some of the hints and tips that will help us when creating our processors. The final step in our journey took a quick look at the CSSStyle library, as a precursor to creating custom syntaxes for PostCSS, which we will explore in the next chapter.

11
Manipulating Custom Syntaxes

Although many developers have moved on from using preprocessors to using PostCSS, it is important to note that PostCSS is not a replacement, just an alternative way of preprocessing CSS styles. To help with the transition, we're not forced to learn a new syntax. Using a handful of plugins, we can take advantage of the speed of PostCSS, while still using syntaxes that we're accustomed to, such as Less, SASS, or Stylus.

In this chapter, we'll take a look at the plugins that make this possible, and work on some simple examples that show you how using a custom syntax that we're all familiar with is still possible when using PostCSS.

This chapter will cover the following technical topics:

- Introducing custom syntaxes
- Implementing examples of custom syntax plugins
- Parsing CSS
- Converting content to strings with the API
- Adding highlighting support to our code

Let's make a start!

Introducing custom syntaxes

W3Schools defines a CSS syntax as follows:

> *"A CSS rule-set consists of a selector and a declaration block: The selector points to the HTML element you want to style. The declaration block contains one or more declarations separated by semicolons."*

We as developers spend many hours crafting sites; this can be something small as a one-page contact card-type site, right through to a large e-commerce website. It does not matter which styles we decide to use, or how we get there: the key is that the final result must use the same standard syntax that we've grown to love over the years.

This does not mean to say that our source should be standard CSS, in fact, it would be very restrictive if this were the only option! We could use libraries such as SASS or Less, but instead, how about using the API and custom syntax plugins to manipulate our styles directly? We touched on some of the principles back in *Chapter 8, Creating PostCSS Plugins*; it's time to revisit this and explore how we can begin to remove this restriction.

Why would we want to do this, I hear you ask? The answer's simple — let's assume for a moment you create themes for WordPress. WordPress' default themes are created using SASS (and PostCSS); this means a dependency on SASS in some form. We can mitigate this a little by using the `gulp-sass` plugin, but this still uses `libsass` to compile code.

What if we could turn this on its head, and use the API and custom syntax plugins that parses SASS code and converts it to PostCSS equivalent? Okay, granted, we may not be able to cover all styles; we can at least make a start on converting some, and reduce our dependency on using SASS. Let's make a start. Before we get stuck into producing code, we have a simple administrative task to perform: we need to install a syntax highlighter first.

Preparing our environment

Throughout the course of this chapter, we will be working directly with the PostCSS API (or a plugin's individual API, if it has one). As we are working directly on CSS (and not simply through a plugin's configuration object), it makes sense to install a syntax highlighter that works with PostCSS.

Not every text editor has one, but if you happen to use Sublime Text, with the Package Control facility installed (and I am assuming this is the case for the demos in this book), then it has a highlighter available for PostCSS that we can install. The plugin is available at `https://github.com/hudochenkov/Syntax-highlighting-for-PostCSS`. Let's get it installed using the following steps:

1. Open up Sublime Text, then press *Cmd + Shift + P* (OS X) or *Ctrl + Shift + P* (Linux/Windows) to open the command palette.

2. From the list that appears, click on **Package Control: Install Package**.

3. After a few moments, it will show a new list; start typing `Syntax Highlighting for PostCSS`:

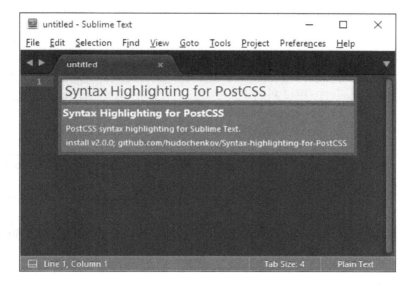

4. When it appears, click on it to install; it takes a couple of moments to complete.

We can of course simply use a highlighter that works with JavaScript; this won't be the same though: having a highlighter designed for PostCSS will make it easier to edit code!

The syntax highlighter that we've just installed comes with its own theme. If you like to roll your own, then you can do so, using the Base16 site at `http://chriskempson.github.io/base16/`.

Okay, let's move on; it's time to get stuck into code. Let's begin by exploring some of the plugins available for parsing code in PostCSS.

Implementing custom syntax plugins

The PostCSS ecosystem contains over 100 plugins at last count; this is on the increase. These plugins will all serve different needs, but will have one thing in common: the process they use to transform our code.

Now, we should be clear that this similarity is at a very high level; we are not referring to the technical details of each plugin! This aside, when creating our own custom syntax, we must follow a three-step process:

1. We first put our code through a parser.
2. We then transform it using anyone of a number of plugins.
3. We finally stringify it, or convert it to valid CSS in string format.

We already have a handful of plugins that allow us to work with other syntaxes within a PostCSS environment; these include languages such as less or JavaScript:

Name of plugin	Purpose of plugin
`sugarss`	This plugin is an indent-based syntax like SASS or Stylus.
	Plugin is available from `https://github.com/postcss/sugarss`.
`postcss-less`	We can use this plugin to transform less into valid CSS. Note: it does not compile code.
	Plugin is available from `https://github.com/webschik/postcss-less`.
`postcss-js`	Anyone working with JavaScript can use this plugin to write styles in JS or transform React Inline Styles, Radium, or JSS.
	Plugin is available from `https://github.com/postcss/postcss-js`.
`postcss-scss`	For those of you using SASS, this plugin is perfect for working with SASS code; it does *not* compile code to CSS.
	Plugin is available from `https://github.com/postcss/postcss-scss`.
`postcss-safe-parser`	This plugin is perfect for finding and fixing CSS syntax errors.It's available to download from `https://github.com/postcss/postcss-safe-parser`.
`poststylus`	We can use this plugin to transform styles created using the Stylus library into valid CSS. Note: it does not compile code.
	Plugin is available from `https://github.com/seaneking/poststylus`.

Although all of these plugins serve a different purpose, they all follow the same principle: they parse the code and transform it, before converting it to a format that can be saved to file as a valid style sheet output.

Leaving aside which parser we use, there is one question though: why would we want to manipulate our code directly? There are a few reasons for needing to alter the code directly; here are a few:

- We may want to create a report that details facts and figures about our code for reference purposes; it is true that there will be plugins or scripts available to do this already, but PostCSS can get us the basics during compilation, and not as a separate process.

- How about this for an idea? If you happen to use an application such as Adobe Color CC, then we can consider using the API to directly transform specific colors into valid RGB(A) or HEX equivalent values. We could use a plugin to achieve this, but performing this directly using the API allows us to retain flexibility with our choice of colors.

- There is nothing stopping us from dissecting existing plugins, and rebasing the tasks they perform into something that we could add to a task runner file, and then adapt to our needs. We might ultimately consider creating a plugin, but if the steps required are very specific to our needs, then a plugin may not be a useful addition.

- There are occasions when error handling can be lacking. The API contains some useful functionality that allows us to add suitably formatted messages on screen, if our process fails.

These are just a few ideas to get started, in addition to manipulating existing non-PostCSS styles (such as those created using SASS, for example).

Enough talking, I feel a demo coming! We've met some of the plugins available, so it's time to put them to good use; two of particular interest are the `postcss-scss` and `postcss-safe-parser` plugins. Let's dive in and take a look at them in more detail, beginning with `postcss-safe-parser`.

Parsing content and fixing errors

Over the next few pages, we'll touch on using a couple of parser plugins, to show how easy it is to transform our code. We will take a look at a plugin that removes the need for SASS (at least at a basic level); before we do so, let's first explore using the `postcss-safe-parser` plugin.

The `postcss-safe-parser` plugin, available from `https://github.com/postcss/postcss-safe-parser`, is perfect for finding and fixing CSS errors. It's a simple plugin to use and install; let's make a start:

1. We'll start by installing the plugin, so go ahead, and fire up a Node.js command prompt session, then change the working directory to the root of our project area.

2. At the prompt, enter this command, then press *Enter* to install the plugin:

   ```
   npm install postcss-safe-parser --save-dev
   ```

3. Next, go ahead and extract a copy of the `T58 - parsing invalid content` folder from the code download that accompanies this book; save it to the root of our project area.

4. Copy the `package.json` and `gulpfile.js` files from it to the root of our project area.

5. Switch back to the NodeJS command prompt session, then at the prompt, enter `gulp` and press *Enter*.

If all is well, we should see a successful compilation: a file marked `output.css` will be created at the root of our project area.

Go ahead and open it. Even though our example only contained one malformed selector, the file contains the same selector, but this time with the missing closing parenthesis added. We can also see the results appear in the console log at the same time as seen in the following screenshot:

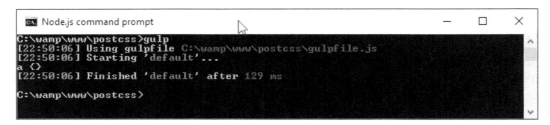

So what's going on here? Well, some of this will be familiar. We're using a standard format task in our Gulp file, along with references to some of the plugins that we've already met, such as `autoprefixer`.

The content that is of interest to us though, is in the default Gulp task as seen in the following screenshot:

```
'use strict';
var gulp = require('gulp');
var postcss = require('postcss');
var safe = require('postcss-safe-parser');
var autoprefixer = require('autoprefixer');
var fs = require('fs');

var badCss = 'a {';

gulp.task('default', function () {
  return postcss([autoprefixer]).process(badCss, { parser: safe }).then(function (result) {
    console.log(result.css); //= 'a {}'
    fs.writeFileSync('output.css', result.css);
  });
});
```

The task may seem a little complex, but in reality, we're parsing our CSS, prior to manipulating it. We start by defining a `postcss` object (into which feeds a request to run `autoprefixer`). This then processes our CSS into an AST, using a parser to find and fix any issues, before piping it out on screen and into a file named `output.css` in our project area.

 Abstract Syntax Trees (AST) are a graphical tree representation of the syntactic structure of our CSS style sheets or code.

Okay, our example was very simplistic, but this was intended to show you how the principle works. In this next example, the same principle has been used to convert standard SCSS code to valid CSS; note, though, that we're not calling SASS (as we have done before), but converting the SCSS code to valid CSS styles.

Parsing SCSS content

In our previous demo, we explored the use of PostCSS to parse our CSS and added the missing closing bracket as a fix for our code. It was a simplistic example; perfect if you're working with standard CSS, but what if your projects are using SASS?

Well, as part of our next example, we'll prove that using a compiler is now old hat; we'll use the `postcss-scss` plugin (from `https://github.com/postcss/postcss-scss`) to directly transform our SASS code, before unwrapping the nesting styles using the `postcss-nested` plugin (available from `https://github.com/postcss/postcss-nested`):

1. We'll start by installing the `postcss-scss` plugin. Go ahead and fire up a NodeJS command prompt session, then change the working directory to the root of our project area.

2. At the prompt, enter this command, then press *Enter*:

   ```
   npm install postcss-scss --save-dev
   ```

   Keep the session open when the plugin has completed installation:

3. From the downloaded code that accompanies this book, go ahead and extract a copy of the `package.json` file from the `T59 - Parsing SCSS` content folder. Save this to the root of our project area.

4. From the same `T59 - Parsing SCSS` content folder, copy the contents of the `src` folder to the `src` folder at the root of our project area.

5. In a new file, add the following code and save it as `gulpfile.js` in the `src` folder at the root of our project area:

   ```javascript
   'use strict';
   var gulp = require('gulp');
   var postcss = require('postcss');
   var fs = require('fs')
   var autoprefixer = require('autoprefixer');
   var nested = require('postcss-nested');

   var scss = fs.readFileSync('src/styles.scss', 'utf-8');
   ```

```
gulp.task('default', function () {
  var syntax = require('postcss-scss');
  postcss([ autoprefixer, nested() ]).process(scss, {
    syntax: syntax }).then(function (result) {
    fs.writeFileSync('dest/styles.css', result.content);
  });
});
```

The keen-eyed amongst you will spot the reference to postcss-nested. We cannot call PostCSS without specifying something, so we'll use this plugin to unwrap the nested statements in our code:

1. Revert back to the NodeJS command prompt session, then add this command and press *Enter*:

   ```
   npm install postcss-nested --save-dev
   ```

2. Once Node has completed installing the plugin, enter gulp at the prompt then press *Enter*:

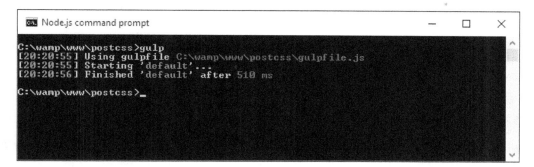

3. If all is well, we will see a compiled file appear in the dest folder:

But hold on a moment: this is a valid *CSS* file, right? Absolutely. But…we've so far had to use a compiler to produce valid CSS code; how come we haven't needed to add one now?

Exploring what happened

Well, the answer lies in the conversion process—traditionally we would have had to compile our code, even though standard SASS files are a superset of current CSS. Instead, we've simply *rewritten* our code using a syntax that translates a standard SCSS file to valid CSS.

If we take a look at our Gulp file in more detail, we can see references to the standard `gulp-postcss` plugin, along with declared instances of the `fs`, `autoprefixer`, `postcss-nested`, and `postcss-scss` plugins. The key for this demo starts on line 10, where we declare an instance of the `scss` variable, and use the **file system (fs)** plugin for Node to read the contents of the file into this variable.

Once into the task, we create an instance of PostCSS as an object, before feeding it the `autoprefixer` and `nested()` plugins (as variables). We then process our SASS code using the syntax that comes with the `postcss-scss` plugin, before piping out the contents as a file into the `dest` folder in our project area.

See? Nice and easy; not a SASS compiler in sight! This simple change removes the need for any dependency on a compiler, after all, SCSS files are just standard CSS text files, so why use a compiler? With all of this talk of parsing CSS (or SCSS for that matter), it's worth spending some time exploring what we mean by this, and how it is important to the whole process.

Parsing CSS

At the heart of writing any custom syntax is the ability to parse content—it doesn't matter whether this is CSS, JavaScript, or something else; we clearly need to understand what we're working with, before we can make changes! At a basic level, these are the steps we must take to transform our CSS when working with PostCSS:

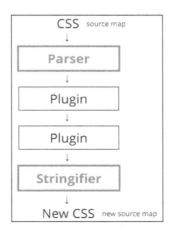

We begin with our source CSS (which comes with or without a source map), which we parse only once, but then put through any number of specified plugins (the example shows two, but we can easily use more). We then convert the output to a string using a stringifier; at this point, we can view the contents on screen or save them to disk.

Let's for a moment take a look at parsing some example code. For this next example, we will use a single CSS rule and parse it using the `postcss-value-parser` plugin (from `https://github.com/TrySound/postcss-value-parser`); the reason for this will become clear shortly:

1. From the code download that accompanies this book, extract and save copies of the `gulpfile.js` and `package.json` files from the T60 - parsing color values folder to the root of our project area; if you want to save any existing files from there, then please do so first.

2. Fire up a NodeJS command prompt session then change the working folder to the root of our project area.

3. We need to install the `postcss-value-parser` plugin, so at the prompt, enter this command and press *Enter*:

```
npm install postcss-value-parser --save-dev
```

NPM will now install the plugin; keep the session open when it has finished:

4. At the prompt, type `gulp` then press *Enter*; gulp will now go away and display the contents, which will look something like this:

```
Node.js command prompt

C:\wamp\www\postcss>gulp
[23:07:47] Using gulpfile C:\wamp\www\postcss\gulpfile.js
[23:07:47] Starting 'default'...
ValueParser {
  nodes:
   [ { type: 'function',
       sourceIndex: 0,
       value: 'rgba',
       before: '',
       after: '',
       nodes:
        [ { type: 'word', sourceIndex: 5, value: '233' },
          { type: 'div', sourceIndex: 8, value: ',', before: '', after: ' ' },
```

Yikes! What does that all mean? Don't worry, it looks worse than it really is; this is an example of an AST, which we discussed earlier in this chapter. This gives us in-depth information on the contents of our CSS, such as the values, types of values, and where they appear in the tree.

The great thing, though, is that once we have all of this content, then we are free to query and manipulate the content at will. Once we have manipulated the content, we then need to convert it to string format, so it can be displayed on screen in a more intelligent format, or saved to disk.

For this demo, we used the `postcss-value-parser` plugin to create our AST; we can also try using the `postcss-safe-parser` plugin (from `https://github.com/postcss/postcss-safe-parser`), or the `postcss-selector-parser` plugin (from `https://github.com/postcss/postcss-selector-parser`), to achieve similar effects.

And the reason why we only used one line of CSS code in our demo? Well, parsing CSS code can get very complex. The example shown in our demo is relatively straightforward; just imagine what it will be like with 2,000+ lines of code!

Let's develop this theme further, and use it to replace some example RGBA values with equivalent HEX-based colors. We can easily do this through the use of the `postcss-unrgba` plugin (from `https://github.com/jonathantneal/postcss-unrgba`), but it weighs in at almost 60 lines; our Gulp file is 43 lines, and a lot of that is comments!

Replacing RGBA colors

Our next example is a relatively straightforward search and replace; it is a perfect example of how it isn't always necessary to use plugins, and that we can parse our code directly to achieve the same effect. Let's make a start:

1. We'll start by extracting a copy of the `T61 - changing colors` folder from the downloaded code that accompanies this book; save the folder to the root of our project area.

2. Copy the `gulpfile.js` and `package.json` files from the `T61 - changing colors` folder to the root of our project area.

3. Copy the `src` folder from the `T61 - changing colors` folder to the root of our project area.

4. Next, fire up a NodeJS command prompt session then change the working folder to the root of our project area.

5. We now need to install an additional plugin, `color-convert` (available from `https://github.com/qix-/color-convert`), which we will use to change the color once we've sucked out the details from within the AST. For this, go ahead and fire up a NodeJS command prompt, then change the working folder to the root of our project area.

6. At the prompt, enter `npm install color-convert --save-dev` and press *Enter*.

7. When the plugin has finished installing, go ahead and enter `gulp`, then press *Enter*. If all is well, we should see the, by now, familiar transformed style sheet appear in our destination folder:

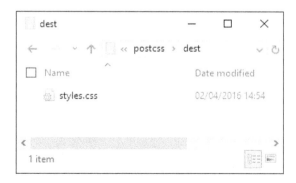

At this point, our style sheet has been transformed. If we preview the results in a text editor, we can confirm that HEX-equivalent values have indeed replaced the original RGBA colors, as shown in the following screenshot:

```
61    #container {
62        background-clip: padding-box;
63        box-shadow: 3px 3px 5px 0px #949494;
64        margin: 5% auto;
65        width: 800px;
66    }
```

Not convinced? Take a look at the same rule within the source file; here it shows the original RGBA value:

```
61    #container {
62        background-clip: padding-box;
63        box-shadow: 3px 3px 5px 0px rgba(148,148,148,1);
64        margin: 5% auto;
65        width: 800px;
66    }
```

See how easy that was? There is one thing note; if we take a look at the Gulp file, it might at first glance look like we still have a few plugins in use. The key here is that three of these are part of Node (`fs`, `path`, and `util`), so we haven't had to install any new ones, over and above the `value-parser` and `color-convert` examples.

Exploring how it all works

It's worth taking the time to consider this code in more detail. This contains some useful techniques that will help get you started on the road to creating custom syntaxes, starting with retrieving the values we need.

We begin with reading the contents of our style sheet file, before parsing it through the `postcss-value-parser` plugin. We walk through each node within the AST, ignoring any that contain a `node.type` of function or a `node.value` of rgba. For any that remain, we collect any that have a node type of word, before mapping them into a single array value which we convert to a number.

This is then transformed from a function node to a word node, before we finally convert the value from an RGBA to HEX color. The contents are converted to a string, and saved to disk in the destination folder, with the same file name.

Node types represent the type of selector we're working with— examples include `root`, `string`, `tag`, and `attribute`. In our example, we've used `node.type` to display a string representation of the selector type, which we can manipulate in code.

Okay, let's move on: the key basis for working with custom syntaxes is to understand the content we need to work with; crack this and you are part of the way to transforming your styles into valid CSS. To help with the process, though, we will need to convert our content to a format that can be saved to disk. It's time to take a look at how, using the PostCSS API.

Formatting the output with the API

When parsing CSS, the output by default is going to resemble something as shown in the following screenshot:

```
Node.js command prompt                                              —    □    ×

C:\wamp\www\postcss>gulp
[23:07:47] Using gulpfile C:\wamp\www\postcss\gulpfile.js
[23:07:47] Starting 'default'...
ValueParser {
  nodes:
   [ { type: 'function',
       sourceIndex: 0,
       value: 'rgba',
       before: '',
       after: '',
       nodes:
        [ { type: 'word', sourceIndex: 5, value: '233' },
          { type: 'div', sourceIndex: 8, value: ',', before: '', after: ' ' },
          { type: 'word', sourceIndex: 10, value: '45' },
          { type: 'div',
            sourceIndex: 12,
            value: ',',
            before: '',
            after: ' ' },
          { type: 'word', sourceIndex: 14, value: '66' },
          { type: 'div',
            sourceIndex: 16,
            value: ',',
            before: '',
            after: ' ' },
          { type: 'word', sourceIndex: 18, value: '.5' } ] } ] }
[23:07:47] Finished 'default' after 44 ms

C:\wamp\www\postcss>
```

It looks a really ugly mess, but is in fact the standard format for an AST tree. The trouble is, it's not very helpful if we want to use details from it in our code! To get around this, we need to convert our content into a string format: the simplest method is to use the `.toString()` method, which is perfect for saving the content to disk.

All of the code for the next exercise is in the T62 - adding a stringifier folder in the code download that accompanies this book.

It's a cinch to use in our Gulp file; let's take a look as part of our next exercise:

1. We'll start by creating a new Gulp task file. In your usual text editor of choice, add the following code; there is a reasonable amount involved, so we will go through it in sections, beginning with the declarations for the plugins used:

```
'use strict';
var gulp = require('gulp');
var postcss = require('postcss');
var util = require('util');
var autoprefixer = require('autoprefixer');
var fs = require('fs');
```

2. We need to set up a few variables; these will be used to store values generated during the compilation process:

```
var newValue = 'white', result, selectors = [], root, decl;
```

3. Next up is the start of our task. The first step is to parse some simple CSS, as a basis for our demo. We then get the first child in our code, and save it to the decl variable:

```
gulp.task('default', function () {
  root = postcss.parse('a { color: black }');
  decl = root.first.first;
```

4. The first piece of information we want is a selector count; this next block will count through each selector using root.walkRules, and push the value into the selectors array:

```
// get a selector count
selectors = [];
root.walkRules(function (rule) {
  selectors.push(rule.selector);
});
```

5. At this point, we're ready to pipe out a summary report of our code — we use console.log to display a number of different values on screen:

```
console.log("\nThe declaration type is: " + decl.type);
console.log("The value of this declaration is: " +
  decl.toString());
console.log("Number of nodes in this CSS: " +
  root.nodes.length);
console.log("Selectors used in this CSS: " +
  selectors.toString());
```

6. We're almost there — in this next block, we do the PostCSS equivalent of a search and replace to update our color from black to white:

```
// Replace color black with white
root.walkDecls(function (decl) {
  if ( decl.value.match(/^black/) ) {
    decl.value = 'white';
  }
});
```

7. We can display our content on screen, but a more useful step is to save it to disk — for this, we can use the `fs` plugin from Node.js to create our transformed CSS file and associated source map:

```
// display content on screen and save to file
result = root.toResult({ to: 'all.css', map: { inline:
  false } });
console.log("Updated color value: " +
  decl.value.toString() + "\n");
fs.writeFileSync('dest/styles.css', result.css);
fs.writeFileSync('dest/styles.css.map', result.map);
});
```

8. Save the Gulp file to the root of our project area, then fire up a Node.js command prompt, and change the working directory to that of our project area.

9. At the prompt, type in `gulp`, then press *Enter* and let the compilation complete.

   If all is well, we should see the results of step 6 appear on screen, like so:

The transformed CSS file and source map will be present in the dest folder:

So, how does this all help us? Well, the ability to parse our code directly opens up some real possibilities; let's pause for a moment to explore what has happened in our demo, and how we can take advantage of this functionality in future projects.

Dissecting our example code

Throughout the book, we've used a variety of plugins to transform our code. These will all make use of the PostCSS API in some form. However, we are not limited to simply using plugins; we can also transform our code directly using the API. At this point, it should be noted that we are not talking about creating a custom parser; indeed, this would easily form enough content for a short book in its own right!

A look through the Gulp file might be enough to put some people off. It is true that creating a custom syntax to parse code created using Stylus or less is not easy, and falls outside the scope of this book. However, we can make use of some of the API to query our content. In our example, there are two blocks of code that are of interest.

The first block parses each selector and keeps a running count. We can use the .walkRules method to iterate through each rule:

```
14    // get a selector count
15    selectors = [];
16    root.walkRules(function (rule) {
17        selectors.push(rule.selector);
18    });
```

Once we have that raw information, we can then stringify it (or convert it to a string), before displaying the content on screen:

```
20    console.log("\nThe declaration type is: " + decl.type);
21    console.log("The value of this declaration is: " + decl.toString());
22    console.log("Number of nodes in this CSS: " + root.nodes.length);
23    console.log("Selectors used in this CSS: " + selectors.toString());
```

It's worth noting that the PostCSS API contains additional functionality to stringify our CSS and assemble it together. These are known as the Stringify and Builder commands; these are only meant for use when creating custom syntaxes. We've simply parsed our content using existing plugins designed for this purpose, so using `toString()` is sufficient for our needs.

Moving on—our example was kept deliberately simple to illustrate the process. We can easily add additional functionality. The API reference documentation at `https://github.com/postcss/postcss/blob/master/docs/api.md` is a good place to start. How about adding error-checking, for example? We've already added one option from it, in the form of source maps; let's briefly cover this in more detail.

Adding source maps

Throughout many of our demos, we've incorporated a task that creates a source map of our CSS styling. It's worked perfectly well so far, but it isn't the final answer—we can do better! To see what is possible, take another look at the last block of code in the Gulp task file used in the previous demo (which should be around lines 33 to 36):

```
// display content on screen and save to file
result = root.toResult({ to: 'all.css', map: { inline: false } });
...
fs.writeFileSync('dest/styles.css', result.css);
fs.writeFileSync('dest/styles.css.map', result.map);
```

Here, we're creating a version of our transformed code that can be saved to file `{inline: false}` prevents the creation of a source map directly in our code. Instead, we use NodeJS' file system to create a source map based on `result.map`; this contains the content of our transformed code.

There are a few points to note when using this method; for more details, take a look at the main PostCSS site at `https://github.com/postcss/postcss/blob/master/docs/source-maps.md`.

Time to change tack: so far we've concentrated on writing our code, but what about presentation? It's not entirely necessary, but setting up highlighting has a twofold benefit: it makes it easier to edit our code, and we can also use it to provide a consistent theme when documenting our code electronically. After all, I'm sure you at least do the latter...don't you?

Highlighting our syntax code

Throughout many of our demos, we've concentrated on using plugins, with minimal changes required to configure the code for use. There is nothing wrong with this, but as always, we can do better. How about installing support for highlighting?

This is an easy way to make it easier to read our code, indeed, we should have installed something like this a long time ago! That aside, it's easy enough to fix; support is available for a wide variety of editors. For the purposes of this chapter, I will assume you are using Sublime Text; this is an example of how it might look (the screenshot shows the Twilight Light theme in use):

```
12    var file = 'src/styles.css';
13    var hexcolor, sourceFile = fs.readFileSync(file, 'utf-8');
14
15    gulp.task('default', function () {
16        var parsedValue = valueParser(sourceFile);
17
18        // walk() will visit all the of the nodes in the tree,
19        // invoking the callback for each.
20        parsedValue.walk(function (node) {
21
22            // Since we only want to transform rgba() values,
23            // we can ignore anything else.
24            if (node.type !== 'function' || node.value !== 'rgba') return;
25
```

Let's dive in and take a look at how to get this set up, using Sublime Text's package manager.

Installing themes

Adding theme support is a cinch when using an editor such as Sublime Text. Let's work through the steps:

1. We'll start by opening a command prompt session. Go ahead and add this command, then press *Enter*:

    ```
    cd %APPDATA%\Sublime Text 3\Packages\User
    ```

2. Next, enter this command, then press *Enter*:

    ```
    git clone git://github.com/chriskempson/base16-textmate.git Base16
    ```

3. Open Sublime Text. If all is well, we should see a new menu entry if we click on **Preferences | Color Scheme | User**:

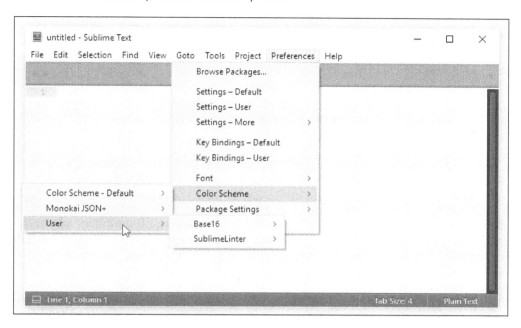

An easy change to make, but a useful one; nevertheless, it's only part of what we can do! To really go to town (figuratively speaking), we can apply similar styling to our CSS styles. This makes it easier to read if we want to document our styles online. After all, color is clearly easier to read than black and white! Let's take a moment to explore what is required to apply a color theme to our documented code.

Creating a HTML display theme

A part of developing code is the need to document it. This is not only for our sanity, but also for future changes, should someone else need to alter our code! Creating printed documentation is now old hat, a better method is to create it online, where we can easily update it without too much fuss. At the same time, we can add some color to it, to make it visually more appealing and provide a more consistent format to our efforts.

We could create this code manually, but that is a resource-heavy process that is prone to error! Instead, we can use the Midas library (available from `http://midasjs.com`) to automate the creation of the basis for our documentation, and we can style it using one of the base16 themes we covered in the previous exercise.

Let's make a start on installing that support:

1. We'll start by firing up a NodeJS command prompt, then changing the working folder to our project area.

2. At the prompt, enter this command, then press *Enter*:

   ```
   npm install midas --save-dev
   ```

3. Once it has finished installing, go ahead and extract the `src` folder and the `gulpfile.js` and `package.json` files from the `T63 - incorporating midas` folder, then save them to the root of our project area.

4. Revert to the NodeJS command prompt, then enter `gulp` and press *Enter*.

5. Gulp will go away and compile a HTML-based extract of our code as `styles.html`, which has been properly formatted with extra markup. The file will appear in the `dest` folder within our project area.

At this point, if we were to view the contents of that file, it will look very plain; this is easy to fix! To do this, we will use the Brewer theme by Timothée Poisot, available from `https://github.com/chriskempson/base16-builder/blob/master/schemes/brewer.yml`; there are a few steps involved to make this happen:

1. Browse to `https://github.com/ben-eb/midas/blob/master/templates/template-light.css`, then save this as a CSS file within the `dest` folder of our project area.

2. Open it in a text editor; it contains a series of placeholders for the base16 themes that are available for use. We would normally use Ruby to generate the CSS for one of these themes, but this isn't entirely necessary; instead, use your editor's search and replace to match up each placeholder with the appropriate color:

```
1    .midas {
2        background: #map(base07);
3        color: #map(base02);
4    }
```

```
5    base01: "2e2f30" #  ---
6    base02: "515253" #  --
7    base03: "737475" #  -
8    base04: "959697" #  +
9    base05: "b7b8b9" #  ++
10   base06: "dadbdc" #  +++
11   base07: "fcfdfe" #  ++++
```

3. Save the result; to make it work, we need to adjust the contents of the `styles.html` file to reference the new style sheet, so that it has the proper HTML structure. Once done, it will look something like this:

```css
footer {
    clear: both;
    font-size: 12px;
    height: 3rem;
    margin-bottom: 5px;
    margin-top: 5px;
}

footer > p {
    padding-left: 2rem;
}

#container {
    background-clip: padding-box;
    box-shadow: 3px 3px 5px 0px rgba(148,148,148,1);
    margin: 5% auto;
    width: 800px;
}
```

This looks far more appealing, I think you'll agree! Although it requires some work to create the initial theme, this will be a one-off process for each theme that you create. Any changes made to the CSS rules or declarations can be generated automatically, and the HTML result updates accordingly.

Summary

We kicked off with a quick introduction to custom syntaxes, before preparing our environment for developing code. We then covered some of the plugins available for parsing content, before exploring some of the reasons as to why we might need to parse custom syntaxes or styles directly before implementing two as examples of how to manipulate our code.

We then dived in and explored how most PostCSS plugins perform changes to our code. We then explored some of the techniques required to alter styles directly, before considering the effects of our changes on the code itself.

Next up, we examined how content can be formatted for screen or to a state ready for saving to disk (including the creation of source maps). We noted that whilst there are some specific methods available, these are reserved for custom syntax development, and that the options we used would suffice for initial manipulation of our code.

We then rounded out the chapter with a look at how we can add highlighting support to our projects—we examined the reasons for adding this, such as making code editing easier, and covered a quick demo that uses the Midas library to create properly laid out documentation for our projects.

The use of different syntaxes is a great way to remove the need for rewriting existing code into valid CSS. There is one thing, though: what happens if we have a mix of both standard CSS and pre-processor code, such as from less or Stylus? Can we work with both at the same time? Absolutely! We will take a look at the Pleeease library, which supports this, in the next chapter.

12
Mixing Preprocessors

Throughout the book, we've explored using PostCSS, and seen how we can build a more efficient preprocessor that meets our needs, without the extra baggage of standard preprocessors. Hold on though—doesn't it take time to build a processor? How do we manage the transition?

No problem, enter the Pleeease library! Throughout this chapter, we'll use the power of Pleeease to combine both preprocessors and postprocessors into one process, mixing existing systems such as SASS, Less, and Stylus. Over the next few pages we take a look at some examples, and show you how easy it is to harness the power of Pleeease.

This chapter will cover the following technical topics:

- Examining the benefits of using the Pleeease library
- Installing and configuring the library
- Exploring some of the features of Pleeease
- Compiling code using Node or the command line
- Setting up a configuration file
- Converting a WordPress installation and testing the results

Let's make a start!

Taking the first steps

When developing a site, developers will nearly always have the opportunity to design and build it from the ground up; we can make decisions regarding the color scheme to use, the structure of the site, and its general appearance.

Sometimes, though, there will be occasions when we want to use a new technology, but have to use an existing site. A question on the minds of many in this position will likely be: where does one start? It will, of course, depend on many factors, of which one is likely to be whether existing processors such as SASS or Less are being used on the site.

The flexibility and power of PostCSS allows us to transition easily from the likes of Less or SASS to using PostCSS—throughout this chapter, we're going to go on a journey to explore some of the tricks we can use to begin that transition process. We'll explore some of the plugin options available, then finish with a look at converting a CMS system such as WordPress to using PostCSS.

 Any reason why WordPress was chosen? It is compiled from SASS, but also uses PostCSS to handle vendor prefixes, we'll build on this with additional plugins later in the chapter.

Let's begin that journey, our first step is to explore some of the plugins we can use to begin that transition process from using SASS to PostCSS.

Exploring the conversion process

Cast your mind back to *Chapter 10, Building a Custom Processor*, for a moment.

The key theme of that chapter was bringing together a number of plugins we covered throughout the preceding chapters, to create what would become our processor. So far, all of the plugins used were based around pure PostCSS, so they wouldn't be able to compile raw SASS code.

We took a brief look at the CSStyle library, as a possible means of getting around this—it's a great library for producing clean code using BEM principles, but it requires that code is written using a specific format. Ordinarily, there is nothing wrong with this at all—every developer's utopia should be to produce clean, efficient code, right?

Yet there is just one small problem, reality! It wouldn't be practical to rewrite a large, complex e-commerce site to use CSStyle without an enormous amount of work; it would require a lengthy transition period to effect such a change. It's not impossible, but using BEM-style notation is better done from ground up, or at least in defined chunks, if your site has multiple style sheets in use.

So if using CSStyle isn't a practical solution for our needs, how can we make that change? There is a more practical solution available to us—it may take longer, but the disruption should be reduced, and allow us to make smaller changes to our code in a more manageable transition process:

- We start by introducing a task runner to compile existing processor code—plugins exist for using libraries such as SASS or Less within runners such as Gulp or Broccoli, to allow us to compile code.

- Once we've transitioned to using a task runner, we can then introduce plugins to handle core processes, such as managing vendor prefixes, creating source maps, and minifying our style sheets.

- We can then break down our existing style sheet into smaller chunks and import each into a master file during compilation. Each can then be converted to use PostCSS plugins that replicate existing processor functionality—for example, we might use `postcss-simple-vars` to create new variables to replace existing SASS-based examples.

The latter step in this process should be iterative, at least until everything has been converted, and allows us to remove any dependency on existing processors. We've used a fair number of Gulp task files to date, so we should be reasonably familiar with the basic use of one by now—here's what a task file might look like, if we were using SASS and Gulp:

```
var gulp = require('gulp');
var postcss = require('gulp-postcss');
var sass = require('gulp-sass');

var autoprefixer = require('autoprefixer');
var cssnano = require('cssnano');

gulp.task('css', function () {
  var processors = [ autoprefixer, cssnano ];
  return gulp.src('./src/*.scss')
    .pipe(sass().on('error', sass.logError))
    .pipe(postcss(processors))
    .pipe(gulp.dest('./dest'));
});
```

In this example, we're using the Gulp plugins for SASS and PostCSS—SASS code is compiled first, before vendor prefixes are added by PostCSS, and the code is minified into the final article.

The benefits of this process, though, mean that we can control the rate of conversion—we are not forced to have to convert everything in one go, and can be selective about what is converted at each point in the process. There will still be a dependency on an external library, but this is temporary; we can remove that dependency when everything has been converted to using PostCSS.

Choosing our plugins

Assuming that we've made the transition process to using a task runner, then where do we go from here?

Well, it's time to choose the plugins we need to use, based on the functionality offered by our site. Some of the more useful plugins to get you started are as follows:

Plugin	Purpose of plugin
postcss-mixins	If your code contains SASS mixins, then this will be essential—the format is very similar, so changes can be made using a search and replace in your editor. The plugin is available from `https://github.com/postcss/postcss-mixins`.
postcss-nested	Nesting code in SASS is a key concept—the `postcss-nested` plugin from `https://github.com/postcss/postcss-nested` is a good choice for replicating this functionality within SASS. Coupled with this, the `postcss-nested-props` and `postcss-nested-vars` plugins can be used to unwrap any properties or variables that are in nested code.
postcss-sassy-mixins	There are occasions when we might have blocks of reusable code; we can use mixins to help reduce the amount of code written in our style sheets. A key concept borrowed from SASS, this plugin replicates the same functionality, and allows us to easily convert from using SASS to PostCSS. The plugin source is available from `https://github.com/andyjansson/postcss-sassy-mixins`.
postcss-simple-extend	If we have styles that share common elements, then we can remove some of this duplication by extending existing styles. This is a common practice when using SASS; the postcss-simple-extend plugin from `https://github.com/davidtheclark/postcss-simple-extend` is perfect for replicating this within PostCSS.

Other plugins are available, depending on your needs. The majority of plugins available are for SASS, but that is simply due to its maturity; others will no doubt become available for processors such as Less or Stylus over time.

 Take a look at the PostCSS plugins catalog available from `http://postcss.parts` for more details.

Adding single plugins is a perfectly acceptable option, but what if we're adding more than just a couple of plugins to mimic SASS code? There are two options that would be useful here, and which we've not covered in our list—using the PreCSS or Pleeease libraries.

The Pleeease library was designed to handle some of the more menial tasks that are a necessary evil when compiling our code. Although not all of the supported tasks will apply, there will be at least three that do—minifying code, adding vendor prefixes, and generating source maps.

In stark contrast, the PreCSS library is likely to be more useful, as it is a collection of plugins that emulate SASS features. The beauty, though, is that we only need to install one plugin to handle changes; PreCSS abstracts the manual conversion of PostCSS styles into valid CSS using a single interface. We will explore using it in more detail a little later on in this chapter, but for now, let's turn our attention to putting the Pleeease library through its paces.

Introducing the Pleeease library

The Pleeease library, available from `http://pleeease.io/`, is designed to simplify the use of preprocessors, and combine the benefits of using multiple tools in one library. It means we can configure it to any one of three processors, such as SASS, Less, or Stylus, in addition to PostCSS, when compiling our code. The compilation can also include all of the typical tasks we might otherwise have to do, such as generating source maps, adding vendor prefixes, and minifying the results.

The library is easy to install—in its simplest format, we can use a configuration file to compile at the command line. Alternatively, we can use any one of several plugins to hook into a task runner, such as Gulp or Grunt. Let's take a moment to explore this in more detail, beginning with installing and configuring the plugin for use.

Installing and configuring the Pleeease library

The Pleeease library is based on Node.js; it is a cinch to install, either for use manually at the command line, or via a task runner such as Gulp. Let's make a start on getting everything set up for use:

1. We'll begin by installing the Pleeease library — for this, go ahead and fire up a Node.js command prompt session, then change the working folder to our project area.

2. At the prompt, enter `npm install -g pleeease-cli`, then press *Enter* — wait for Node to complete the installation.

At this point, the Pleeease library is installed and configured for use from the command line — if Node complains of elements that need to be updated, then it may be necessary to run `npm update -g n` to bring your version up to date. If you are a Windows user, then there is a handy PowerShell script available at `https://github.com/felixrieseberg/npm-windows-upgrade` to help with this process.

> You may get a couple of warnings about deprecated modules for `graceful-fs` and `lodash`: these can be ignored for the purposes of the demo.

Assuming we did not encounter any issues with installing Pleeease (over and above some deprecation warnings, as already mentioned), then we are now ready to use Pleeease in anger. Over the next few pages, we will take a look at compiling manually as well as using Gulp as our favored task runner. Let's begin by exploring how easy it is to perform a basic compilation at the command line using a `.pleeeaserc` file.

> For the purposes of this chapter, we will concentrate on using SASS; if your preference is to use Less, you can use the `gulp-less` plugin as an alternative. Likewise, if your desire is to use Stylus, then the `gulp-stylus` plugin will work equally well with Pleeease.

Compiling code manually

The simplest way to compile code using the Pleeease library is with a `.pleeeaserc` configuration file.

This resembles a (simplified) JSON file, and will look something like this:

```
{
  "in": ["foo.css", "bar.css"],
  "out": "baz.css",
```

```
    "browsers": ["last 3 versions", "Android 2.3"]
}
```

Looks pretty straightforward, doesn't it? We simply need to specify our source files (in), and what we should get (out). In this example, we've gone one step further, to specify the level of browser support needed—this is mainly to ensure that the right vendor prefixes have been applied.

This setting uses the same configuration as Autoprefixer: we can equally pass it a valid query from the Browserslist query list at https://github.com/ai/browserslist#queries.

This is a useful method for compiling if our requirements do not stretch to using a task runner, or we want to keep our processes simple. The only downside is that we can't tie in any other tasks that could be automated, such as renaming the compiled style sheet with a .min.css extension—for this, we will need to use a task runner such as Gulp.

If we do use a task runner, this opens up all kinds of possibilities, such as automating processes to resize images, renaming compiled style sheets, and checking our code for consistency. Before we do so, let's just cover a useful tip—the Pleeease site includes an online playground (available at http://pleeease.io/play/). We can use this to help familiarize ourselves with using the library before committing ourselves to compiling code for a production site:

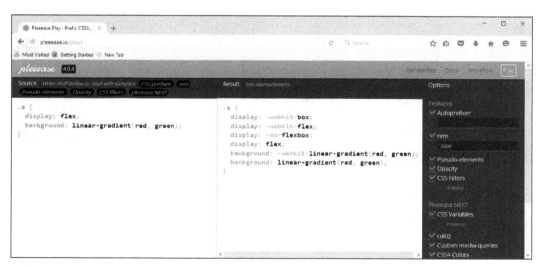

Okay, enough chitchat: it's time to get practical, so to speak! For some, compiling at the command line might be enough, but in this modern age of automation, why spend time performing manual processes that can easily be automated?

Compiling using a task runner

If you haven't already guessed by now, I'm a big fan of using Node.js — my task runner of choice is Gulp. It used to be Grunt, but there is something about Gulp that I find is easier to use — I'm not sure why! Anyway, either can be used with Pleeease, so if your preference isn't Gulp, then please feel free to alter the code accordingly.

Let's work through the steps needed to use Gulp to run our compilation process:

1. Fire up a Node.js command prompt session, then change the working folder to our project area.

2. At the prompt, enter these commands, pressing *Enter* after each:

    `npm install gulp-pleeease`

    Keep the Node.js command prompt session open — we will need it shortly.

3. Extract a copy of the T65 - using gulp-pleeease folder from the code download that accompanies this book to the root of our project area.

4. Copy the package.json and gulpfile.js files to the root of our project area, then copy example.css from the src folder under T65 - using gulp-pleeease to the src folder at the root of our project area.

5. Revert to the Node.js command prompt session, then at the prompt enter gulp and press *Enter*:

```
gulp                                                    —    □    ×

C:\wamp\www\postcss>gulp
[22:35:42] Using gulpfile C:\wamp\www\postcss\gulpfile.js
[22:35:42] Starting 'styles'...
[22:35:42] Finished 'styles' after 216 ms
[22:35:42] Starting 'rename'...
[22:35:42] Finished 'rename' after 23 ms
[22:35:42] Starting 'sourcemap'...
[22:35:42] Finished 'sourcemap' after 34 ms
[22:35:42] Starting 'default'...
[22:35:42] Finished 'default' after 59 µs
```

Assuming compilation is successful, Gulp will produce the now familiar files within the dest folder at the root of our project area. If we take a look at the results, we should see that it has minified the file, added vendor prefixes, and converted the blue and red color attributes to their equivalent HEX values.

Let's put this technique to good use and create a simple web page as an example of how we can use Pleeease. When checking our Gulp file, we will see that we don't need to use half of the plugins we've used in previous exercises, as Pleeease adds that support from within its plugin.

Building an example using Pleeease

Throughout many of the demos in this book, we've had to import a series of plugins to manage different tasks such as minifying code, or checking it for consistency.

There is nothing technically wrong with this approach, but it is inefficient—after all, why use six tools when one will suffice, so to speak? We've tried to maintain a one plugin—one job rule throughout the book, so why are we breaking with convention?

The great thing about using Pleeease is that it already contains support for some of these tasks that would otherwise require separate plugins; this means we can remove some of the plugins referenced in the Gulp task file. Pleeease is simply a layer that abstracts support for six other plugins through one common interface.

Let's put that to use in the form of compiling styles for a simple web page:

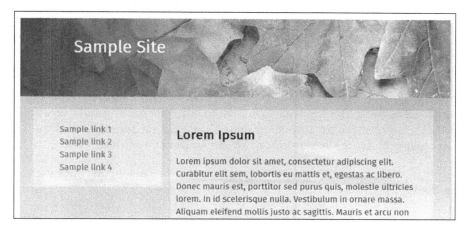

Let's make a start:

1. We'll start, as always, by extracting a copy of the `TXX - creating a page using pleeease` folder from the code download that accompanies this book; save it to the root of our project area.

2. From the `css - completed version` folder, copy the `styles - pre compile.css` file to the `src` folder at the root of our project area; rename it `styles.css`.

3. Copy the `gulpfile.js` and `package.json` files from the root of the `tutorial` folder to the root of the project area—these should replace any already present at the root of our project area.

4. Fire up a Node.js command prompt session, then change the working folder to the project area.

5. At the prompt, type `gulp` then press *Enter* — Pleeease will now go away and compile our code, and spit out valid style sheet files in the `dest` folder at the root of our project area.

6. Once completed, copy the contents of the `dest` folder to the `css` folder within the `tutorial` folder.

If we try previewing the results of our work by double-clicking on `webpage.html`, we should see a web page appear, similar to the screenshot at the start of this demo. The real proof, though, is in the Gulp task file — in comparison to other examples we've created in earlier demos, we've managed to remove one task completely, and reduce the number of plugins referenced by over half!

Compiling with other preprocessors

Yet there is one problem — so far, all of our work using Pleeease is PostCSS-based; what if we had been using a processor such as SASS as the basis for producing our code?

Unfortunately, this is where Pleeease falls down — although it does include support for SASS, Stylus, and Less, it is still very experimental. An example of where this causes an issue is in nesting; Pleeease has yet to support nesting when configured to use SASS. This reduces the appeal of using Pleeease — after all, one of the key reasons for using PostCSS is to remove any dependency on libraries such as SASS!

To get around this means using the `gulp-sass` plugin. This is a wrapper for the `libsass` library. To achieve this, we would add a task such as this to our Gulp task file:

```
20  gulp.task('sass', function () {
21    return gulp.src('src/*.scss')
22      .pipe(sass().on('error', sass.logError))
23      .pipe(gulp.dest('dest/'));
24  });
```

When using this method, we can pre-compile our SASS code to valid CSS before transforming it with PostCSS plugins. The trouble is, it seems an inefficient way to compile our code — there is a better alternative, in the form of the PreCSS library.

Using the PreCSS library

Okay…so why is it better, I hear you ask?

The simple answer to this is that we can compile SASS-like code directly without using an external library such as libsass. The distinction here, though, is that it works on SASS-*like* code, not direct SASS.

This isn't an issue though—we can easily perform a search and replace using a text editor to make the minor formatting changes required to make it compatible for PreCSS. The library source is available at `https://github.com/jonathantneal/precss`; the developer has even provided an online playground for our use, at `https://jonathantneal.github.io/precss/`, so that we can try out changes before committing to code.

At this point, we're going to break with convention—rather than produce a simple web page, let's push the boat out and use a content management system such as WordPress. Why? Well, for two reasons: WordPress already uses both PostCSS and SASS—it makes perfect sense to continue using the same tools! On this basis, let's dive in and take a look at using both in more detail.

Converting a WordPress installation

All of our existing examples have so far been based around single pages; many developers are likely to use content management systems such as WordPress.

Thankfully, we can apply many of the same principles we've used so far to styling WordPress—in fact, there are some plugins we can use that mimic SASS, which is used to create core style sheets for themes that come as part of each WordPress download. The theme we will use is Twenty Sixteen, which comes with current versions of WordPress downloaded since December 2015; it can also be downloaded from `https://wordpress.org/themes/twentysixteen/`.

For the remainder of this chapter, we're going to explore some of the tips and tricks we can use to incorporate PostCSS into a WordPress theme. A key point of note here, is that we've already covered some of the tasks that can be used—with care and planning, some can easily be reused when creating style sheets for CMS applications. We'll explore some of the tips and tricks we can use—although these will be geared towards the Twenty Sixteen theme, they can equally be used in other themes that are developed for WordPress.

> This next example does assume a certain amount of knowledge of WordPress, and ideally some of the basics around using SASS or Less — I would recommend reading around these topics if you are new to either application.

Let's get started. Our first task is to set up our environment, ready for use. Before we set up our environment, though, I would strongly recommend you have a copy of the code download for this chapter handy — much of what will be discussed will make reference to the code!

Setting up our environment

To get the best out of this chapter, we need to set up an installation of WordPress — for the uninitiated, there are two ways to achieve this:

*   We can install WordPress as a locally hosted application using a web server such as WAMPSever (`http://www.wampserver.com/en`) or Apache (`http:/www.apachefriends.org` — if you are a Linux or Mac user)
*   We can use a version of WordPress installed on our own web space online

For the purposes of this book, we will use the former — to get hold of WordPress, head over to `http://www.wordpress.org` and hit the blue **Download WordPress** button on the right side of the screen (near the top).

I will assume our version of WordPress has been installed locally under `C:\wamp\www\wordpress`, using your local web server of choice, following the instructions available at `https://codex.wordpress.org/Installing_WordPress`. My preference is to use WAMPServer (available from `http://www.wampserver.com/en`), but if you would like to use a different web server or folder, then please adjust the steps accordingly.

Okay, with WordPress installed, configured, and ready to go, let's crack on. The next step is to take a look at the options available to us for beginning the transition process.

> The steps given throughout the remainder of this chapter will be geared towards Windows, as this is the platform normally used by the author; please adjust accordingly, if you use Linux or Mac devices.

Considering the conversion process

Where does one start, when working with an average WordPress style sheet, I hear you ask?

Well, the first thing we should not do is be put off by its size. Yes, I know this might sound crazy (after all, the Twenty Sixteen theme weighs in at 3920 lines!), but with some planning, we can easily break this into something more manageable.

If we only achieve one task with PostCSS, then that task must be to make use of the `postcss-import` plugin to help break our code into more manageable principles. If you happen to have used processors such as SASS or Less, then it's the same principle—in our master `style.css`, we can create a series of import statements, and hive off each block into separate files.

Once we've broken the style sheet into more manageable chunks, there are a fair few things we can implement in our code; we should always consider it an iterative process, until such time as we exhaust all possible alternatives, the site is no longer required, or we migrate to a different solution. Over the next few pages, we'll cover some of the ideas and considerations that are likely to crop up—this should help get you started with making the changes to your theme. So without further ado, where do we start?

Well, the obvious one is using Autoprefixer; WordPress makes good use of CSS3 styles, of which a fair number still require vendor prefixes. A consideration here, though, is that as we will be working backwards from the original style sheet, we will need to strip out existing vendor prefixes and set our task runner to add these in automatically. It's a necessary evil of working with existing style sheets in WordPress, but at least we should only have to do it once! There may be a temptation to create a mixin to manage vendor prefixes, but this is not considered best practice—Autoprefixer will update styles at each compilation.

We're already familiar with using Autoprefixer from earlier examples—in the same vein, we can also consider minifying our code, which will help reduce bandwidth usage. Adding such a facility should be a cinch—we can use the same tasks from earlier demos, as long as we set the right order of tasks. We will need to alter it to compile `style.css` directly (this is the main file for WordPress style sheets), but as our processor will be geared towards using WordPress, this won't be an issue.

Another area we can look at is rem unit support, with pixel fallback. Many developers have their own views on using rem as a unit of measure; some say pixel values work just as well, but its suitability will depend on where it is being applied. This aside, Gulp has a suitable plugin we can use to help provide this functionality, if we need it.

One way to really make an impact on our code is to use nesting — this is a common technique for preprocessors such as SASS, and involves writing code in a nested format. The key benefit is to remove code that is duplicated — consider it a form of shorthand (in a manner of speaking), which will be transformed into valid CSS at compilation.

A useful technique to also look at is the use of variables; these work in much the same way as scripting or programming languages. Now before you go running for the hills, don't worry: they are easy to use. We need to provide a list of placeholder names, and the values they represent; we can then do a search and replace throughout our code for each value, and replace it with the appropriate variable. Why do this, I hear you ask? Well, it's simple: if you change a color in the future, you only need to change it in one place; PostCSS will automatically change all other instances for you at the compilation stage.

If you would like to really get stuck into the core code for WordPress, then it's always worth exploring the code repository at `https://core.trac.wordpress.org/browser/trunk/`. If you look carefully, you should even see where PostCSS is being used!

Okay, enough chitchat: let's get stuck into some code! The changes we will make as part of our next demo are just some of the ways in which we can incorporate the use of PostCSS plugins (or Gulp, for that matter), into our process. We'll begin by exploring the changes we need to make, and follow this with some ideas for you to try out as part of using PostCSS.

Making changes to our code

Although we've only covered a few ideas, there are nevertheless a fair few steps to go through; the key to this (and keeping your sanity!) is to complete each in blocks, and not all in one go.

The bulk of our changes will use existing tasks we've created in earlier demos; to this we will add the PreCSS library (from `https://github.com/jonathantneal/precss`), along with postcss-import and gulp-pixrem plugins. With this in mind, we'll make a start — our first task is to split the code into more manageable style sheets.

Splitting our style sheet

The critical part of this process is to split our style sheet—for this, we will use the `postcss-import` plugin, from `https://github.com/postcss/postcss-import`:

1. We'll start, as always, by firing up a Node.js command prompt, then changing the working folder to the root of our project area.

2. At the prompt, go ahead and enter this command, then press *Enter*:

   ```
   npm install postcss-import --save-dev
   ```

3. Wait for Gulp to complete the installation process.

Next, we need to split our style sheet into separate blocks; the most convenient way to do this is split it into sections according to the list at the top of `style.css`:

1. In the `src` folder at the root of our project area, create a new folder called `css`.

2. Go ahead and open up a copy of `style.css` from within the Twenty Sixteen folder—it's located at `C:\wamp\www\wordpress\wp-content\themes\twentysixteen\`.

3. Save this to the `src` folder at the root of our project area.

4. On or around line 53, add this line: `@import "css/variables.css";`. Don't worry for now what it will be for—this will become clear later in this chapter.

5. Find lines 54 to 252, then copy them to a new file—save this as `normalize.css` in the `css` folder within the root `src` folder.

6. In the `style.css` file within the `src` folder, add these import statements, as indicated:

```
47    *     14.3 - >= 910px
48    *     14.4 - >= 985px
49    *     14.5 - >= 1200px
50    * 15.0 - Print
51    */
52
53    @import "css/variables.css";
54    @import "css/normalize.css";
55    @import "css/genericons.css";
56    @import "css/typography.css";
57    @import "css/elements.css";
58    @import "css/forms.css";
59    @import "css/navigation.css";
60    @import "css/accessibility.css"
61    @import "css/alignments.css";
62    @import "css/clearings.css";
63    @import "css/widgets.css";
64    @import "css/content.css";
65    @import "css/media.css"
66    @import "css/multisites.css";
67    @import "css/queries.css";
68    @import "css/print.css";
69
```

7. Repeat the process until you have extracted all sections into their own files (1 to 15). Save them with the same names as each main section.

 Note, when saving the files, you *don't* need to split sections 11 to 15 into their sub-sections — keep these within their respective files.

8. We have one last step to perform: we need our Gulp task file! From the code download that accompanies this book, go ahead and extract a copy of `gulpfile.js` and `package.json` from the `T68 - converting a WordPress theme` folder, then save both to the root of our project area.

9. Take a quick look at the `gulpfile.js` file, in particular, at lines 31 to 35:

```
31    gulp.task('styles', function () {
32        return gulp.src('src/style.css')
33            .pipe(postcss([ atImport(), precss(), autoprefixer() ]))
34            .pipe(gulp.dest('dest/'));
35    });
```

Notice how we are compiling directly to `style.css`, unlike previous exercises? It's not ideal, but as WordPress themes use `style.css` by default, this is something we can live with as part of our compilation process.

Adding support for vendor prefixes

Our next task is to install support for adding vendor prefixes — in a sense, we've already covered how to achieve this. Most, if not all, of our previous demos already include support for vendor prefixes, using the Autoprefixer plugin.

As a reminder, Autoprefixer is available from `https://github.com/postcss/autoprefixer`; there is an online version we can use to test changes at `https://autoprefixer.github.io/`.

If we take a look at the Gulp task file we downloaded in the previous example, we can see the autoprefixer plugin has been called as part of firing PostCSS:

```
31    gulp.task('styles', function () {
32        return gulp.src('src/style.css')
33            .pipe(postcss([ atImport(), precss(), autoprefixer() ]))
34            .pipe(gulp.dest('dest/'));
35    });
```

There are, however, a couple of key points we should note at this stage.

When using the Autoprefixer plugin, it uses data from the Can I Use site (`http://www.caniuse.com`) to update any vendor prefixes it finds that are out of date. It is worth spending time going through your style sheet to ensure that it does not already include vendor prefixes—if it does, these need to be removed.

We can remove them manually, or a more effective route is to use the `postcss-remove-prefixes` plugin, available from `https://github.com/ohnotander/postcss-remove-prefixes`. We can add it to our Gulp task file, or run it directly from the command line. The key here is to complete the removal first, so that Autoprefixer can then be used to manage vendor prefixes.

WordPress already uses Autoprefixer to manage vendor prefixes—you can see evidence of it in the `Grunt` file at `https://core.trac.wordpress.org/browser/trunk/Gruntfile.js`. Granted, it is using Grunt, but the process is very similar for those of you using Gulp or one of the other task runners available that are compatible with PostCSS:

```
23        grunt.initConfig({
24            postcss: {
25                options: {
26                    processors: [
27                        autoprefixer({
28                            browsers: [
29                                'Android >= 2.1',
30                                'Chrome >= 21',
31                                'Edge >= 12',
32                                'Explorer >= 7',
33                                'Firefox >= 17',
34                                'Opera >= 12.1',
35                                'Safari >= 6.0'
36                            ],
37                            cascade: false
38                        })
39                    ]
40                },
```

Although setting up Autoprefixer in our Gulp task file is very easy—at least the basics—it will only be successful if we spend time removing any vendor prefixes that can then be added automatically at compilation. The `postcss-remove-prefixes` plugin will remove simple examples such as the following one, so that we are left with unprefixed versions that Autoprefixer can then update during compilation:

```
149    hr {
150        -webkit-box-sizing: content-box;
151        -moz-box-sizing: content-box;
152        box-sizing: content-box;
153    }
```

The final core task we should perform is to check our code for consistency—by now, this should be an all-too familiar task, as we've already set up a suitable task from earlier demos that can easily be reused for compiling WordPress themes. It's time to revisit this task. To ensure it works correctly, we will need to amend the settings slightly, so let's cover that now.

Checking our code for consistency

If we take a look at the Gulp task file we saved at the start of these changes, we should see this configuration object:

```
17    var stylerules = {
18        "color-no-invalid-hex": 2,
19        "declaration-colon-space-before": [2, "never"],
20        "indentation": ["tab"],
21        "number-leading-zero": [2, "always"]
22    };
```

A little further down is the task, there are two changes here: we've hardcoded the `destination` file, and the order which has been adjusted, to allow for the presence of the `pxrem` task. The indentation setting has also been changed within the configuration object—when compiled, the style sheet uses tabs for indentation.

This will throw up a host of warnings, we can either manually alter 3000+ entries, or alter how the indentation is checked. Hopefully it's a no-brainer as to which we would prefer to do, at least in the short term!

Leaving aside these two changes, the remainder of the linting task has not changed:

```
43    gulp.task('lint', ['pxrem'], function() {
44        return gulp.src("dest/style.css")
45            .pipe(postcss([ stylelint({ "rules": stylerules }),
46        reporter({ clearMessages: true })
47        ]))
48    });
```

Okay, let's change tack: there is one more core task which we should run, which is to minify our code. We've already used it in a number of demos, but let's take a moment to just revisit it within the context of compiling WordPress themes.

Minifying our code

If we had to rank the top four key tasks that could be performed using PostCSS, then this next task should definitely be at the top of that list. Minifying our code is key to conserving bandwidth usage — WordPress themes are no lightweights!

Our Gulp file already has this built in: the `package.json` file will have the appropriate reference set. If we take a look at the task file in more detail, we should see something akin to this:

```
57    gulp.task('minifyCSS', ['sourcemap'], function () {
58        return gulp.src('dest/*.min.css')
59            .pipe(nano({ autoprefixer: false }))
60            .pipe(gulp.dest("dest/"));
61    });
```

Looks familiar? It should — it's an almost direct copy of the existing task we've used from earlier demos. We've switched off `autoprefixer`, as this is being used elsewhere in our Gulp file.

Let's move on. WordPress uses SASS as its main pre-processor; we could use the Pleeease library to compile both SASS and PostCSS code, but a cleaner option is to use the PreCSS library. This abstracts support for a number of plugins that emulate SASS code (but without the SASS baggage, so to speak). Let's dive in and take a look at this in more detail.

Creating variables

One of the key features of SASS (and other processors) is the ability to use variables as placeholders for values—these are transformed into valid CSS styles at compilation.

Why use them, I hear you ask? Simple, if you decide to change a font family, or color, do you want to wade through thousands of lines of code to update any instance where it has been used? I would hope the answer is no—and quite rightly so: we have better things to do! One of those, is to install the plugin that will add variable support in the form of PreCSS.

We've already installed PreCSS from an earlier demo, so all that remains to do is to ensure it is added to our Gulp task file accordingly (it's already in ours, and in the accompanying `package.json` file):

```
31   gulp.task('styles', function () {
32       return gulp.src('src/style.css')
33           .pipe(postcss([ atImport(), precss(), autoprefixer() ]))
34           .pipe(gulp.dest('dest/'));
35   });
```

The real work comes in changing our style sheet—let's take a look at what is required:

1. First, we need to create a file to store our variables—go ahead and create a blank file in the `css` subfolder under the `src` folder at the root of our project area, and label it `variables.css`.

2. Open up the `variables.css` file. Go ahead and add these values:

```
/**
 * 0 - Variables
 */

/**
 * 0.1 - Colors
 */
$lightgray: #d1d1d1;
$almostblack: #1a1a1a;
$verydarkgray: #686868;
$white: #ffffff;
$verylightgray: #f7f7f7;
$strongblue: #007acc;
```

```
/**
 * 0.2 - Fonts
 */
$Monserrat: Montserrat, "Helvetica Neue", sans-serif;
$OpenSans: "Open Sans", sans-serif;
$Merriweather: Merriweather, Georgia, serif;
$Inconsolata: Inconsolata, monospace;

/**
 * 0.3 - Font Sizes
 */
$baseSize: 16px;
```

3. Save the file, if we take a look back at *Splitting our style sheet*, you will notice that we've already included a link to it from our master style sheet:

```
47    *        14.3 - >= 910px
48    *        14.4 - >= 985px
49    *        14.5 - >= 1200px
50    * 15.0 - Print
51    */
52
53    @import "css/variables.css";
54    @import "css/normalize.css";
55    @import "css/genericons.css";
56    @import "css/typography.css";
57    @import "css/elements.css";
58    @import "css/forms.css";
59    @import "css/navigation.css";
60    @import "css/accessibility.css"
61    @import "css/alignments.css";
62    @import "css/clearings.css";
63    @import "css/widgets.css";
64    @import "css/content.css";
65    @import "css/media.css"
66    @import "css/multisites.css";
67    @import "css/queries.css";
68    @import "css/print.css";
69
```

4. Values from this file will replace placeholders within our code, to produce valid CSS.

5. The next task is a necessary evil, we have to work our way through each style sheet to be imported, and replace existing values with the variable equivalents. This screenshot shows a part example — here, the `font-family` value has been updated, but the `border` value has yet to be changed:

```
101    /* Tag Cloud widget */
102    .tagcloud a {
103        border: 1px solid #d1d1d1;
104        border-radius: 2px;
105        display: inline-block;
106        font-family: $Monserrat;
107        line-height: 1;
108        margin: 0 0.1875em 0.4375em 0;
109        padding: 0.5625em 0.4375em 0.5em;
110    }
```

6. Once each file has been changed, then save each, ready for the next exercise.

There is no easy way to get around it, but altering WordPress theme style sheets can require lots of patience! The best way to manage it is to use your editor's search and replace function — editors such as Sublime Text 3 (the author's editor of preference) have a very useful facility to replace text in multiple files; making use of this will help reduce the manual effort required to update each file.

Adding support for rem units

This next task is one that is likely to cause debate — altering our code to use rem units, with pixel fallback added automatically.

Some developers claim that pixel values work just as well; others say that it all depends on where you need to specify a value, as to which unit of measure to use. Either way, we can use PostCSS to add pixel fall-back support automatically. The source for this plugin is available from `https://github.com/gummesson/gulp-pixrem`. Let's explore what is needed to add support for rem units:

1. Open up a Node.js command prompt session, or if the one from the previous session is still available, then revert to it.

2. Ensure that the working folder is set to the root of our project folder, then at the prompt enter this command and press *Enter*:

   `npm install gulp-pixrem --save-dev`

3. Gulp will go away and install the plugin — wait for it to complete before continuing.

4. We already have our Gulp task file in place—if we look at it in detail, we can see it being called at line 39:

```
37   gulp.task('pxrem', ['styles'], function() {
38       return gulp.src("dest/style.css")
39         .pipe(pixrem())
40         .pipe(gulp.dest('dest/'));
41   });
```

At this point, we have everything in place - the next task is to work our way through the various style sheets that we've created, and replace any instance of pixel values with rem equivalents.

This is a thankless but necessary task—the plugin works by adding pixel fallback values for any instances of rem units that it finds within our code. It is up to us to do as much or as little as we want, in terms of changing values—it is worth making some changes to ensure that the code compiles, but the remaining changes can be done over time.

When compiling the code, we will end up with code similar to this example—this extract comes from the Widgets section (section 10):

```
1426   .widget .widget-title {
1427       font-family: Montserrat,"Helvetica Neue",sans-serif;
1428       font-size: 16px;
1429       font-size: 1rem;
1430       letter-spacing: 0.046875em;
1431       line-height: 1.3125;
1432       margin: 0 0 1.75em;
1433       text-transform: uppercase;
1434   }
```

It's easy to simply convert our style sheet to use pixel fallback support—the key here is that we need to decide where we want to be using rem unit support, and where existing values such as pixels or em units would be preferable.

Moving on, there are two more tasks we can set up as part of our compilation process—how about mimicking the ability to nest styles from SASS, or creating mini loops to automate generating certain styles? Don't worry if this is not something that you're familiar with—let's dive in and see what these mean in action.

Nesting rules in our style sheet

The nesting of styles is a common feature when using processors such as SASS—if we have a bunch of styles that have very similar selectors, then it creates a degree of unwanted duplication.

We could stick with this duplication, but a more sensible option is to take the core part of the selector, then nest descendants within that block—this example is taken from the `typography.css` file:

```
50  blockquote {
51      &:before, &:after {
52          content: "";
53      }
54
55      p {
56          margin-bottom: 1.4736842105em;
57      }
58
59      cite, small {
60          color: $almostblack;
61          display: block;
62          font-size: 16px;
63          line-height: 1.75;
64      }
65
66      cite:before, small:before {
67          content: "\2014\00a0";
68      }
69
70      em, i, cite {
71          font-style: normal;
72      }
73
74      strong, b {
75          font-weight: 400;
76      }
77
78      & > :last-child {
79          margin-bottom: 0;
80      }
81  }
```

The idea is to avoid having to write the same duplicated parent styles—we can concentrate on the children instead! While the code may look longer, it is definitely easier to read; we can group together styles that have a common parent.

The technique is easy to pick up, but can be deceptively hard to get right; if you are not familiar with it, then I would recommend taking a look at my two books on SASS *SASS Essentials* and *SASS CSS How-to*, available at `https://www.packtpub.com/`.

Once compiled, the code will appear as normal CSS. There's one thing to note, though: resist the temptation to nest everything; nesting is really best kept to where you can see a real difference in the amount of code used!

Looping through styles

There is one more change we can make to our code—take a look at the `media.css` file that we created earlier in this chapter, in particular around lines 158 to the end:

```
158    @for $i from 6 to 9 {
159        .gallery-columns-$(i) .gallery-caption {
160            display: none;
161        }
162    }
```

I can already hear the next questions coming, what is that meant to be, and why are we using what looks like a programming loop in our code? In this instance, we're borrowing a principle from SASS, namely creating loops; this, coupled with string interpolation allows us to create the rules automatically.

 String interpolation is creating a placeholder in our code, which will be transformed with values at compilation.

When the code is compiled, this is how the code will look:

```
2560    .gallery-columns-6 .gallery-caption,
2561    .gallery-columns-7 .gallery-caption,
2562    .gallery-columns-8 .gallery-caption,
2563    .gallery-columns-9 .gallery-caption {
2564        display: none;
2565    }
```

It's a more advanced principle to grasp, but certainly one worth spending time getting up to speed—if applied correctly, it can save a lot of time with creating styles!

Let's change tack at this point—we've covered a number of concepts that will help get you started; there are a few more ideas that we can follow up at a later date, once the basics are in place. Let's take a moment to consider these in more detail.

Considering future possible ideas

Over the last few pages, we've covered a number of areas where PostCSS can be used to help better manage our WordPress style sheets. It's important to bear in mind that there are no hard and fast rules on what should be used, but that each style sheet will have its own requirements.

The options we've covered only scratch the surface of what is possible — for those of you who are familiar with SASS, you may well be asking why we didn't use SASS mixins, for example. The simple reason is that there is nothing stopping us from doing so: it was all about providing options that give us a quick and easy win at the conversion stage.

Let's pause for a moment and consider some other ideas that will help get you started on updating our style sheet:

- **Adding mixins**: This is the obvious choice, but one that needs planning; this will be all about creating blocks of code that can be reused at will throughout our code.

- **Color fallback**: Although not part of the PreCSS package we've been using to date, color fallback is another option to consider. The core WordPress themes use standard HEX notation; we can update it to use RGB equivalents and use a PostCSS plugin to add in HEX values. If we prefer, we can even use a plugin such as postcss-rgba-hex to convert from using RGBA colors to plain HEX — you may prefer working with the former, or have processes that require the use of the former format.

- **Font support**: How about incorporating the font-magician plugin for PostCSS? If we look at the `variables` file created earlier, it will contain a number of fonts that are not standard (at least to Windows); it means that our WordPress theme will look a little plain, to say the least! Fortunately, we can use the font-magician plugin to provide font-face support for the non-standard fonts; most, such as Inconsolata, Open Sans, and Merriweather, are available from the Font Squirrel website at `http://www.fontsquirrel.com`.

We've picked on just three ways to help extend your theme — with the use of a task runner such as Gulp, we are really only limited by the extent of what is available as plugins for Gulp. We don't have to limit ourselves to PostCSS plugins only; this will restrict what we can do, and mean that we're missing out on useful functionality. The key here is to consider what changes you want to make, and plan how and when you will make them — the process should be iterative, which will help with managing the changes!

Compiling and testing the changes

Over the last few pages, we've covered a number of key tasks that would be perfect for compiling WordPress themes.

In an ideal world, we would automate as much as possible, or at least tasks where it would make sense—to remove tasks that give little value when done manually, for example. The key, though, is to give plenty of thought as to which order these tasks should be carried out; getting the order right can be the difference between receiving a valid style sheet file ready for use, and getting…well, what can only be classed as rubbish! Yes, that might seem a little extreme, but if the task order isn't right, then you can get compiled files that break your theme.

Leaving this aside, let's take a look at compiling our code—for the purposes of this exercise, we will use a copy of the pre-edited files that are available in the code download that accompanies this book.

 Before continuing, you may like to save copies of the source files you've created in the `src` folder that sits at the root of our project area, for safe keeping.

To get a feel for what we will be discussing, this is a screenshot excerpt of the Twenty Sixteen theme in action:

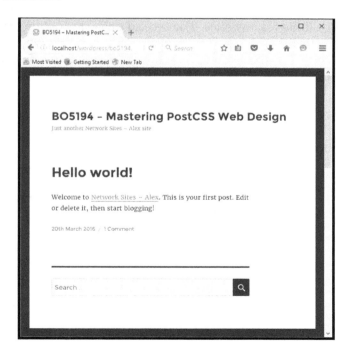

Let's make a start:

1. We'll start by downloading and extracting a copy of the `src` folder that is under `T68 - converting a WordPress theme` in the code download; save this to the root of our project area. Make sure there are *no* other files present in this folder first!

2. Next, make sure that the `gulpfile.js` and `package.json` files that we downloaded earlier are still present—we will need both during compilation.

3. Go ahead and fire up a Node.js command prompt session, then change the working folder to the root of our project area.

4. At the prompt, enter `gulp` then press *Enter*; Gulp will run through each task and spit out a compiled theme file in the `dest` folder at the root of our project area.

5. Copy this to the root of the `Twenty Sixteen` folder, which can be found at `C:\wamp\www\wordpress\wp-content\themes\twentysixteen`—if you use Linux or OSX, then please alter the path accordingly.

We now have a fully compiled style sheet! There are some points of note though—for example, the order of tasks that we covered earlier in this section doesn't match the order shown in the `gulpfile.js` file. Let's cover these points now:

- The type of tasks you include can be split into two groups—those that I would describe as core, such as minifying files or providing source maps; these can be done for any sites. The second ones are custom tasks—these will be specific for each site, and might include requests to compile variables or nested code. It's up to you to plan how these are created, so that you can reuse them for future projects.

- There is no right or wrong answer as to what should be included in a Gulp task file; the tasks you want to include, and the order they are called, will ultimately be determined by your own requirements. In our example, we used this order, from top to bottom:

Name of task	Purpose
`styles`	This compiled the raw code—merging the rules into one file, running PreCSS through the code, and updating vendor prefixes where needed.
`pxrem`	With the base code in place, we can now run through it and add pixel fallback for rem units, where appropriate.
`lint`	In this task, we're checking the compiled code for consistency.

Name of task	Purpose
`rename`	We then rename our base compiled file to have a `.min.css` extension; this is in preparation for minifying our code.
`sourcemap`	At this stage, we want to produce a source map, so this task kicks in to create a suitable map file for us.
`minifyCSS`	The final task is to minify the CSS style sheet file—it already has the right extension in place.

We've done the hard work—it's time to see the fruits of our labor in action. The style sheet is now in the `theme` folder within our WordPress installation—all that remains is to test it! We could get into using automated testing facilities such as Quixote (available from `http://www.quixote-css.com/`), but this would fall outside of the scope of this book. Instead, we can simply launch our local WordPress installation and check to see what it looks like—this is a useful way to gauge if there is anything amiss with our theme.

For our demo, we used the Twenty Sixteen theme. Out of the box, this is a very bare theme. Although this may not seem much, we've done most of the hard work needed to implement a PostCSS workflow when working with WordPress. A key measure of success is that the base theme should be identical to the original version that came with WordPress. If this is the case, it then means we can now concentrate on manipulating our style sheet over a period of time to further develop the styles within this (or any other) theme.

Summary

The success of using PostCSS will be partially determined by how well your code comes across from existing processors such as SASS—this will come from planning and taking an iterative approach to converting code. We've covered a lot of tips and ideas to help with the process, so let's take a moment to review what we've learnt.

We kicked off with a look at exploring the conversion process, and covered some of the plugins we might use to help with the process. We then moved on to covering the Pleeease library, with a look at installing and configuring it before using it in a quick demo.

Next up came a quick discussion about why Pleeease may not be as useful as we first thought; we then covered using the PreCSS library as a better alternative for transitioning to PostCSS.

We then explored using PreCSS in some depth by working through making changes to a standard theme for WordPress—we discovered some of the tips and tricks we can use to score quick wins when making the initial changes. We then rounded out the chapter with a look at compiling our code, and checking it in a standard WordPress installation to ensure it is still working as we would expect to see it operating.

Phew, we've covered a lot! With careful planning and using an iterative approach, we can transition from using processors such as SASS, and move to using PostCSS. However, sometimes our code may not work as expected—there are a few places where our code may trip up, so we'll cover them in the next chapter.

13
Troubleshooting PostCSS Issues

For many readers, PostCSS can be a little confusing—after all, it's still a relatively new library that is unlike other processors! Throughout the book, we've been on a journey of discovery—we'll finish with a look at some tips and tricks for best practice, along with some pointers for troubleshooting if we should find ourselves stuck.

Throughout the course of this chapter, we will take a look at some common issues you might experience when creating PostCSS processors. We'll see how easy it is to fix them, and discover what to do next if issues are not as easy to solve as we might have expected…

We will cover a number of topics throughout this chapter, which will include the following:

- Fixing some common issues
- Exploring some common issues in detail
- Getting help from others

Let's make a start!

Fixing some common issues

In an ideal world, any processor we build will work flawlessly, irrespective of which task runner or method we use to process each PostCSS task. Our aim is to end up with one or more successfully compiled files, as shown in this example:

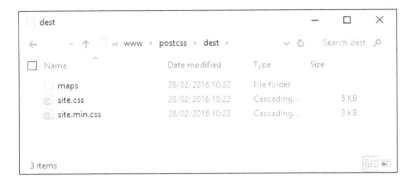

But as we all know, not everything goes well 100% of the time; if it did, we would either be exceptionally lucky, or things would begin to get mundane!

Being a pragmatist, I suspect most people will have some form of issue crop up as they get to grips with PostCSS; throughout the course of this chapter we will explore some of the more common issues, how to resolve them, and bring together some of the tips and tricks we can use to help make our lives a little easier when using PostCSS. Let's begin with a look at some of the more common issues we might face, in more detail.

Exploring some common issues

PostCSS as a processing system is easy to set up and use, but occasionally we may come across issues during development. The issues will vary, of course, but to help you along, we can explore some of the more common issues we may face during development.

For the purposes of this chapter, we will assume that the Gulp task runner has been used — you will likely see similar issues with other task runners such as Grunt or Broccoli. It's time to explore some of these issues in more detail.

Not compatible with your operating system...

The beauty of PostCSS is that we can install any one of dozens of plugins available — if we're using a task runner such as Gulp, then we can easily extend this to cover the vast array available for use.

In most instances, plugins will install without a hitch; you may find that you see this appear occasionally:

```
npm WARN optional Skipping failed optional dependency /chokidar/fsevents:
npm WARN notsup Not compatible with your operating system or architecture: fsevents@1.0.6
```

The warning message that is of most importance to us is not the ENOENT messages, but this one:

```
notsup: Not compatible with your operating system or architecture:
fsevents@1.0.6
```

It should be noted that this is only a warning, and not an error (as such) — it is caused by the use of fsevents, which is MacOSX only and will not work on Windows or Linux environments. In most cases this can be ignored, although it would be wise to test your processor to ensure it has not had any detrimental impact on your code.

[This error is not limited to fsevents — it can apply to any package, which is not supported in the environment you use.]

Task '<name of task>' is not in your gulpfile

We've created a Gulp task file with a number of tasks within, and run it to compile our style sheet. Instead of getting our processed files, we end up with this message:

```
Node.js command prompt                                        —    □    ×

C:\wamp\www\postcss>gulp
[15:48:44] Using gulpfile C:\wamp\www\postcss\gulpfile.js
[15:48:44] Task 'rename' is not in your gulpfile
[15:48:44] Please check the documentation for proper gulpfile formatti
ng

C:\wamp\www\postcss>
```

This is caused by the Gulp task not being present in the gulp file — in this declaration example, we're calling the `rename` task:

```
43    gulp.task('sourcemap', ['rename'], function () {
44        return gulp.src('dest/*.css')
45            .pipe(sourcemaps.init())
46            .pipe(sourcemaps.write('maps/'))
47            .pipe(gulp.dest("dest/"));
48    });
```

But a look through the gulp file shows that there is no `rename` task in sight:

```
gulpfile.js - Notepad                                              —  □  ×
File  Edit  Format  View  Help
'use strict';

var gulp = require('gulp');
var postcss = require('gulp-postcss');
//var autoprefixer = require('autoprefixer');
var cssnano = require('cssnano');
var sourcemaps = require('gulp-sourcemaps');
var rename = require('gulp-rename');
var stylelint = require('stylelint');
var reporter = require('postcss-reporter');
var rucksack = require('rucksack-css');


gulp.task('styles', function () {
  return gulp.src('src/*.css')
    .pipe(postcss([ rucksack({ fallbacks: true, autoprefixer: true }) ]))
    .pipe(gulp.dest('dest/'));
});

gulp.task("lint-styles", ['styles'], function() {
    return gulp.src("dest/*.css")
    .pipe(postcss([ stylelint({
        "rules": {
            "color-no-invalid-hex": 2,
            "declaration-colon-space-before": [2, "never"],
            "indentation": [2, 2],
            "number-leading-zero": [2, "always"]
        }
    }),
    reporter({
        clearMessages: true,
    })
    ]))
});

gulp.task('sourcemap', ['rename'], function () {
  return gulp.src('dest/*.css')
    .pipe(sourcemaps.init())
    .pipe(sourcemaps.write('maps/'))
    .pipe(gulp.dest("dest/"));
});

gulp.task('default', ['styles', 'lint-styles', 'rename', 'sourcemap']);

var watcher = gulp.watch('src/*.scss', ['styles', 'lint-styles', 'rename', 'sourcemap']);
watcher.on('change', function(event) {
  console.log('File ' + event.path + ' was ' + event.type + ', running tasks...');
});
```

This is a simple fix—just rename the task so that the names match, and retry the compilation. Note, though—if more than one task is incorrectly named, then the process will fail but will only show the name of the first one that is at fault. Make sure that each task name is entered correctly in the file to ensure successful compilation.

Cannot find module '<name of plugin>'

If any error is likely to catch us out, then it is this one—let me explain:

As you get to grips with installing PostCSS plugins, you will see many that use the naming convention `postcss-<name of plugin>`. It seems a sensible proposition, but beware – not every PostCSS plugin uses this naming convention!

A great example is Rucksack – one would expect to use `postcss-rucksack` (and yes, that includes me!), but we will get this error if we do:

It turns out that Rucksack is one of those examples that doesn't use the same naming convention that many people would expect it to use. Instead, it uses `rucksack-css`, as the name we would expect to use had already been taken.

This is one of those instances where it pays to read the documentation, if only to save a lot of embarrassment later:

It clearly states what name to use when installing the plugin! Yes, it happens to the best of us...

ReferenceError: <name of task> is not defined

Let us assume that we have a series of tasks in our gulp file, but for some unknown reason, we're getting this error when we compile our code:

```
C:\wamp\www\postcss>gulp
[11:47:54] Using gulpfile C:\wamp\www\postcss\gulpfile.js
[11:47:54] Starting 'styles'...
[11:47:54] 'styles' errored after 34 ms
[11:47:54] ReferenceError: rucksack is not defined
    at Gulp.<anonymous> (C:\wamp\www\postcss\gulpfile.js:33:21)
    at module.exports (C:\wamp\www\postcss\node_modules\gulp\node_modu
les\orchestrator\lib\runTask.js:34:7)
    at Gulp.Orchestrator._runTask (C:\wamp\www\postcss\node_modules\gu
lp\node_modules\orchestrator\index.js:273:3)
    at Gulp.Orchestrator._runStep (C:\wamp\www\postcss\node_modules\gu
lp\node_modules\orchestrator\index.js:214:10)
    at Gulp.Orchestrator.start (C:\wamp\www\postcss\node_modules\gulp\
node_modules\orchestrator\index.js:134:8)
    at C:\Users\alex\AppData\Roaming\npm\node_modules\gulp\bin\gulp.js
:129:20
    at nextTickCallbackWith0Args (node.js:419:9)
    at process._tickCallback (node.js:348:13)
    at Function.Module.runMain (module.js:444:11)
    at startup (node.js:136:18)
```

What could be causing it? Well, there are at least two possible causes:

- We include the plugin within the task itself, but forget to include a reference to it within the declarations at the top of our file
- We do manage to include both the plugin within the task and its associated declaration, but somehow manage not to give the same declaration name

The fix for this is to make sure that when we include the declaration at the top of the Gulp task file, that the same name is used when calling the task later in the file.

Please provide array of postcss processors!

This next error is one that can catch anyone out, but is easy to fix—as time goes by you will develop your own processor; you will likely reach a point where you start to move some of the PostCSS processor tasks out from the main PostCSS call into their own task.

Imagine that you have a PostCSS task similar to this:

```
31    gulp.task('styles', function () {
32        return gulp.src('src/*.css')
33            .pipe(postcss([ rucksack({ fallbacks: true }), autoprefixer(), shortcolor, nesting, pixrem ]))
34            .pipe(gulp.dest('dest/'));
35    });
```

There is a natural temptation to split this task into separate ones; after all, I extolled the virtues of keeping a 1:1 relationship between the task name (that is, styles), and what it does in the task! If, however, you take things a little too far, and think that you don't need to have a PostCSS processor in the task, then you may come unstuck, and land up with an error similar to this screenshot:

A quick check in your Gulp task file will likely show something akin to this:

```
31    gulp.task('styles', function () {
32        return gulp.src('src/*.css')
33            .pipe(postcss())
34            .pipe(gulp.dest('dest/'));
35    });
```

We have a `postcss` task, but without any processors within it! Although it is tempting to rework processors to ensure we maintain that 1:1 relationship, we must always leave one processor in the `postcss()` task, to ensure it operates correctly.

 You will hear talk of the term processor used in several different ways — they can equally apply as a generic term for what is our Gulp task file. It can also apply to the processor tasks that should be added to any `postcss()` task.

Entries failing to appear in the package.json file

This next error is a little trickier to catch, but the fix for it is easy — over time, you will likely make changes to your Gulp task file; this of course means that new plugins will need to be added from another `package.json` file (if already installed), or added afresh, if they haven't already been installed.

As the Gulp task file is just a plain text file, we can edit it in any text editor — my personal favorite is Sublime Text 3 (http://www.sublimetext.com/3), but any will suffice. Notepad isn't a good one, as it will fail to handle the line-endings correctly!

This aside, if we edit our `package.json` file to remove an entry, then add a new one, we might come across this warning:

```
npm WARN optional Skipping failed optional dependency /chokidar/fseven
ts:
npm WARN notsup Not compatible with your operating system or architect
ure: fsevents@1.0.8
npm WARN Failed to parse json
npm WARN Trailing comma in object at 28:3
npm WARN       }
npm WARN       ^
npm WARN File: C:\wamp\www\postcss\package.json
npm WARN enoent ENOENT: no such file or directory, open 'C:\wamp\www\p
ostcss\node_modules\cls\package.json'
```

The cause of this little gem is a really irritating one—it's amazing how one single character can cause all these warnings! The culprit is the extraneous comma at the end of a line where there *isn't* another plugin listed immediately after, as shown on line 27 in this screenshot:

```
24        "postcss-pxtorem": "^3.3.1",
25        "postcss-reporter": "^1.3.0",
26        "postcss-short-color": "^1.0.0",
27        "stylelint": "^2.3.7",
28      }
29    }
30
```

If we remove the comma and retry the installation, we will soon see that the error has disappeared.

Output of compiling results is not as expected

This final error can be deceptive—it's not strictly speaking even an error! Imagine we've created a killer processor application using Node and Gulp; it contains a number of tasks similar to the ones we created earlier, and have since used throughout this book.

We enter the relevant command and hit *Enter*. PostCSS starts the compilation: so far so good. A look in the dest folder shows this—where's our minified file and source map?

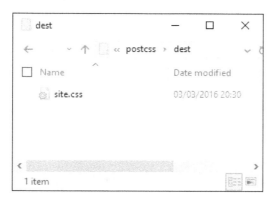

But hold on – where's the error? A check of the output from the compilation process shows no error, so what gives?

This little oddity is caused by miscalculating the order in which tasks should run— although the screenshot clearly says an error, it's not an error in the true sense. Let me explain.

The key to a successful compilation process (and by default, a working processor), lies in the need to make sure that each task we run is fired in the right order. To generate this error, I removed the constraint on our rename task in the Gulp file from the T45 - converting to use Rucksack demo, thus:

```
gulp.task('rename', function () {
  return gulp.src('dest/*.css')
    .pipe(postcss([ cssnano() ]))
    .pipe(rename('style.min.css'))
    .pipe(gulp.dest("dest/"));
});
```

The task looks perfectly acceptable, but introduces a problem—instead of just one starting task, we now have two!

The net result of this is that the styles task is run first (as it is called first in the default task from line 36). It's quickly followed by the rename task (no constraint on it), then sourcemap and lint-styles (following the constraints set against each task).

We end up with just one compiled file in the `dest` folder — the rename and styles tasks are both run at the same time; as the latter isn't completed, the former can't produce any content!

Let's move on. If all else fails, and you find problems you can't fix, then it is time to seek help....here's a quick rundown of the options available to you as a beginner to using PostCSS.

Getting help from others

At this stage, you've tried fixing an issue, but failed – you're not quite sure where to go next…

Don't worry, there are plenty of people who have been there, and needed help! A good start is the main documentation, which is available at `https://github.com/postcss/postcss/tree/master/docs`. If this draws a blank, then Google is a good option; in addition, there are a couple of other options that may help.

Logging issues at Stack Overflow

If you spend time researching Google and don't find anyone who has had this problem before, then you can try logging a question on Stack Overflow:

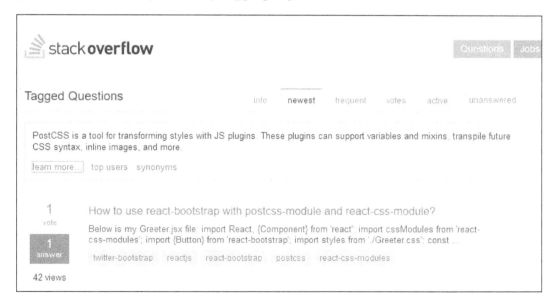

The URL is `http://stackoverflow.com/questions/tagged/postcss` — this lists all of the questions tagged with the name `postcss`, and is open to anyone to suggest a course of action or hopefully a tip that will get you back in business. If you do find yourself logging an issue, please try where possible to give details of the system you use (Windows, Mac, or Linux), any screenshots or details of the error, and the steps you were taking to arrive at the error.

Finding a bug with PostCSS

Taking things a step further, you can also log a development request, or an issue that requires a change to the code — to do this, please browse to the issues log on the GitHub site, at `https://github.com/postcss/postcss/issues`:

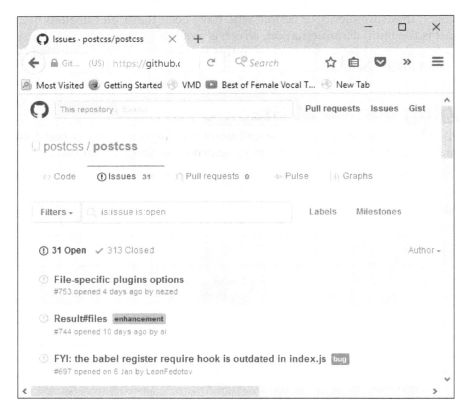

There are a few things to bear in mind:

- Don't be alarmed if you are advised to log the issue on the plugin's website, and not in GitHub for PostCSS – many issues are not as a result of a problem in PostCSS, but in the plugin itself.

- It helps to show a copy of your task runner's task file and `package.json`, just in case—some of the issues that people experience are as a result of (known or unknown) compatibility issues between plugins, or where a certain order must be followed to ensure plugins can be used.

- PostCSS plugin developers frequently develop on the Apple Mac or Linux platforms—it means that some errors you may see are as a result of using a platform that doesn't support one or more commands in the plugin.

- If you do come across problems when using one or more plugins, try to strip back your processor tasks to those that include the plugins that are causing issues. Even if this doesn't eliminate the issue, it will help narrow the cause and avoid unnecessary checks by others during the troubleshooting process.

- The license used by PostCSS is the MIT license—it effectively means that you can do as you like with the software, as long as the copyright notice remains with the library.

- It's worth noting that CodePen supports the use of PostCSS—you may find it useful to try out code online (and have it compile automatically), rather than running your processor manually. CodePen only supports a limited range of plugins, so it won't be useful for all occasions—but hopefully some!

> For more details, take a look at this blog posting on the CodePen site: `https://blog.codepen.io/2015/07/14/postcss-now-supported-on-codepen/`.

- The downside of open source software (and plugins created for PostCSS) is the varying levels of support offered by plugin developers—whilst support for the core system is very good, you may find support for individual plugins to not be quite so active! Don't rely on plugin developers to respond quickly if you have a critical issue—please log it via Stack Overflow first, before raising it on the plugin site. The latter should be used if the issue is identified to require further development.

With these in mind, good luck! PostCSS is fast gaining ground—with some big name companies using it, such as WordPress and Google, it is sure to become very popular. It would be a shame to give up on something if you come across a problem with using a plugin!

Remember, if one plugin doesn't work, then look around—others may well be available that can take their place. It's a dog eat dog world, where those plugins that are not supported are likely to fall by the wayside, leaving those where support is active and problems are resolved efficiently and promptly.

Summary

When learning a new topic, it is highly likely that we will have questions — throughout the course of this chapter, we've looked at some of the common errors you might experience, and listed solutions to help get back on track. We then explored what might happen if you have issues that can't easily be resolved with help from other developers.

Okay, let's move on: we've covered a lot of ground throughout the book, so it's time to look forward and see what CSS may bring. The great thing about PostCSS is that plugins already exist that allow us to use tomorrow's features today — we'll cover this and more in the next chapter.

14
Preparing for the Future

Mastering CSS is an essential skill—the technology is continually evolving, so in order to succeed, we must keep abreast of changes. PostCSS is a great tool that allows us to not only use CSS rules of today, but work with rules of the future. In this chapter, we'll take a look at some of the CSS syntax that makes up what is frequently referred to as CSS4, and how we can provide equivalent support using current CSS3 classes.

We will cover a number of topics throughout this chapter, which will include the following:

- Understanding some of the risks of supporting future CSS standards today
- Exploring using `cssnext` to provide support for future CSS syntax
- Working with some of the existing plugins to convert CSS4 standards into current CSS3 code
- Examining how we can change existing plugins to add more support for new CSS4 selectors

Let's make a start!

Supporting CSS4 styles today

Style sheets have been in existence for over 35 years, with the original version of what we now know as CSS dating from the days of SGML in the 1980s.

We have come a long way since the original CSS standard was released in 1996—over the last few years, the standard for CSS4 has been developed, with new features such as `:not` or `:matches` pseudo-classes to better target elements, custom properties (or variables), and location-based links, such as `local-link`. Over the course of the next few pages, we're going to explore a few of these CSS4 features, and see how we can introduce support for them using current CSS3 equivalent code.

There is one small thing that we need to clear up first — CSS4...does not exist. What? I hear you say. Surely it must, I've seen plenty online about it! Yes, it is true: CSS4 as a standard does exist, but *not as a single unique entity*. Let me explain.

Previous iterations of CSS have been based around creating a single global standard, irrespective of how browser manufacturers decide to support elements that make up standard. It's for this reason that we had to rely heavily on vendor prefixes for some years, we still do, but most vendors have since removed prefixes from many of the more common attributes such as `border-radius` or `box-shadow`.

The key difference here, though, is that a decision was taken to deliver CSS4 as a series of modules — CSS as a standard has become very heavy, with the resulting increase in time required for development becoming unsustainable. This is why we will see talk of CSS Modules, such as Custom Properties or Selectors — these can evolve as independent standards to a point that we may no longer refer to CSS as version X, but just CSS.

 Any reference to CSS4 within this chapter is purely to identify next generation styles we can implement using PostCSS plugins and CSS3 current standards.

Okay, this aside, it's time to get stuck in: PostCSS offers good support for some of the more common elements of we collectively call CSS4. Let's take a look to see what is available.

Converting CSS4 styles for use

The idea behind basing CSS4 around a series of modules was aimed at making it easier (and ultimately quicker) to update each standard; it does mean that modules will be in a state of flux, at least for the time being!

This said, there are some clear styles we can recreate using current CSS3 styles — one such example is CSS4 Selectors. Even though it is still in draft at the time of writing, a PostCSS plugin is available in the form of `postcss-selector-not` (from `https://github.com/postcss/postcss-selector-not`). A sister style that is also available as a PostCSS plugin is `postcss-selector-matches` (available from `https://github.com/postcss/postcss-selector-matches`) — these two are intended to replicate the `:not` negation and `:matches` pseudo-selectors that are coming as part of the new CSS4 standard.

For more information on individual CSS4 selectors, take a look at the full list available at `http://css4-selectors.com/selectors/`. This will also give you an indication of available browser support—this list will be updated with changes as selectors are ratified for use.

Looking further afield, there are a small handful of plugins that provide support for upcoming CSS4 standards—in addition to the `:matches` and `:not` plugins, we can use any of the following:

Name of plugin	Purpose of plugin
`mq4-hover-shim`	Currently in beta, this plugin provides limited support for the Media Queries Level 4 hover media feature—it is available from `https://github.com/twbs/mq4-hover-shim`.
`host`	Working with the Shadow DOM? If you need to make `:host` selectors work properly with pseudo-classes, then this plugin is for you—the source is available at `https://github.com/vitkarpov/postcss-host`.
`pseudo-class-any-link`	How many times have you had to add pseudo-selectors such as `:link` or `:visited` to your code? This PostCSS plugin fixes that—we can now use the proposed `:any-link` pseudo-class in CSS. Head over to `https://github.com/jonathantneal/postcss-pseudo-class-any-link` for more details.
`postcss-initial`	The PostCSS Initial plugin resets a specified property's value to what it was initially set in code (and not by the browser). For more details, head over to `https://github.com/maximkoretskiy/postcss-initial`.
`font-variant`	This plugin transforms `font-variant` settings to the equivalent `font-feature-settings value`—it is designed for special cases, when it is not possible to reproduce using normal means, for example, a slashed zero to differentiate between a 0 and an O—the former equates to zero. The source for the plugin is available at `https://github.com/postcss/postcss-font-variant`.
`postcss-input-range`	This plugin allows us to style input range elements. We need to provide unprefixed CSS styles, and the plugin will automatically handle support for all of the various prefixes required to allow this element to be styled across different browsers. The source for this plugin can be downloaded from `https://github.com/jonathantneal/postcss-input-range`.

Okay, let's move on: I feel a demo coming! Let's take a look at using the `postcss-selector-matches` property, to see how we can use it in action.

Validating e-mail addresses

How many times have you come across e-mail submissions from your site, where you aren't 100% sure your visitors have left a valid e-mail address?

If we leave aside exact numbers, it goes without saying that any requests submitted from any website must have a valid e-mail address; with the plethora of top level domains that are now available, it's even more critical that they be valid!

To help with this, we can use the `:invalid` and `:valid` attributes to style `<input>` fields — whilst they may not be able to tell if `.design` is a valid TLD (and yes, it is), they can at least cope with the basics of ensuring that you have a TLD present, an @ symbol, and the name of a recipient.

> You can perform a test in your browser to gauge support for these and other CSS4 selectors — check out the CSS4 Selectors site, at `http://css4-selectors.com/`.

Let's knock up a simple example using the `postcss-selectors-matches` plugin for PostCSS, to see how we can style such fields:

1. We'll start as always by firing up a Node.js command prompt session, then changing the working folder to our project area.

2. At the prompt, go ahead and enter this command, then press *Enter*:

   ```
   npm install postcss-selector-matches --save-dev
   ```

   Keep the window open, we will need it shortly. If all is well, we should see this appear:

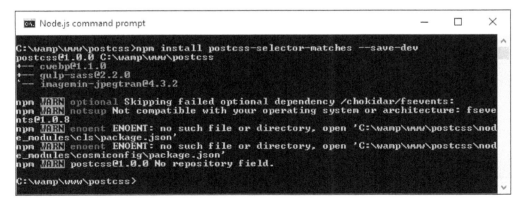

3. Next, extract a copy of the `T69 - matches pseudo-selector` folder from the code download that accompanies this book, and save it to the root of our project area.

4. Copy `matches - pre-compile.css` from the `css`—completed version folder within `T69 - matches pseudo-selector`, and save it to the `src` folder at the root of our project area.

5. Copy the `gulpfile.js` and `package.json` files from the `T69 - matches pseudo-selector` folder to the root of our project area, and rename it `matches.css`

6. Revert to the Node.js command prompt session from earlier, then at the prompt enter `gulp` and press *Enter*.

7. If all is well, PostCSS will go away and compile our code into valid CSS—we should see the now familiar files appear in the `dest` folder.

8. Copy the contents of this `dest` folder to the `css` folder underneath `T69 - matches pseudo-selector`, then try previewing the `matches.html` file in a browser. If all is well, we should see something akin to this:

It's a simple demo, and yes, somewhat contrived. At this level, it wouldn't be necessary to use `:matches`, as it ends up generating more code than is necessary! But it does show how easy it is to apply the technique, and have it provide valid CSS, as in the case of our example:

```
1   :valid, :invalid {
2       border: 2px solid;
3   }
4
5   :valid {
6       border-color: green;
7   }
8
9   :invalid {
10      border-color: red;
11  }
```

Okay, let's change tack: we will stay with the range theme for our next demo, but this time look at a more stylish example, where we can really go to town on transforming the appearance of our selected element.

The range input element is one that has been traditionally hard to style, more often than not, we may end up resorting to using jQuery UI to change its appearance! Not so with CSS4—we can use a series of new CSS attributes to apply styles, without the use of any additional libraries. Let's take a look at this in more detail.

Supporting the new range input

A quick question, how many times have you had to create a site where you needed to choose a value, say from 1 to 100? Or pick a specific opacity of color, from almost transparent to completely opaque?

Okay, perhaps they're an odd couple of questions to ask, but the eagle-eyed should spot that I am of course referring to using sliders, which we can adjust to select a specific value. There are different ways to add these to a page, but which in the main will require some help to style, perhaps the most recognizable tool being jQuery UI!

This is fine if we need to use jQuery UI in our pages to provide other functionality, but what if we only needed it for the slider? It's a bit of overkill—thankfully, we can fix that with the use of the `postcss-input-range` plugin, available from `https://github.com/jonathantneal/postcss-input-range`. It's time for that demo, so let's knock up a quick example of how one can be styled to represent a progress bar:

1. We'll start by installing the `postcss-input-range` plugin, for this, go ahead and fire up a Node.js command prompt, then change the working folder to our project area.

2. At the prompt, enter the following command, then press *Enter*:

   ```
   npm install postcss-input-range --save-dev
   ```

   If all is well, we should see something akin to this screenshot:

```
Node.js command prompt                                    —    □    ×

Your environment has been set up for using Node.js 4.3.2 (x64) and npm.

C:\Users\alex>cd \wamp\www\postcss

C:\wamp\www\postcss>npm install postcss-input-range --save-dev
postcss@1.0.0 C:\wamp\www\postcss
+-- cwebp@1.1.0
+-- gulp-sass@2.2.0
+-- imagemin-jpegtran@4.3.2
`-- postcss-input-range@2.0.0

npm WARN optional Skipping failed optional dependency /chokidar/fsevents:
npm WARN notsup Not compatible with your operating system or architecture: fseve
nts@1.0.8
npm WARN enoent ENOENT: no such file or directory, open 'C:\wamp\www\postcss\nod
e_modules\cls\package.json'
npm WARN enoent ENOENT: no such file or directory, open 'C:\wamp\www\postcss\nod
e_modules\cosmiconfig\package.json'
npm WARN postcss@1.0.0 No repository field.

C:\wamp\www\postcss>
```

3. Next, extract a copy of the `T70 - using range input` folder from the code download that accompanies this book. Go ahead and save it in our project area.

4. In the `css` folder of `T70 - using range input`, copy the `range - precompile.css` file to the `src` folder of our project area, and rename it `range.css`.

5. Copy the `gulpfile.js` and `package.json` files from the `T70 - using range input` folder to the root of our project area.

6. Revert to the Node.js command prompt window, then at the prompt enter `gulp` and press *Enter*.

7. Gulp will now run our compilation process, if all is well, we should see the now familiar style sheet files appear in the `dest` folder, along with a map file in the maps subfolder. Copy these to the `css` folder under `T70 - using range input`.

8. If all is well, we should see something akin to this screenshot when previewing the results in a browser:

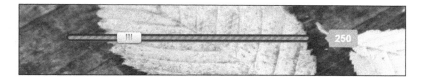

There is nothing complicated in this demo, even though we've only scratched the surface of what is possible when styling the range element—for example, we can add datalists to define certain values to scroll through, such as specific times of the day.

Browser support is still limited, but for an idea of what is possible, check out `http://demo.agektmr.com/datalist/`; the CSS guru Chris Coyier also has a couple of articles on the use of range inputs on his site at `http://www.css-tricks.com`.

The real magic in our demo appears when we take a look at the compiled code—one of the key elements for styling a range input is the `range-thumb` attribute, which is the knob we use to select a value on the slider. Here are two examples of how our code now looks, with support added for Firefox:

```
37   ::-moz-range-thumb {
38     width: 2.5em;
39     height: 1.125em;
40     border-radius: 0.25em;
41     box-shadow: 0 1px .125em #000;
```

This has support for Internet Explorer (which has been superseded by Edge):

```
52    ::-ms-thumb {
53        width: 2.5em;
54        height: 1.125em;
55        border-radius: 0.25em;
56        box-shadow: 0 1px .125em #000;
```

When using this plugin, we don't have to worry about adding vendor prefixes—our original code contains just the unprefixed versions; the relevant prefixes will be added at compilation, until such time as they are no longer needed for styling our input element.

 If you would like help with styling the new range input element, then check out http://danielstern.ca/range.css/—it's a useful tool!

Over the course of the last two demos, we've briefly scratched the surface of what is possible when using PostCSS—we've used the same format of Gulp task file to incorporate support for each plugin, which when run, has produced the requisite CSS style sheet for each demo. Nothing outrageous here, right? After all, it's followed the same principles we covered earlier, such as one plugin for one task…or can we do better?

Yes, by now you should know that I always like to go one better if I can. Remember how I said it is preferable to create tasks in our runner that worked on a one-to-one basis? Was each task in our (Gulp) file related to a specific plugin? Well, as someone once said, rules are meant to be broken—it's time to throw out the rulebook, and consider a different approach, at least for future syntax…

Supporting future syntax with cssnext

A key part of supporting CSS4 is the constant state of flux that we must deal with, until such time as modules have been standardized. If we maintained our current approach, it would entail constant updates of any plugins we decided to use that relate to CSS4 attributes—this is clearly not sustainable!

Instead, we can use a single plugin pack, in this case `cssnext`, to manage support for a range of new features. The beauty, though, is that all of the features are enabled by default, and will only kick in when needed in the code. There will of course come a time when new features are supported natively, at this point, we can simply discard the compilation process without impacting the final result.

It's worth taking the time to get to know `cssnext` — let's dive in and take a look in more detail.

Creating a site template with cssnext

The `cssnext` plugin is one of those exceptions to our guideline of one plugin per task; we call it using the plugin name, but in reality, it will perform a number of transformations at the same time.

The plugin is available from `http://cssnext.io/`. It is worth noting that an older version exists; we're using the newer version in this demo. The `cssnext` plugin was originally a complete system in its own right, before PostCSS became as popular as it is now.

The plugin contained options which didn't really belong to a plugin focused on the future of CSS, so the developers rewrote it to make `cssnext` simpler. At the same time, it was designed to be integrated into PostCSS, where we can use it at the same time as other plugins within our processor.

 The plugin even has its own playground, which we can use to test if changes will produce the desired effect — check it out at `http://cssnext.io/playground/`.

Let's explore this plugin in more detail — we'll begin by installing it, before setting up code for our next demo.

Setting up our demo

For this next demo, we're going to set up a basic template that can be used for a site — it's not going to win any awards for style, but the aim here is to explore how easy it is to make the changes, not become top billing at the next awards ceremony! Let's dive in and take a look at what we need to do:

1. We'll start by firing up a Node.js command prompt session then changing the working folder to the root of our project area.

2. At the prompt, enter this command, then press *Enter*:

   ```
   npm install postcss-cssnext --save-dev
   ```

If all is well, we should see something akin to this screenshot:

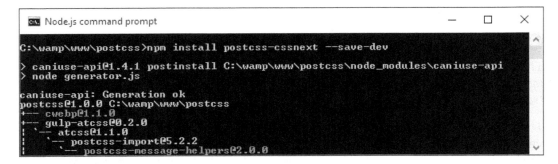

3. Next, go ahead and extract a copy of the T71 - working with cssnext folder from the code download that accompanies this book – save it to the root of our project area.

4. From the T71 - working with cssnext folder, save copies of the *styles.css* file to the src folder at the root of our project area, then package.json and gulpfile.js to the root of our project area.

5. Revert to the prompt we had open, then enter gulp and press Enter.

6. Gulp will go away and compile our file, when it has completed, we will see the now familiar files appear in the dest folder at the root of our project area.

7. Copy the contents of the dest folder at the root of our project area to the css folder within T71 - working with cssnext folder at the root of our project area.

8. Go ahead and preview sitepage.html from within the T71 - working with cssnext folder in a browser – if all is well, we should see something akin to this screenshot:

We've now seen the template for our site — there are several places where we have made changes to take advantage of the power of `cssnext`. For this, go ahead and open up a copy of the file `stylescss` from within the `css` folder of `T71 - working with cssnext` folder that we saved to our project area — let's explore what changes have been made:

- **Autoprefixer**: The plugin covers support for providing vendor prefixes for any future styles; any in the base file have been removed, and will be added during compilation.

- **Media query ranges / custom queries**: Instead of using the existing format, which isn't always clear, we can begin to use `>=` or `<=` to better express the range that we're applying as part of our query. At the same time, we can use a custom query to define preset ranges at the top of our file, which can be used throughout the style sheet.

- **Nesting**: Fans of existing preprocessors such as SASS or Less will be familiar with the nesting principle; put simply, this allows us to nest styles inside each other. We can then adjust the selectors used for these rules, so that when compiled, each rule is transformed into valid CSS.

- **Custom selectors**: Staying with the preprocessor theme, we can create custom values at the top of our code, and apply them as appropriate throughout.

- **#rrggbbaa colors**: Traditionally, hex colors have been expressed as either three or six digit values; using `cssnext`, we can expand them to either four or eight digit values. The `cssnext` plugin will transpile them into standard RGBA values, with equivalent HEX values provided as a fallback mechanism.

- **rem units**: Traditionally, developers have used pixel values to apply sizes to elements or fonts. Pixel values don't respect user settings in a browser, so may not resize as expected. To work around this, `em` units were introduced; the math behind calculating `em` values was simplified with the introduction of rem units. Today, some developers argue that pixel values should reign supreme; the `cssnext` plugin provides both pixel and rem units, which can be used where supported by browsers.

At first thought, you might expect to have to include a number of plugins, or a detailed configuration object; not so! Instead, all we need in our Gulp task file is this:

```
27   gulp.task('styles', function () {
28     return gulp.src('src/*.css')
29       .pipe(postcss([ cssnext() ]))
30       .pipe(gulp.dest('dest/'));
31   });
```

I've always been a keen fan of keeping things simple—the `cssnext` plugin is a perfect example! Whilst we may need to update the plugin regularly to keep abreast of changes, we don't need to change our Gulp file.

The plugin will simply transform those styles it finds that are supported by the plugin, and leave alone any not covered by the plugin. The beauty of this is that we can either let it run as is, or if we want disable functionality that is no longer needed, then we simply disable it within the configuration object:

```
cssnext(input, {
    features: { customProperties: false }
})
```

To prove that the changes we made work, we've turned our (non-responsive) template from this:

...to this view, where our content clearly fits the smaller screen better:

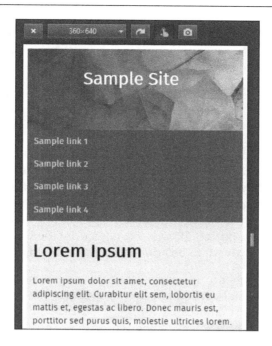

Even though it's only a small part of the changes made, is directly responsible for making our template responsive, it goes to show that incorporating `cssnext` into our processes is easier than you might think!

Okay, let's move on: we're going to take a look at a couple more plugins, but with a twist. We'll first look at using a plugin to provide support for a new color being introduced as part of CSS4, before using it as a basis for fixing a keyword issue that should have been fixed a long time ago!

Creating plugins to provide extra CSS4 support

Throughout the course of this chapter, we've covered a number of plugins that handle support for the upcoming CSS4 standards, and explored how we can use the `cssnext` plugin pack to manage the transition to using these new styles.

There is more out there that we can do—the great thing about PostCSS is that we can absolutely write our own plugins to help bolster support for CSS4 attributes. To help prove this, over the next few pages we'll work our way through fixing some issues in CSS, and altering an existing CSS4 color plugin to add support for a different color; we'll start with adding a little color to our next demo, if you pardon the pun!

Adding future color support to CSS

"She made it to six. For almost twelve hours, she was six..."

There is something of a poignant twist to this next demo—the color `rebeccapurple`, which forms the basis for this next exercise, came about as a tribute to Eric Meyer's daughter, Rebecca, who passed away on her sixth birthday in June 2014, due to cancer.

As anyone who spends any time developing CSS styles will know, Eric has been a major advocate of web standards, and in particular CSS—it is often said that one would be hard pushed not to read a book about CSS during their development that had not been written by Eric! The community proposed the addition of `rebeccapurple` as a color in Rebecca's memory (it was her favorite color), and in recognition of Eric's contribution. It was announced by the CSS Working Group that the change had been approved, to be added as part of the upcoming CSS4 standard.

To help support the change for browsers that have not yet caught up, the developer Maxime Thirouin created a PostCSS plugin to transform the `rebeccapurple` color to the more compatible format of `rgb(102, 51, 153)`—the source for this plugin is available at `https://github.com/postcss/postcss-color-rebeccapurple`.

Let's take a look at the plugin in more detail:

1. We'll start by installing the `postcss-color-rebeccapurple` plugin, so go ahead and fire up a Node.js command prompt, and change the working folder to our project root.

2. At the prompt, go ahead and enter the following command:

   ```
   npm install postcss-color-rebeccapurple –save-dev
   ```

   Then press *Enter*—if all is well, we should see something akin to this screenshot:

```
Node.js command prompt                                    —    □    ×

C:\wamp\www\postcss>npm install postcss-color-rebeccapurple --save-dev
postcss@1.0.0 C:\wamp\www\postcss
+-- cwebp@1.1.0
+-- gulp-sass@2.2.0
`-- imagemin-jpegtran@4.3.2

npm WARN optional Skipping failed optional dependency /chokidar/fsevents:
npm WARN notsup Not compatible with your operating system or architecture: fseve
nts@1.0.8
npm WARN enoent ENOENT: no such file or directory, open 'C:\wamp\www\postcss\nod
e_modules\cls\package.json'
npm WARN enoent ENOENT: no such file or directory, open 'C:\wamp\www\postcss\nod
e_modules\cosmiconfig\package.json'
npm WARN postcss@1.0.0 No repository field.

C:\wamp\www\postcss>_
```

Keep the window open—we'll need it shortly.

3. Next, go ahead and extract a copy of the T72 - adding rebeccapurple color folder from the code download that accompanies this book—save the folder to the root of our project area.

4. Copy the styles - pre-compile.css from within the T72 - adding rebeccapurple color folder to the root src folder of our project area, and rename as styles.css

5. Copy the gulpfile.js and package.json files from the T72 - adding rebeccapurple color folder to the root of our project area.

6. Revert to the Node.js command prompt session, then enter gulp at the prompt and press *Enter*.

7. When compilation has finished, copy the contents of the dest folder from the root of our project area to the css folder under T72 - adding rebeccapurple color.

8. Try previewing the results—if all is well, we should see this simple box, which has been backfilled with the color rebeccapurple:

To prove it works, have a look at the .css file from within the css folder under T72 - adding rebeccapurple color—we should see the compiled RGB value within:

```
styles.css                           ✕

1   #box {
2       background-color: rgb(102, 51, 153);
3       height: 10rem;
4       width: 10rem;
5       margin: 3rem;
6       padding: 1rem;
7       color: #fff;
8       font: 1.4rem Arial, sans-serif;
9       box-shadow: 5px 5px 6px 0px rgba(192,192,192,1);
10  }
```

We can also validate this with a quick check using a site such as *ColorHexa.com*—check out `http://www.colorhexa.com/663399`; searching for `rebecca purple` will show the same page.

There is a perfect opportunity here—I believe that there is always something good that can come from something tragic. Leaving aside the *raison d'être* for this plugin, we can use it as a basis for adding support for additional colors from the CSS4 Color Module standard.

The changes we need to make are relatively straightforward, and can easily form the basis for a new plugin. Let's take a look at what's involved; for this demo we will use `burlywood`, which is a light shade of brown:

1. We'll start by editing our CSS file—open up `styles.css` in the `src` folder under the root of our project area and change the highlighted line as indicated:

   ```
   #box {
      background-color: burlywood;
      height: 10rem;
   ```

2. Next, we need to update the `rebeccapurple` plugin file to change existing color references to use the new color—we'll start with the initial declaration:

   ```
   var postcss = require("postcss")
   var color = require("color")("burlywood").rgbString()
   ```

 The plugin `index.js` file can be found within the `node_modules\ postcss-color-rebeccapurple\` folder.

3. We then need to change the check made in the code that changes each instance of the color:

   ```
   if (value && value.indexOf("burlywood") !== -1) {
      decl.value = value.replace(/(burlywood)\b/gi, color)
   }
   })
   ```

4. For now, go ahead and save the file—yes, the plugin name doesn't represent the color, but this is only a test, so it won't matter.

5. Fire up a Node.js command prompt, then change the working folder to our project area. At the prompt, enter `gulp` then press *Enter*.

6. Copy the contents of the root `dest` folder to the `css` folder in the `T73 - adding support for new color` folder.

7. Run `testpage.html` — if all is well, we can see the compiled RGB value within, as before:

```
 1    #box {
 2        background-color: rgb(222, 184, 135);
 3        height: 10rem;
 4        width: 10rem;
 5        margin: 3rem;
 6        padding: 1rem;
 7        color: #fff;
 8        font: 1.4rem Arial, sans-serif;
 9        box-shadow: 5px 5px 6px 0px rgba(192,192,192,1);
10    }
```

8. Try re-running the `testpage.html` file from within the `T73 - adding support for new color` folder; we should see the change in color (and yes, it's definitely not purple!):

We can verify that the color displayed is indeed `burleywood`, using the same principle as before. This time check out `http://www.colorhexa.com/deb887`, which clearly shows the HEX and RGB values:

#deb887 Color Conversion

The hexadecimal color #deb887 has RGB values of R:222, G:184, B:135 and decimal value is 14596231.

Hex triplet	deb887		CIE-LAB
RGB Decimal	222, 184, 135		XYZ

All that remains for you now is to convert this into a plugin. This should be easy to do: try taking a copy of the existing `rebeccapurple` plugin, then performing a search and replace with the color of your choice. It's not perfect, but will give you a head start — the next part will be to use what we learnt back in *Chapter 8, Creating PostCSS Plugins*, to turn it into a fully-fledged plugin available in the NPM repository.

To get a list of the CSS4 Module colors, have a look on Google—there are plenty of links; try this as a start: `https://github.com/segundofdez/css4-colors/blob/master/less/colors.less`.

Okay, time to change focus: although this chapter is meant to be about looking forward, we're going to change direction and look backwards for a moment.

The reason for this? A number of mistakes in the design of CSS have been acknowledged by the CSS Working Group. A PostCSS plugin by Jonathan Neal provides a short-term fix for a number of these issues—some which could well be fixed properly in a future version of CSS!

Going back in time

When developing code, I'm a great fan of only developing for modern browsers as a rule—ideally *n-1*, or current plus one previous version. In the main, this isn't an issue for the likes of Firefox or Chrome, but it's a different story for IE. Where possible, older versions of IE will very likely be left by the wayside…but that's another story!

The one exception we can make though is not around browser support, but trying to correct some issues with attribute naming. The CSS Working Group have acknowledged that some of the attribute names weren't defined correctly when they were released—you can see a complete list at `https://wiki.csswg.org/ideas/mistakes`, which is regularly updated.

To help with this, and as a precursor to the second demo in this section, we're going to install the Time Machine plugin for PostCSS (hence the title of this section!). This provides a short-term fix for some of the bugs in CSS. We will then use this as inspiration to design a quick and dirty plugin to fix another bug that is listed on the CSSWG site, but which is not fixed by the Time Machine plugin.

The source for this plugin is available from `https://github.com/jonathantneal/postcss-time-machine`.

For this demo, we will reuse the simple demo created to display the `rebeccapurple` color from *Adding future color support to CSS*. The compiled results from that demo use an RGBA function—the CSSWG have stated that RGBA should not exist, and instead the alpha channel should have been added as the fourth channel for the `RGB()` function. We'll fix that as part of our demo—the plugin will allow us to write what was intended, whilst compiling it to code that can be understood by any browser.

Let's make a start on installing the plugin for use in our demo:

1. We'll start by installing the plugin, so go ahead and fire up a Node.js command prompt session, then change the working folder to our project area.

2. At the prompt, enter this command and press *Enter*:

   ```
   npm install postcss-time-machine --save-dev
   ```

   If all is well, we should see something akin to this screenshot — keep the session open, as we will need it shortly:

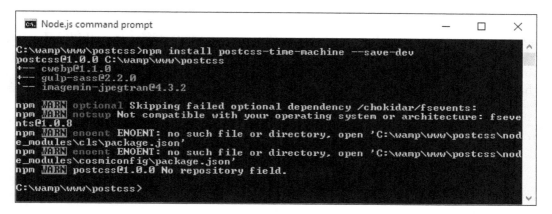

3. Next, go ahead and extract a copy of the T74 - going back in time folder from the code download that accompanies this book — save the folder to the root of our project area.

4. Copy the styles - pre-compile.css from within the T74 - going back in time folder to the root src folder of our project area, and rename it styles.css.

5. Copy the gulpfile.js and package.json files from the same T74 - going back in time folder to the root folder of our project area.

6. Revert to the Node.js command prompt, then at the prompt, enter gulp and press *Enter*.

7. If all is well, we should see our usual compiled files appear in the dest folder — copy these to the css folder under T74 - going back in time.

At this point, try previewing the results of our demo, if all is well, we should see the same box as before, but this time with a slightly lighter shade of rebecca purple as its color:

This is a box colored rebecca purple

If we take a look at the CSS styles though, the keen-eyed may spot something — how come we're using 194 as our alpha value, yet the code shows 0.8? The answer is simple: this plugin was designed to use 0 to 255 for each value, including the alpha channel. Simply divide 194 by 255:

```
1    #box {
2        background-color: rgb(102, 51, 153, 194);
3        height: 10rem;
4        width: 10rem;
```

The answer is 0.8. Okay, you will actually get something like 0.76078, but if we round up to one decimal place, this will become 0.8:

```
1    * {
2        box-sizing: border-box;
3    }
4    #box {
5        background-color: rgba(102, 51, 153, 0.8);
6        height: 10rem;
```

Now, before we continue, there is something we should consider: the practical application of this plugin. It's not meant to pour cold water on a nice idea, but adoption may take a little time — developers in a team will be used to writing styles that include functions such as rgba(), background-blend-mode, or hsla(), so it may take some time to change the mindset!

This said, it is a useful fix if we want to adhere to the intended standards, and can manage the change of mindset to not type function names that we may have been doing for some time. We can even take things a step further and create our own plugin — Time Machine doesn't include fixes for all of the attributes, so let's take a look at creating one to manage the bug that surrounds the background-blend-mode attribute in CSS.

Creating our own plugin

One of the attributes not fixed by the Time Machine plugin is the `background-blend-mode` function — this is normally used to calculate the final color pixel when layers overlap each other.

The bug that was introduced relates to the name — the **CSS Working Group (CSSWG)** have acknowledged that all blend-mode variants should be written without -mode in the name, so that in our case, background-blend-mode would be written as `background-blend`.

It's an easy fix to make, here's a perfect opportunity for you to try creating your own plugin! We're going to take a different route at this point — time for some audience participation, so to speak!

To help you along the way, it's worth taking another look at *Chapter 8, Creating PostCSS Plugins*; when creating the plugin, we can use this code:

```
var postcss = require('postcss');

module.exports = postcss.plugin('backgroundblend', function
backgroundblend(options) {
  return function (css) {
    options = options || {};

    // Processing code will be added here
    css.eachDecl('background-blend', function (decl) {
      if (decl.prop.indexOf('background-blend') !== -1) {
        decl.prop = 'background-blend-mode';
      }
    });
  };
});
```

Most of this code is boilerplate, but the key to making this work is this excerpt:

```
css.eachDecl('background-blend', function (decl) {
  if (decl.prop.indexOf('background-blend') !== -1) {
    decl.prop = 'background-blend-mode';
  }
});
```

In a nutshell, we parse each CSS rule in turn — if any contain background-blend, we simply replace each instance with background-blend-mode.

To prove it works, we can use the following code to test if our plugin works:

```
<!DOCType html>
<head>
  <meta charset="utf-8">
  <title>Demo: Creating new plugin to change blend-mode</title>
  <link rel="stylesheet" type="text/css" href="css/styles.css">
</head>
<body>
  <div id="div"></div>
</body>
</html>
```

If all is well, we should get something akin to this screenshot:

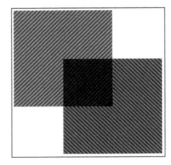

If you get stuck, then a completed version is available in the code download that accompanies this book; a quick peek in the `T75 - back in time change` folder for `styles - pre-compile.css` will show this:

```
1  #div {
2      width: 300px;
3      height: 300px;
4      background: url('../img/br.png'),
5                  url('../img/tr.png');
6      background-blend: multiply;
7  }
```

When compiled, we can clearly see it shows the version we will be used to seeing:

```
1  #div {
2      width: 300px;
3      height: 300px;
4      background: url('../img/br.png'),
5                  url('../img/tr.png');
6      background-blend-mode: multiply;
7  }
```

It's a quick and dirty plugin, which will likely need a little more development before putting it into production use—for example, it caters purely for background-blend-mode, whereas we should support any attribute that contains blend-mode within the name!

Summary

Creating CSS styles opens up a world of possibilities: we are only limited by what we must support! Throughout the course of this chapter, we've explored some of the possible options we can use when working with the newer CSS4 styles—let's take a moment to review what we have learnt.

We kicked off with a quick introduction to what we know as CSS4—we then moved on to explore some of the plugins that cater for supporting newer styles with more compatible CSS equivalent code.

Up next came a simple demo that explored some of the new CSS4 pseudo-classes, and how we might use them in a (theoretical) context. We then moved onto something more practical, in the form of styling the new range input using just CSS.

Moving swiftly on, we then took a look at the cssnext plugin pack, which provides an abstract layer for supporting CSS4; we saw how easy it is to implement, and that we can easily switch off functionality if it is no longer needed in our projects.

Our next demo came in the form of working with color—we used the `rebeccapurple` plugin to show firstly how easy it is to add support for one of the new colors within CSS4, then to modify it to provide support for other colors as needed in our projects. We then rounded out the chapter with a look back in time at some of the mistakes made when CSS was released, and how (with a little imagination), we might provide a temporary workaround until such time as these mistakes are fixed in a future version of CSS.

We've now come to the end of the book - I hope you've enjoyed our journey through the world of PostCSS, and that hopefully this book will help improve your skills as a future developer or user of PostCSS.

Index

Symbols

663399 color information
reference link 372
#deb887 Color Information
reference link 373
@each statements
iterating through 45-48

A

Abstract Syntax Trees (AST)
about 22, 295
URL 22
animated gallery
creating 178-181
animations (T41)
about 165, 166, 192
own animation plugin (T41), using 193, 194
plugin, exploring 195, 196
Apache webserver
URL 5
API reference documentation
reference link 307
architecture, standard plugin
classes, in API 203
exploring 198, 199
index.js file 199
List module 202
methods, in API 204, 205
nodes, in API 204
package.json file 199
package.json, using 200, 201
reference link 198
test.js file 199
test.js file, exploring 201, 202

Vendor module 202
asset
links, automating 106-109
links, maintaining 106
AtCSS
reference link 229
autoprefixer plugin
reference link 267
AVA test runner
reference link 209

B

Base16
reference link 291
Block Element Modifier (BEM)
about 68, 69
changes, exploring 76, 77
code, compiling 72
code, linting 72
errors, fixing 77, 78
simple message boxes, creating 70, 71
support, installing 72-75
boilerplate
reference link 198
Bourbon Neat
about 139
demo, exploring 148, 149
used, for creating example 145-147
Brewer theme
reference link 310
Browserslist query list
reference link 251
URL 319
bxSlider plugin
reference link 95

C

preprocessors
other preprocessors, compiling with 322
processing 2
processor
creating 255, 256
creating, tips 282, 283
exploring 256
extending 276-279
Gulp task file, exploring 257-259
issues, dissecting 260
package.json file, dissecting 256, 257
promises
reference link 203
pseudo-class-any-link plugin
about 359
reference link 359

Q

quantity queries
reference link 87
Quixote
URL 341

R

range input element
reference link 364
rebeccapurple color
reference link 370
reload capabilities
adding 274, 275
rem units
support, adding for 334, 335
responsive capabilities
adding 159
design, correcting 160-162
responsive design
avoiding 101, 102
responsive text support
adding 96-98
Rucksack
about 229, 282
alias functionality 231
automatic prefixing 238
clearfix functionality 231

code, dissecting 241, 242
demo, exploring 236, 237
easings 238
font src expansion 231, 238
Hex RGBA shortcuts 238
installing, as plugin 233
legacy fallbacks 239
property aliases 238
reference link 231
responsive typography 238
shortcuts, adding 231
shorthand positioning 238
slider conversion, for using 238-241
used, for animation 235, 236
used, for easing 233, 234
runner.md
reference link 224

S

SASS
animated gallery, creating 178-181
finishing touches, adding 181-184
setting up 26-28
switching to 176, 177
URL 26
Sassmeister
URL 140
sassy-mixins plugin 316
separation of concerns 37
short
reference link 229
shortcut plugins
postcss-border 228
postcss-border, reference link 228
postcss-focus 228
postcss-focus, reference link 228
postcss-short-data 228
postcss-short-data, reference link 228
using, in PostCSS 228
shortcuts
adding, with Rucksack 231
demo 232
Shorthand Color
about 282
reference link 282

www.ingramcontent.com/pod-product-compliance
Lightning Source LLC
Chambersburg PA
CBHW081504050326
40690CB00015B/2917